Advancing a Jobs-Driven Economy:
Higher Education and Business
Partnerships Lead the Way

Book Contributors
Senior Leaders

Rob Denson, Chair, STEM Higher Education Council (SHEC)

Dr. Martha Kanter, Senior Advisor, SHEC

Luminaries in Education and Business

- Alamo Colleges, The
- Alcoa
- American Association of University Women (AAUW)
- Amgen Foundation
- Apollo Education Group
- Arizona State University (ASU)
- Association of Community College Trustees (ACCT)
- Austin Community College (ACC)
- Business Roundtable and E3 (Engage, Educate, Employ)
- Center for American Progress (CAP)
- Chattanooga State Community College
- Chicago State University (CSU)
- Citizen Schools
- College for America
- CollegeWeekLive
- ConsultEdu (Cisco)
- Cumberland Center
- Dassault Systèmes
- Delta College
- Des Moines Area Community College (DMACC)
- EverFi

- Gateway Technical College
- Grinnell College
- Harper College
- Hope Street Group
- Howard University
- Innovate+Educate
- Iowa, Lt. Governor
- Jobs for the Future
- Madison Area Technical College (MATC)
- Manufacturing Institute, The
- Maricopa County Community College District (MCCCD)
- Mathematics Engineering Science Achievement (MESA) Pennsylvania
- Michigan Technological University
- Mike Rowe, TV host, Writer, Narrator, Producer, Actor and Spokesman
- Million Women Mentors®
- My College Options (NRCCUA)
- National Association for Equal Opportunity in Higher Education (NAFEO)
- National FFA Organization (FFA)

- Oak Ridge Associated Universities (ORAU)
- Olin College of Engineering
- Organization for Economic Co-operation and Development (OECD)
- PepsiCo
- Rose–Hulman Institute of Technology
- Saudi Arabian Ministry of Higher Education
- Society of Hispanic Professional Engineers (SHPE)
- Sodexo
- STEMconnector®
- Taft College
- Tata Consultancy Services (TCS)
- TE Connectivity
- Thinking Media
- Tuskegee University
- U.S. Chamber of Commerce Foundation
- United Negro College Fund (UNCF) with the Association for Public and Land-Grant Universities and White House Initiative on Historically Black Colleges and Universities
- University of California, Davis with Workforce Magazine, University of Houston-Downtown, and Baylor University
- University of Central Missouri
- University of Colorado, Colorado Springs
- University of Maryland, Baltimore County
- Western Governors University
- Youth Service America (YSA)

Quote Contributors

Apollo Education Group
CHS
Colorado Technical University
Gallup
Monsanto
Teach for America
Washington State University – Tri Cities

And all CEO STEM trailblazers who lead the way for advancing STEM in higher education and the workforce. Additional quotes from *100 CEO Leaders in STEM,* a publication by STEMconnector®, can be found in the Appendix. Endorsements can be found on subsequent pages.

www.STEMconnector.org

Endorsements

"Advancing a Jobs–Driven Economy is important to us as a business because it provides an opportunity to partner with higher education institutions across the country, share feedback about the needs that exist in different sectors and use that as a vehicle to create a collaboration between the industry and academia."

– Balaji Ganapathy, Head of Workforce Effectiveness
Tata Consultancy Services (TCS)

"Advancing a Jobs–Driven Economy is a vital resource for catalyzing innovation in STEM education and workforce development. STEMconnector® is uniquely positioned to highlight the partnerships needed to address complex challenges."

– Dr. Dean Evasius, Director of Scientific Assessment and Workforce Development
Oak Ridge Associated Universities (ORAU)

"Advancing a Jobs–Driven Economy is important because it brings together both educators and the business community. Businesses know what they need in order to be competitive. The only way to ensure that we have the workforce to enhance America's long–term competitiveness is to have partnerships and collaborations between business and our educational institutions…What is needed now is bold leadership and transformational change."

– John R. McKernan, President
U.S. Chamber of Commerce Foundation

"Advancing a Jobs–Driven Economy is the nexus between the worlds of business and academia. It brings the complete human capital value chain together. It's here where knowledge, experience and talent meet the critical challenges of the marketplace."

– Dale E. Jones, President
Diversified Search

"The University of Central Missouri is excited about *Advancing a Jobs–Driven Economy* and participating in the national dialogue regarding STEM education. We look forward to working with other colleges and universities nationwide to promote stronger collaboration between institutions of higher education, industry, and government to improve access to new STEM career pathways."

– Dr. Charles Ambrose, President
University of Central Missouri

"Science, technology, engineering, and mathematics are fundamental to assuring our national competitiveness and embodied by many leading community college programs. The Association of Community College Trustees is proud to be a part of *Advancing a Jobs–Driven Economy* to improve STEM education throughout the United States."

– J. Noah Brown, President and Chief Operating Officer
Association of Community College Trustees

"This book addresses strengthening the presence of Innovation Excellence in education and workforce development, which are key and fundamental to unlocking the advancement of a jobs-driven economy."

– Dr. Heidi Kleinbach-Sauter, Senior Vice President Global Foods R&D
PepsiCo

"Advancing a Jobs–Driven Economy and STEMconnector® are tremendous vehicles to link Historically Black Colleges and Universities/Predominantly Black Institutions with various stakeholders, and to educate the wider community about their amazing return on investment."

– Lezli Baskerville, President and Chief Operating Officer
National Association for Equal Opportunity in Higher Education

"As a founding member of the STEM Higher Education Council, Arizona State University (ASU) is dedicated to evolving the higher education experience so that we can develop more innovative pathways to better connect students to STEM careers. *Advancing a Jobs–Driven Economy* provides the framework to build new relationships with businesses, government and foundations to find opportunities for collaboration in building the next generation of STEM professionals."

– Dr. Mitzi Montoya, Vice President and University Dean of Entrepreneurship and Innovation
Arizona State University

"As a leader in undergraduate STEM education, Rose–Hulman Institute of Technology is uniquely positioned to help shape the next generation of scientific and engineering problem solvers with the institute's environment of individualized student attention and support. We salute *Advancing a Jobs–Driven Economy* in addressing those STEM issues that are important to keeping America competitive in the global innovation economy and addressing the grand challenges of the future."

– Dr. Phillip Cornwell, Vice President for Academic Affairs
Rose–Hulman Institute of Technology

"Western Governors University is pleased to be part of *Advancing a Jobs–Driven Economy.* It is only through productive collaborations like this one that higher education can fully achieve the goals for STEM education that we all know are crucial to the country's future."

– Dr. Phil Schmidt, Vice President for Compliance and Accreditation and
Dean of the Teacher's College
Western Governors University

Advancing a Jobs-Driven Economy: Higher Education and Business Partnerships Lead the Way

STEMconnector®

Advancing a Jobs-Driven Economy:

Higher Education and Business Partnerships Lead the Way

© 2015 by STEMconnector® All rights reserved.

Published in New York, New York, by Morgan James Publishing. Morgan James and The Entrepreneurial Publisher are trademarks of Morgan James, LLC.
www.MorganJamesPublishing.com

The Morgan James Speakers Group can bring authors to your live event. For more information or to book an event visit The Morgan James Speakers Group at
www.TheMorganJamesSpeakersGroup.com.

A free eBook edition is available with the purchase of this print book.

CLEARLY PRINT YOUR NAME ABOVE IN UPPER CASE

Instructions to claim your free eBook edition:
1. Download the BitLit app for Android or iOS
2. Write your name in **UPPER CASE** on the line
3. Use the BitLit app to submit a photo
4. Download your eBook to any device

ISBN 978-1-63047-542-0 paperback
ISBN 978-1-63047-543-7 eBook
Library of Congress Control Number:
2015900105

Cover Design by:
STEMconnector® Team
Carmellita Green

Edited by:
STEMconnector® Team

Interior Design by:
Carmellita Green
carmellita.green@ebsbalt.com

In an effort to support local communities and raise awareness and funds, Morgan James Publishing donates a percentage of all book sales for the life of each book to Habitat for Humanity Peninsula and Greater Williamsburg.

Get involved today, visit
www.MorganJamesBuilds.com

Habitat for Humanity®
Peninsula and
Greater Williamsburg
Building Partner

Dedication

This book is dedicated to those higher education and business leaders and organizational advocates who are driving change and stepping up as revolutionaries to challenge the status quo. These leaders believe that employers and educational leaders must together own STEM education as a career pathway. Employers today know that STEM Education is a critical driver of their own growth and innovation, and educators must be partners to prepare students for the 21st century workforce.

STEMconnector® and its STEM Higher Education Council (SHEC) salute the change agents represented in *Advancing a Jobs-Driven Economy* and the thousands of individuals committed to gaining the skills for good jobs.

A special tribute to the SHEC Chair, Rob Denson, President of Des Moines Area Community College (DMACC), Dr. Martha Kanter, SHEC Senior Advisor, and others who stand together with our STEMconnector® team and advisors.

We salute the day when we witness hundreds of partnerships and a million success stories. A special thanks to the college teachers and leaders who understand the importance of bridging the skills gap. Our dedication is to all who are committed to preparing our students and driving our economy.

We urge all to join the STEM Higher Educational Council and STEMconnector®, use this book to move forward using best practices and programs and we encourage you to provide your success stories on our Virtual Community of Practice website (book. STEMconnector.org/SHEC) so that *Advancing a Jobs-Driven Economy* and the initiatives it describes can live on at the speed of life and business.

Sincerely,

Edie, Talmesha, Ted and The STEMconnector® Team

TABLE OF CONTENTS

CHAPTER TWO – NURTURING INNOVATION

CHAPTER THREE – PARTNERSHIPS THAT DRIVE SUCCESS

CHAPTER FOUR – INDUSTRY MODELS

CHAPTER FIVE – AN INSIDE LOOK AT THE INFORMATION TECHNOLOGY SECTOR

CHAPTER SIX – BUILDING THE WORKFORCE OF TOMORROW THROUGH MANUFACTURING

CHAPTER SEVEN – K–12 STEM EDUCATION: LAYING THE FOUNDATION

CHAPTER EIGHT – CONNECTING TEACHERS AND STUDENTS TO STEM OPPORTUNITIES

CHAPTER NINE – CAREER FOCUSED EXPERIENTIAL LEARNING

CHAPTER TEN – LIFELONG LEARNING AND COMPETENCY BASED EDUCATION

CHAPTER ELEVEN – THE DIVERSITY OPPORTUNITY

CHAPTER TWELVE – DEVELOPING STEM HUMAN CAPITAL THROUGH STATE AND FEDERAL ACTION

FOREWORD

It's a New Day, Leadership Urgency

By: Rob Denson, Chair, STEM Higher Education Council, President, Des Moines Area Community College and Edie Fraser, Chief Executive Officer, STEMconnector®

Higher education should be very concerned. According to the Lumina study, *What America Needs to Know about Higher Education Redesign,* there is a substantial gap between business and academic leaders' assessment of the workforce preparedness of today's college graduates.

> *In a recent survey done by Gallup for Inside Higher Ed, 96% of college and university chief academic officers said they are extremely or somewhat confident in their institution's ability to prepare students for success in the workforce. By comparison, the Gallup/Lumina Foundation Poll found just 11% of business leaders strongly agree today's college graduates have the skills and competencies that their business needs.*

This Misalignment Must Be Changed

"Students want to know their investment in a postsecondary degree or certificate will lead to a good job," said Brandon Busteed, Executive Director of Gallup Education. "And employers want institutions to deliver graduates who have the skills and experience necessary for work success. But something is very wrong when you see the academic leaders of higher education giving themselves an A+ on this while business leaders give them an F. We all have a shared responsibility to fix this fast."

Progress Will Require Partnerships Between Business, Education and Policy Makers

Further, Accenture's *Bridge the Gap: Rebuilding America's Middle Skills,* Burning Glass Technologies, and Harvard Business School recommend that:

- Business leaders must champion an employer-led skills-development system, in which they bring the type of rigor and discipline in sourcing middle-skills talent applied to their supply chains. This includes workforce planning to identify skills gaps, ongoing and preferred relationships with talent sources, especially community and technical colleges, and building robust internal training and internship/apprenticeship programs.

- Educators from community and technical colleges must embrace their roles as employment partners helping their students realize their ambitions by being attentive to developments in the jobs market and employer needs.

- Policymakers must actively foster collaboration between employers and educators, investing in improving publicly available information on the jobs market, revising metrics for educators and workforce development programs so that success is based on placing students and workers in meaningful employment, and championing the crucial role that middle skills jobs play in a competitive U.S. economy."

Action Requires Meeting the Demand Side – Jobs and STEM 2.0

STEMconnector® and its STEM Higher Education Council (SHEC) are addressing this issue directly as it relates to STEM-skill careers and endorsing a call to action. The SHEC is composed of Public and Land-Grant universities, for-profit and non-profit private colleges and universities, Hispanic Serving Institutions (HSIs), Historically Black Colleges and Universities (HBCUs), and community colleges. The Council understands:

- Science, technology, engineering, and math are at the heart of the 21st century jobs-driven economy

- The essential role of business in any solution to what seems to be an insatiable skills-gap in America

- STEM 1.0, today's STEM education system within the current general momentum and environment, is not effective.

- Without dramatic and intentional change, businesses may eventually be forced to "off-campus" the preparation of the workforce and move away from traditional modes of higher education and training

- The associated risk to education, as we know it, of becoming irrelevant, if we are not immediately responsive. As one of our SHEC members stated, "We will not allow ourselves to be disrupted out of business."

Education must embrace the STEM 2.0 model STEMconnector® and its STEM Innovation Task Force have created. STEM 2.0 is the next stage for our students in preparation for the future workforce, mastering context. STEM 2.0, which seeks to define and find solutions for future critical career capabilities beyond a STEM 1.0 education, provides the capabiolities that our future workforce must possess. STEM 2.0 doesn't seek to reform or recreate the education system. Its unique advantage is to leverage existing programs and initiatives and add new elements from an employer perspective.

To that end, the first SHEC Summit's focus was on Advancing a Jobs-Driven Economy. This Summit was not a cloister of academics; we also brought our most engaged business partners into the room to share best practices and their needs. Our book, *Advancing a Jobs-Driven Economy,* is an outcome and extension of that collaborative effort.

Advancing a Jobs-Driven Economy will introduce you to the term "Boundary-Breaking Collaboration," connecting education and business in new and high impact driven ways. Business leaders expressed that the solution lies in better aligning our skills with their needs, progressing from STEM 1.0 to STEM 2.0.

Meeting the needs of business also meets the needs of students. *Advancing a Jobs-Driven Economy* takes on the challenge of showcasing effective business-education relationships. This compilation of contributions from thought leaders in higher education provides insight and suggestions as to how successful best-practice initiatives can be scaled-up.

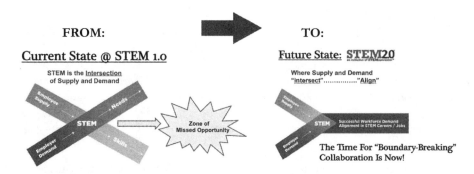

The Significance of this Book

We commend the business and education champions who have contributed to *Advancing a Jobs-Driven Economy*. New models of partnership drive scalable solutions that engage underrepresented communities and equip students with the skills and competencies that companies demand. These partnerships deserve our attention and many initiatives can be scaled up. More than sixty-six thought leaders have made a strong call to action. In each of the submissions, we see there is hope for a skilled workforce to meet current and future job needs and an "evolution" led by these partnerships.

Change and Disruption are Evidenced Everywhere but Need to be of Major Proportions

There are numerous pathways to jobs. Among the developments are job applicants arriving at colleges and businesses with skills training and certificates from high school, technical schools, the military and other endeavors. Applicants have been exposed to environments of experiential learning. Whether it's producing stackable credentials for demonstrating career assistance or internships and apprenticeships, change and disruption are occurring across the country. Things are moving, but not nearly fast enough based on what we are hearing from business. We must have more than a jobs-driven beginning. We need focused energy toward the advancement of a jobs-driven economy.

Aligning corporate, education, and community partners requires that we rethink and redesign the system that supports STEM education and workforce preparedness. The sustainability of our schools, the innovative engines of our businesses, the prosperity of communities, and the global competitiveness of our economies are at stake.

Join the Advancing a Jobs-Driven Economy Movement and thank you for being a part of the STEM Workforce Solution!

Let's Act! We need innovative and qualified students to fill the jobs of the 21st Century.

Call to Action

- Share copies of this book to promote open discussions for a "Call to Action"

- Add to the stories and post your case studies on our *Advancing a Jobs-Driven Economy's* Virtual Community of Practice website at **book.STEMconnector. org/SHEC**

- Partner up! Form partnerships to advance STEM and report the results.

- Get engaged and spearhead a campaign.

- Join STEMconnector® and our STEM Higher Education Council, if you have not already done so, to stay up to date on all the latest in STEM.

Contributor Highlights

Foreword
*"Institutions must understand the employee skills needs of the business community and align these and assign faculty to fulfill the demand such as the experience with Accumold."

\- Rob Denson, Chair, **STEM Higher Education Council** and
President **Des Moines Area Community College** and
Edie Fraser, Chief Executive Officer
STEMconnector®

Preface
"We must ensure that we are effectively connecting students with internships, jobs, and careers …We argue that quality is not measured by how many students you weed out, but by setting a high standard and then supporting your students so they can attain and surpass that standard."

\- Dr. Freeman A. Hrabowski, President
University of Maryland, Baltimore County

Introduction
"Let us close the achievement gap and get business to create pipeline programs from high school through graduate school. To supply the needs, community colleges and universities join with business and government to rethink, redesign and provide the relevant educational programs and services and build sustainable relationships."

\- Dr. Martha Kanter, Distinguished Visiting Professor of Higher Education and
Senior Fellow, **New York University** and
Senior Advisor, **STEM Higher Education Council**

Chapter 1: Aligning Skills to Jobs
"A new approach is organized innovation. Three pillars that comprise the network are Channeled Curiosity, Boundary-breaking collaboration and Orchestrated Commercialization. Innovate while insuring interdependence to ensure all parties participate. If we build a re-energized American innovation ecosystem, we will gain high-paying jobs."

\- Dr. Steven Currall, Chancellor's Advisor, **University of California, Davis;**
Ed Frauenheim, Associate Editorial Director, **Workforce Magazine;**
Sara Jansen Perry, Assistant Professor of Management in the Department of
Management, Marketing, and Business, **University of Houston – Downtown;** and
Emily Hunter, Assistant Professor in the Department of
Management and Entrepreneurship, **Baylor University**

"Drawing on lessons learned from supply chain management, talent pipeline management offers a promising new approach that is demand-driven and transformative for how employers engage education and workforce partners."

\- John R. McKernan, President
U.S. Chamber of Commerce Foundation

"While there is much debate about the wisdom of importing talent from other countries, it is universally agreed that it is our collective responsibility to prepare as many of our own citizens for these positions as is possible. This is a responsibility that is shared between higher education and industry itself."

- Steven M. Rothstein, CEO
Citizen Schools

"The Board has a strong role in Advancing a Jobs-Driven Economy, both in the community and institutional community."

- J. Noah Brown, President and Chief Executive Officer
Association of Community College Trustees

"Teach kids that there is no such thing as a bad job and that any job can be done with passion and enthusiasm....Accept that the concept that "I will never stop learning." And with it, understand hard work or "I choose to work my butt off."

- Mike Rowe, TV host, Writer, Narrator, Producer, Actor and Spokesman

Chapter 2: Nurturing Innovation

"Our commitment, as a nation, to inculcate in students a deep culture of Innovation Excellence will require actions between educators and the private sector to offer a portfolio of "career focused experiential Learning: opportunities to enable a jobs-driven economy."

- Dr. Heidi Kleinbach-Sauter, Senior Vice President of Global Foods R&D
PepsiCo

"We must double our efforts to ensure that those who access college cross the finish line with a degree in four years or perhaps less. And most important, within a jobs-driven economy, we are required to define student success in terms of skills and competencies required in a future-focused world."

- Stan Elliott, Director, Missouri Innovation Campus
University of Central Missouri

"What we need is an infrastructure that allows partnerships to scale and multiply. The STEM 2.0 initiative of STEMconnector® provides an excellent framework for building these partnerships. Let's get started!"

- Dr. Dean Evasius, Director of Scientific Assessment and Workforce Development
Oak Ridge Associated Universities

"As a physical embodiment of the maker movement, ASU focuses on Innovations and with TechShop, opportunities to replicate."

- Dr. Mitzi Montoya, Vice President and University Dean of
Entrepreneurship & Innovation
Arizona State University

Chapter 3: Partnerships that Drive Success

"Supply schools with the content to teach the skills they seek in their employees."

- Mary Wright, Program Director
Jobs for the Future

"Collaborations and partnerships are essential in STEM fields, with the rapidity at which technology evolves. Through the agreement with the business and the community, we bought a mall, and built a curriculum and offerings that will remain on the leading edge of developments in the information technology sector and ensure a new generation of tech workers with the skills and training in demand by today's employers."

- Dr. Richard Rhodes, President and Chief Executive Officer
Austin Community College

"It takes an Industry, Higher Education, and Public Education STEM Collaborative. The model is Applied STEM dual credit pathway programs. This collaboration with a dual credit pathway program starting with high school students engaged and the partnerships with business give us evidence of success."

- Dr. Bruce H. Leslie, Chancellor
The Alamo Colleges

"Employers are looking for workers with specific skills. The call to action means that higher education institutions must be willing to respond to business and respond "Just in time" with training to skill up the workforce."

- Dr. Jean Goodnow President
Delta College

"Going forward… (we must) Understand the employee skill needs of the business entity."

- Rob Denson, President
Des Moines Area Community College and
Chair, **STEM Higher Education Council**

"Provide a roadmap that any higher learning institution can use to build the workforce that business needs with three elements: Support economic development in your community; create and provide the training that business requires and make sure that graduates have content mastery."

- Dr. Jim Catanzaro, Former President
Chattanooga State Community College

To prepare a workforce it takes hands-on practical experience and instructors with the experience, education and skills from industry

- Dr. Dena Maloney, Superintendent-President
Taft College

Chapter 4: Industry Models

"Partnerships are what create the pipeline to jobs and with a variety of companies and the USDA, as well as partnerships with other universities, we now launch the next 125 years of excellence."

- Dr. Walter A. Hill, Provost and
Dr. Olga Bolden–Tiller, Associate Professor, Agricultural Science
Tuskegee University

"Young leaders within FFA are developing skills that make them solidify college ad career ready. These will be the workers, managers and leaders we must have for agriculture to grow."

- Dr. W. Dwight Armstrong, Chief Executive Officer
National FFA Organization

"Action points we cite are that institutions of higher education can provide resources to support the areas of need such as STEM Cell Technologies and that takes partnership."

- Dr. Thomas Tubon, Project Director, Co–PI
Human Stem Cell Technologies Education Initiative
Madison Area Technical College

"To succeed in winning, we need to ascertain needs as higher education works with business. We emphasize work-based learning; and we add Accessibility as business and higher education become more proactive."

- Dr. Wayne Watson, President
Chicago State University

Chapter 5: An Inside Look at the Information Technology Sector

"If industry and education can create Digital Fluency skill sets, the resulting workforce can fully participate in the jobs of the digital era, and exponentially impact economic growth."

- Balaji Ganapathy, Head of Workforce Effectiveness, **Tata Consulting Services** and
Co-Chair, **STEMconnector® STEM Innovation Task Force**

"Impart real skills to real people who can fill jobs in high demand fields and make the necessary advancement to help close the skills gap and gain jobs."

- Mark Brenner, Chief of Staff to the Chief Operating Officer and
Senior Vice President of Corporate Communications and External Affairs
Apollo Education Group

"There a myriad of uses of technology in education, but much of the use is piecemeal, ad hoc and with little 'joined-up' thinking; IoT (the Internet of Things) has the potential to bring that all together."

- Dr. Michelle Selinger, Education Technology Specialist
ConsultEdu (Cisco)

"The digital moments that are the foundation of the new economy represent the opportunities of the new economy, which means jobs for future generations. Higher education leaders and business leaders need to recognize that these opportunities are the jobs of tomorrow, and they need to build an acceptable product – a well-educated student – who is prepared to be a part of the workforce to leverage the opportunities of the digital economy."

- Earl Newsome, Corporate Chief Information Officer
TE Connectivity

Chapter 6: Building the Workforce of Tomorrow through Manufacturing

"The skills gap might be called "the training gap." Schools and institutions should be the first place manufacturers are looking for supplying talent."

- Jennifer McNelly, President
The Manufacturing Institute

"To advance a Jobs-Driven economy, we need to do a much better job of working together across sectors."

- Martin Scaglione, President and Chief Executive Officer
Hope Street Group

"Digital technologies are rapidly transforming virtually every aspect of work; built the skills. Other areas include energy, auto and trucking; aerospace and transportation, medical care, biotechnology, additive and sustainable manufacturing."

- Jerry Jasinowski, Chairman of Critical Skills Initiatives
EverFi

"Building an unprecedented collaboration is what is essential in our call to action. These leaders are united in their commitment to help individuals understand and gain the skills they need to enter into and advance in the jobs of today and tomorrow. There is a call to action to develop a National Learning Economy."

- Emily DeRocco, Director, National Network of Business and Industry Associations,
Business Roundtable and Founder and Chief Executive Officer,
E3 (Engage, Educate, Employ)

"Communicating Talent Pipeline Priorities creates a pull-model driven by Alcoa's four talent pipelines: Potential (K-12 grades); Entry-level (10+year pipeline); Mid-level (5 year pipeline) and Experienced (current pipeline). This takes collaboration mixed with competency-based communication"

- Greg Bashore, Global Director, Talent Acquisition and Workforce Development
Alcoa

Chapter 7: K–12 STEM Education: Laying the Foundation

"The "pipeline" moving students through high school, into college and graduate programs, then providing them with access to research and training so that, in the end, we have a workforce ready to enter the job market, is a virtual sieve."

- Don Munce, President and Ryan Munce, Vice President
My College Options (NRCCUA)

"As higher education seeks to increase the diversity, quantity and quality of our incoming students, we must be equally committed to retaining and further cultivating them once they become our customers."

- Dr. Jamie M. Bracey, Director of STEM Education Outreach and Research,
Temple University's College of Engineering and Executive Director
Pennsylvania Mathematics, Engineering & Science Achievement (MESA)

"In order to effect real change, we will need to take some risks and try new things."

- Evan Weisenfeld, Vice President of Strategic Partnerships
CollegeWeekLive

"Building partnerships with other public sector institutions as well as private enterprises is key to success, collaborate partnerships to drive a results-driven approach. When we enlarge the K-pipeline, we enhance collaborative partnerships between 2 and 4 year institutions."

- Dr. Pamela Shockley–Zalabak, Chancellor and Professor of Communication
University of Colorado, Colorado Springs

"Students, when given a personal and social context for learning, have fun in figuring out possible solutions to real-world applications, through tacit and explicit understanding of STEM concepts. Partnerships are key, with business, with universities and community colleges and across to local K-12. Partner with corporate America in Science and Engineering Festivals while focusing on demand of STEM 2.0."

- Dr. John Lehman, Associate Vice President for Enrollment,
Marketing, and Communications
Michigan Technological University

"K-12 and Higher Education Partnerships play a critical role in an effective STEMester of Service."

- Scott Ganske, Education Director
Youth Service America (YSA)

"Colleges and K-12 districts must continue to forge collaborative relationships to ensure the transition from high school to college to the workforce is seamless."

- Dr. Kenneth Ender, President
Harper College

Chapter 8: Connecting Teachers and Students to STEM Opportunities

"For innovation to be sustainable and lead to economic growth, we need another element: inclusions of diversity. Everyone in the pool."

- David Bergeron, Vice President for Postsecondary Education Policy
Center for American Progress

"Liberal arts colleges offer a very distinctive educational experience, and the opportunity to partner with leaders and innovators from STEM-related organizations will only enhance our student's readiness for the 21st century marketplace."

- Mark Peltz, Associate Dean and Director of Career Development
Grinnell College

"We understand and value our responsibility in contributing to the goal of creating a K-12 system capable of training the next generation of STEM professionals."

- Dr. Philip Schmidt, Vice President for Compliance and
Accreditation and Dean of the Teachers College
Western Governors University

Chapter 9: Career Focused Experiential Learning

"As employers, we have seen that new employees with rich, experiential learning projects in their backgrounds are better prepared for the workplace and are productive more quickly."

- Al Bunshaft, President and CEO
Dassault Systèmes Americas

"Higher education and industry need to have clear lines of communication so higher education is aware of the knowledge, skills, and abilities needed by industry and so industry has a better appreciation for the education we provide our students."

- Dr. Phillip Cornwell, Vice President for Academic Affairs and
Professor of Mechanical Engineering
Rose–Hulman Institute of Technology

"Higher education and businesses must continue to partner if we are to advance a jobs-driven economy. One path towards this is to fully participate in effective large-scale partnerships committed to strengthening education and building the future workforce."

- Scott Heimlich, Vice President
Amgen Foundation

"Our call to action is for everyone concerned about our economic prosperity, our education competitiveness and our ability to sustain career opportunities for future generations to get involved by becoming an learner and champion for STEM in your local school and community....It is imperative that education and business work together to advance a common agenda to drive local economies as we do...Up-Skilling the workforce is a shared responsibility."

- Dr. Bryan Albrecht, President and Chief Executive Officer
Gateway Technical College

Chapter 10: Lifelong Learning and Competency Based Education

"A call to action to challenge business and industry, higher education and national partners to focus on a new model of education to employment—with a demand driven focus on the key "win" at the end.... This new system must be demand driven and will require systemic change from the demand side players (businesses small to large) for true success."

- Jamai Blivin, Chief Executive Officer
Innovate+Educate

"Establish training partnerships between community colleges and local businesses that focus on high-demand jobs."

- Dr. Dane Boyington, Co–founder and Chief Technical Officer and Sheila Boyington, Co–founder and President
Thinking Media

"Today's employers expect practical skills, not just theory—proof of both the ability to learn and the ability to execute. And they aren't getting it."

- Melissa Goldberg, Senior Workforce Strategist and Julian L. Alssid, Chief Workforce Strategist
College for America

Chapter 11: The Diversity Opportunity

"Actively recruit more women into nontraditional and STEM fields... while developing educational and career pathways to help students navigate STEM curricula and partner with local employers to connect these students to available opportunities."

- Linda Hallman, Executive Director and Chief Executive Officer
American Association of University Women (AAUW)

"Mentoring is a vital tool in recruiting women and minorities for STEM."

- Julie Kantor, Vice President and Chief Partnership Officer and MacKenzie Moore, Associate, Business Development
STEMconnector® and Million Women Mentors®

"We need to create partnerships aligning skills to careers, always look for developing new programs and then partner on infrastructure investments and research in STEM."

- Dr. Wayne Frederick, President
Howard University

"Research continues to show that Latinas, as compared to other underrepresented females, are less likely to enroll in STEM, despite being a part of the largest minority group in the US. Industry and Education alike are also finding that there are, and continue to be, many social and cultural barriers that make it especially difficult for young Latinas to break into male-dominated STEM career paths."

- Dr. Maria Harper–Marinick, Executive Vice Chancellor and Provost
Maricopa County Community College District

"Diversity fosters innovation and innovation drives business success."
- Richard Morley, Chief Executive Officer
Society of Hispanic Professional Engineers (SHPE)

"Develop more tech jobs for minorities. Commit to innovation and scale up success."
- Dr. Chad Womack, National Director, STEM Initiatives and
UNCF–Merck Science Initiative
United Negro College Fund;
Dr. John M. Lee, Vice President, Office for Access and Success
Association for Public and Land–Grant Universities;
Ken Tolson, Member, President Board of Advisors
White House Initiative on Historically Black Colleges and Universities; and
Dr. George Cooper, Executive Director
White House Initiative on Historically Black Colleges and Universities

Chapter 12: Developing STEM Human Capital through State and Federal Action

"OECD has synthesized research across policy areas such as employment, entrepreneurship and economic development to show how policymakers across governance levels can better align their efforts to boost job creation from the bottom up. It shows not only "what needs to be done", for example to improve skills utilization in firms or promote lifelong learning, but also the governance mechanisms of "how it can be done", from injecting local flexibility into national policy frameworks to improving horizontal accountability at the local level."
- Anna Rubin, Policy Analyst
Organization for Economic Co-operation and Development (OECD)

"We understand that STEM collaboration is key. Our stakeholders are diverse and passionate about being involved"
- Kimberly K. Reynolds
Lieutenant Governor of Iowa

"The STEM community needs federal and state action. We advocate for our HBCU's Centers of Excellence and more private and public sector action."
- Lezli Baskerville, President and Chief Executive Officer,
National Association for Equal Opportunity in Higher Education

Chapter 13: A Global Perspective

"Clearly, the key to effecting change, spurring progress and creating long-term success lies in a strategy based on and driven by meaningful engagement."
- Michael Norris, Chief Operating Officer, President of the Corporate Services Market
Sodexo North America

"The future welfare of both human beings and the planet depend on a distinctly human resources – innovation."

- Dr. Scott T. Massey, Chairman and Chief Executive Officer
Cumberland Center

"The Kingdom of Saudi Arabia shoulders the burden of a continuous need to nurture a futuristic climate ripe for entrepreneurial innovative overtures that will catapult their ambitious youth into the next technology-based millennium."

- Dr. Amal Fatani, Consultant and General Supervisor of Female Affairs
Saudi Arabian Ministry of Higher Education

PREFACE

Changing the Culture of STEM Education to Improve Student Success
By: Dr. Freeman A. Hrabowski, President, University of Maryland, Baltimore County

A few years ago, I chaired a study committee at the National Academies that wrote *Expanding Underrepresented Minority Participation: America's Science and Technology Talent at the Crossroads.* The committee was tasked with examining how to improve the participation and success of underrepresented minorities in STEM as a follow–up to the Academies' Rising Above the Gathering Storm. While examining that problem, we uncovered another: colleges and universities are failing students in STEM from all racial and ethnic groups.

Of course, it did not surprise people that underrepresented minorities did not fare well in undergraduate STEM. Only about 20 percent of Blacks and Hispanics who start as STEM majors graduate with degrees in these fields. What did surprise people was that the numbers for white and Asian American students – 32 percent and 41 percent, respectively – were not much higher.

When shown these numbers, university faculty and administrators typically argue that the problem lies with preparation and K–12 needs to fix it. But researchers have probed further into the data and found, when considering student success in STEM, that the higher the SAT scores, the larger the number of AP credits earned, and often the more prestigious the institution, the greater the chance that a student who starts in STEM will leave it within the first year or two.

I noted this recently at a meeting with a federal agency, and later one of the top executives came up to me and said, "You just told my story. I was the valedictorian of my high school class, I had near perfect SATs, I chose to major in chemistry in a very prestigious university, and I had planned to go to medical school. By the end of my first semester in college, I had earned an A in each of my classes but Chemistry, in which I earned a C. When I went home at the end of the semester I told my parents and everyone else that I loved English and was changing majors."

We need to look in the mirror and acknowledge that while there are problems with pre–college preparation, the high attrition rates in STEM pose a major problem for undergraduate STEM education. We all know that in most colleges and universities, introductory courses in mathematics and the natural sciences are seen as "weed out" courses. We've all heard the statement, "Look at the student to your left and now look at the student to your right. One of you will not succeed in this course." On our campus, we say, "Look at the student on your left and now look at the student on your right. Our goal is to make sure all three of you succeed and if we don't, then we fail. And we don't plan to fail."

As a nation, we are falling behind. If you look at the proportion of 24–year–olds who have earned a first university degree in the natural sciences or engineering, several European and Asian countries are at 10 percent or higher for this demographic group. In the U.S., we are at just 6 percent. We must act in tackling the problem of attrition from undergraduate STEM majors; this is the place to start.

Course Re–design

On a recent flight, I read a short piece by Gary Kelley, Chief Operating Officer of Southwest Airlines, in which he described his company's *secret sauce*. He said, "Your business plan is what you are, but culture is who you are." Indeed, your culture embodies the values you hold, the assumptions you make, the questions you ask, and what you reward and what you don't reward. For colleges and universities, our challenge is to put students first. In order to address this critical problem of attrition in undergraduate STEM education, faculty and administrators need to change the culture of teaching and learning in our institutions to support student success.

At UMBC and other institutions in the University of Maryland System, we are changing this culture by better understanding how students learn, and redesigning our introductory courses to facilitate better teaching and deeper learning. We argue that quality is not measured by how many students you weed out, but by setting a high standard and then supporting your students so they can attain and surpass that standard.

The classroom approaches we are employing as we re–design our courses include supplementing or even replacing lectures with active, group learning that involves discovery through solving hands–on problems. In fact, we use real problems from the companies in our research park. These approaches encourage students to take greater responsibility for their own learning as they take turns serving, within their groups, as manager, data analyst, recorder, and blogger. These changes can be difficult for students who prefer to work independently or want to passively attend lecture courses, but we have found that they learn more by working in groups, and that this approach better prepares them for careers in which they will likely need to work in teams.

We, in academia, often base decisions on anecdotal information as opposed to making data–driven, evidence–based decisions. The kind of culture change reflected in course re–design and other innovations begins by identifying a problem, and it continues through the process of collecting and examining relevant data. It is furthered by engaging stakeholders – students, faculty, and staff – in conversations about the problem, the data, and possible solutions, and it succeeds as we develop a common understanding of the problem and agree to a solution that reflects our values and the data.

Understanding the data is critical. We have built an evaluation component into our initiatives so that we can understand whether they are succeeding and what we might do to change course, if needed. We also use data analytics at the course and student level, to explore and assess overall performance trends and also to identify students who would benefit from early intervention. All of these approaches are important to improving student success.

Partnerships

As we work to increase the number of students succeeding in STEM, we must also ensure that we are effectively connecting students with internships, jobs, and careers. Partnerships are central to this. On our campus, we are partnering with other colleges and universities, government agencies and laboratories, and companies. In this way, we can play a stronger role in an "ecosystem" encompassing education, training, internships, hiring, research, and technology commercialization.

Our partnerships with corporations are valuable and multi–faceted. The defense industry leader, Northrop Grumman, for instance, is supporting our students in cyber–security. We have partnerships with start–ups and smaller companies, including over 100 biotechnology and IT companies on campus in our research park. These partnerships provide students with internship opportunities, contributing to their overall education and their development as professionals while also helping them establish the networks that will get them jobs. Students often ask, "How am I going to use what I'm learning?" Giving college students a chance to work in cyber–security or biotech labs provides an answer to that question.

It is critical that we focus on the skills people need in order to be effective. Are we educating engineering, computing, and science majors who communicate effectively, who know how to work in teams, and who can put their knowledge and skills to productive use? Sometimes my humanities majors who take a few computer science or information systems courses go up the ladder in tech careers faster than our technology majors because they know how to speak and write well, and how to work effectively with people.

This is where companies can help. We need more connections and better communication between our faculty and their corporate counterparts. It helps our faculty to listen to companies to understand the skills that employees need and understand how graduates are faring after they are hired. What can we do to better prepare them for the work, for their first jobs, and for their careers in the long–run?

Professionals serve as excellent mentors for STEM students, guiding them through their studies and helping them navigate their way to jobs and careers. Students profit from having all types of mentors, including men and women and people from all social and other backgrounds. Mentors can emphasize to students that while the work is often hard, they will do well if they persevere.

We believe in multilevel partnerships. It enriches the academic environment for faculty and students to work collaboratively with researchers in companies on corporate projects. It strengthens our curricula for professionals from national agencies and companies to sit on advisory committees. Their advice and suggestions are invaluable.

Success is Never Final
U.S. News and World Report has ranked UMBC #1 in its annual list of "up and coming national universities" each of the past six years. Someone joked that eventually we should actually "arrive." But I tell people on my campus that we need to be careful about that. The moment you arrive is the moment you stop innovating. Redesigning courses and strengthening partnerships are two steps along the road to changing our culture and improving student outcomes, but we need many more. Success is never final.

About The University of Maryland, Baltimore County

The University of Maryland, Baltimore County was born amid the turbulent swirl of the 1960s, and had to cut her own path in a field of older, established institutions. From the beginning, UMBC believed that a university could be innovative, interdisciplinary, inclusive – and great. UMBC believed that groundbreaking research and a relentless focus on undergraduate success could go hand–in–hand. To this day, UMBC's faculty, staff and students work and create, outside traditional structures. It's not happenstance that UMBC had the first university research park in Maryland, dedicated to growing ideas into thriving businesses.

UMBC is a dynamic public research university integrating teaching, research, and service to benefit the citizens of Maryland. As an Honors University, the campus offers academically talented students a strong undergraduate liberal arts foundation that prepares them for graduate and professional study, entry into the workforce, and community service and leadership. UMBC emphasizes science, engineering, information technology, human services and public policy at the graduate level. UMBC contributes to the economic development of the State and the region through entrepreneurial initiatives, workforce training, K–16 partnerships, and technology commercialization in collaboration with public agencies and the corporate community. UMBC is dedicated to cultural and ethnic diversity, social responsibility, and lifelong learning.

About the Author

Dr. Freeman A. Hrabowski, III, has served as President of UMBC (The University of Maryland, Baltimore County) since 1992. His research and publications focus on science and math education, with special emphasis on minority participation and performance. He chaired the National Academies' committee that produced the recent report, *"Expanding Underrepresented Minority Participation: America's Science and Technology Talent at the Crossroads."* He also was recently named by President Obama to chair the newly created President's Advisory Commission on Educational Excellence for African Americans.

In 2008, he was named one of America's Best Leaders by U.S. News & World Report, which ranked UMBC the nation's #1 "Up and Coming" university the past five years (2009–13). During this period, U.S. News also consistently ranked UMBC among the nation's leading institutions for "Best Undergraduate Teaching" – in 2013, other universities on the list included Duke, Cal–Berkeley, Princeton, and Brown. TIME magazine named him one of America's 10 Best College Presidents in 2009, and one of the "100 Most Influential People in the World" in 2012. In 2011, he received both the TIAA–CREF Theodore M. Hesburgh Award for Leadership Excellence and the Carnegie Corporation of New York's Academic Leadership Award, recognized by many as the nation's highest awards among higher education leaders.

Acknowledgments

Advancing a Jobs-Driven Economy would not be possible without the hard work and dedication of all of STEMconnector®'s loyal staff and supporters. We would like to give a special thank you to: Edie Fraser, Chief Executive Officer, Dr. Talmesha Richards, Chief Academic and Diversity Officer, Dominik Sauter, Associate, Special Projects, Ashley Post, Director, Projects, Ted Wells, Vice President and Chief Strategy Officer, and Brian Jackson, Director, Strategic Initiatives.

STEMconnector® Senior Advisors: Rob Denson, President of Des Moines Area Community College and Chair of the STEM Higher Education Council; Sheila Boyington, Co-founder and President, Thinking Media; Dr. Dane Boyington, Co-founder and Chief Technology Officer, Thinking Media; Alex Belous, Education Portfolio Manager of Cisco Public Benefit Investments & Cisco Foundation; Dr. Heidi Kleinbach–Sauter, Senior Vice President Global Foods R&D, PepsiCo; Michael Norris, Chief Operating Officer North America, Sodexo; Jane Oates, Vice President, Apollo Education Group; Dr. Martha Kanter, Distinguished Visiting Professor of Higher Education and Senior Fellow, New York University; and Dr. Freeman Hrabowski, President, University of Maryland, Baltimore County

Diversified Search: Dale Jones, President

STEMconnector® Consultants: Morgan James Publishing, Laura Clise, and Book Designer, Carmellita Green

STEM Higher Education Council Members (as of January 15, 2015):

- Alabama State University
- Alamo Colleges, The
- Apollo Education Group
- Arizona State University
- Association of Community College Trustees
- Austin Community College
- Brandeis University
- Chattanooga State Community College
- Chicago State University
- CollegeWeekLive
- Colorado Technical University
- Cumberland Center
- Delta College
- Des Moines Area Community College
- Gateway Technical College
- Grinnell College
- Harper College
- Howard University
- Iowa State University
- Madison Area Technical College
- Maricopa Community College
- Mathematics Engineering Science Achievement (MESA)
- Michigan State University
- Michigan Technology University
- Morehouse College
- My College Options (NRCCUA)
- National Association of Equal Opportunity in Higher Education (NAFEO)
- National FFA Organization
- Oak Ridge Associated Universities
- Olin College of Engineering
- Rose–Hulman Institute of Technology
- Taft College
- Tuskegee University
- United Negro College Fund
- University of Central Missouri
- University of Colorado, Colorado Springs
- University of Florida
- University of Iowa
- University of Massachusetts, Boston
- University of Nebraska
- Washington State University - Tri Cities
- Western Governors University

INTRODUCTION

Closing the Achievement Gap to
Deliver a High–Performing 21st Century Workforce

By: Dr. Martha Kanter, Distinguished Visiting Professor of Higher Education and Senior Fellow, New York University and Senior Advisor, STEM Higher Education Council

Now more than ever, America needs well–educated, competent graduates from our community colleges and universities to fill the jobs of today and tomorrow. Increasing and ensuring this pipeline is the shared responsibility of higher education, business, and government leaders. In partnership, these sectors – together – have the opportunity to deepen their investments of time, effort, and money to close the achievement gap and produce the 21st century workforce needed to propel the nation's innovation, competitiveness, and influence in our fast–moving, geopolitical world.

Labor economists estimate that in the decade ahead, more than 25 million positions, or nearly half of job openings, will be in the middle–skills range with an increasing number requiring expertise in STEM. Think about how many technicians, laboratory specialists, machine operators, administrative assistants, customer response managers and other mid–range skilled workers it takes to serve the needs of our nation's corporations, small and medium–sized businesses, non–profits and government at the local, state and federal level. Georgetown University's Center on Education and the Workforce confirms that more than 60 percent of our nation's workforce will need an associate's, baccalaureate or advanced degree to meet the middle and high skill needs of business, industry and government between now and 2020.[1] Today, only 15 percent of undergraduates are STEM majors, not enough to meet our nation's demand for graduates in these fields of study.

> *The lockstep march from school to work and then on to retirement no longer applies for a growing share of Americans.*
>
> – Anthony P. Carnevale, Director, Georgetown Center on Education and the Workforce

To supply these needs, it is of critical importance that community colleges and universities join together with business and government to rethink, redesign and provide the relevant educational programs and services to meet the full range of STEM jobs regionally and globally in the years ahead. Building sustainable relationships and breaking boundaries to leap across the status quo will be key to ensuring the high performing workforce that is sorely needed for our nation to compete and succeed as a fully informed, democratic society.

The Challenge

Whether we call it the "skills gap" or the "achievement gap," the truth is that we don't have enough young adults prepared with the critical thinking, problem–solving, communications, analytical capacities and technical skills that employers want and that our nation needs. While we're seeing increases in the overall high school graduation rate (80 percent today is the highest it's been in decades), students from low–income families, who are underrepresented in American higher education, lag too far behind their higher income counterparts. Sadly, this has been the case for more than 50 years. In fact, by age

24, less than 9 percent of students from families in the lowest income quartile obtain their bachelor's degrees while more than 75 percent of students from the highest income quartile graduate from college.[2] For all college students, only a third of students from low–income families will earn their degrees today, while more than two–thirds will graduate from higher income quartiles.[3]

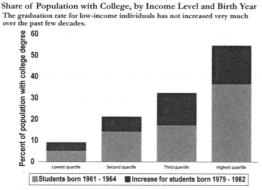

Share of Population with College, by Income Level and Birth Year
The graduation rate for low-income individuals has not increased very much over the past few decades.

Source: Bailey and Dynarski (2001)
Note: Original data come from National Longitudinal Survey of Youth, 1979 and 1997.

Upward social and economic mobility is a hallmark of the American dream, and obtaining education beyond high school will be key to financial self–sufficiency for the majority of Americans in the 21st century. With the expected population increases of Latino and African American families in the decades ahead, closing the achievement gap with attention to race and ethnicity must also be a focus of higher education, business and government partnerships. Right now, college graduates who are White graduate at twice the rate of Black and three times the rate of Hispanic students in the United States. STEM graduates will have numerous opportunities for employment, but as the National Academies report: "At present, just 26 percent of African Americans, 24 percent of Native Americans and Pacific Islanders, and 18 percent of Hispanics and Latinos in the 25– to 34–year–old cohort have attained at least an associate's degree.[4] The news is even worse in Science, Technology, Engineering, and Mathematics (STEM) fields, the subject of this report."

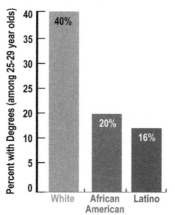

White Students Attain Bachelor's Degree at Nearly Twice the Rate of African Americans and Three Times the Rate of Latinos

Bachelor's Degree Attainment of Young Adults (25-29) years old, 2013

Source: U.S. Census Bureau, Educational Attainment in the United States 2013

Two additional challenges help to frame the national imperative to close the achievement gap. First, as Carnevale et al. report, "young adults' labor force participation rate has returned to its 1972 level, a decline that started in the late 1980s and has accelerated since 2000" and "there are more job openings created from retirements per young person today than there were in the 1990s." It's also taking longer for college graduates to reach the middle of the wage distribution, especially for students of color. Second, of the 93 million adults in the U.S. population, more than 40 percent, lack the reading, writing and computation skills expected of a high school graduate, including those who earned high school diplomas in the 20th century.[5]

When we examine all of these challenges and look ahead with the knowledge that underrepresented students will become the majority of college–going adults in the decades ahead, it is of utmost importance that we close the achievement gap as soon as possible.

The Opportunity

We have an unprecedented opportunity before us: to create a vibrant, high performing workforce for the 21st century – especially in STEM, a call to action that is urgently needed for our nation's success. To harness this opportunity, we have an evidence base of high impact practices drawn from education–industry–government partnerships, we have data and strategies on how to close the achievement and skills gaps, and we have a shared interest in tackling this problem from prominent leaders in business, higher education and government. Members of STEMconnector®'s Higher Education Council have come together to take advantage of this opportunity – to show how these challenges are being addressed. They know that we must increase the percentage of Americans with community college and university degrees from 40 percent to more than 60 percent in the decade ahead to make sure that our nation remains innovative, competitive and prosperous. America's future success must be driven by the values of our democracy that include high standards, hard work, equal opportunity and a strong ecosystem built on the foundation of education, business and government working together toward common goals.[6, 7]

The Time Is Now

To advance our jobs–driven economy and maintain the widest set of opportunities for Americans to contribute to the social, civic and economic prosperity of our nation, it is imperative that colleges and universities advance deeper partnerships with business and government. The following actions would help to close the achievement gap, fill the middle–skill and high–skill demands of our nation's workforce and enable millions more students and their families to realize the American Dream.

- **State and federal government** should support the expansion and deepening of higher education–business partnerships by simplifying and re–engineering government work–study, cooperative education, internships, scholarships and loan forgiveness programs that incentivize college enrollment, persistence and completion for success in career and community.

- **Business should create pipeline programs** from high school through graduate school that provide every student who works hard and stays on course to graduate with paid internships, service opportunities and tuition reimbursement programs.

- **Higher Education should take bold steps** to strengthen partnerships between high schools, community colleges and universities by streamlining articulation, by implementing high–impact, evidence–based remediation and retention practices, by clarifying all educational costs, and by simplifying the higher education pathways to middle and high skill jobs.

These actions have the power to bring the highest impact STEM partnerships and strategies to scale across our nation and to transfer to other non–STEM pipelines to meet the diversity of America's workforce needs. Accordingly, these steps would advance the U.S. imperative to retain its pre–eminence in higher education and the workforce for the generations ahead. We must overcome these disparities and join in the call to action for our nation to thrive in the 21st century. The time is now.

About the Author

Dr. Martha J. Kanter is a Distinguished Visiting Professor of Higher Education and Senior Fellow at New York University. Her academic interests include: The Confluence of Access, Equity and Excellence; The Intersection of Policy and Politics in American Higher Education; and The Contributions of America's Community Colleges to the Nation's Social Fabric, Civic Future and Economy.

In 2009, President Barack Obama nominated Kanter to serve as the U.S. Under Secretary of Education, with oversight responsibility for all federal postsecondary statutory, regulatory and administrative policies and programs for the U.S. Department of Education, including the $175B annual federal student aid programs, higher education, adult education, career–technical education, international education and 6 White House Initiatives. Through the first term of the Obama Administration, Kanter and her team focused on increasing college access, affordability, quality, and completion to implement President Obama's goal, "to have the best educated, most competitive workforce in the world by 2020." She oversaw the simplification and successful implementation of the Direct Student Loan program that resulted in a 50 percent increase in college enrollment, growing the number of Pell Grant recipients from 6 to more than 9 million students.

CHAPTER ONE

Aligning Skills to Jobs

"Industry must take a stronger stake in education by taking part in developing school's curriculum, creating internships for talented students and supporting communities with valuable education opportunities and resources...education is the single most important factor in achieving US innovative competitiveness globally."

-Tom Linebarger, Chairman and Chief Executive Officer
Cummins

Excerpt from *100 CEO Leaders in STEM*, a publication by STEMconnector®

Organized Innovation for a Jobs–Driven Economy:
The Role of Boundary–Breaking Collaboration

By: Dr. Steven Currall, Chancellor's Advisor, University of California, Davis;
Ed Frauenheim, Associate Editorial Director, Workforce Magazine;
Sara Jansen Perry, Assistant Professor of Management in the Department of
Management, Marketing, and Business, University of Houston – Downtown; and
Emily Hunter, Assistant Professor in the Department of Management and
Entrepreneurship, Baylor University

Today, many Americans remain pessimistic about our economic future. Despite a recovery with stock market highs, the creation of high–skill, high–paying jobs during the past few years has been disappointing. Our ability to get better at basic research and then translate it into prototypes, commercial products, companies, and industries will determine, to a large degree, our level of economic prosperity in the future.[8] New approaches to innovation will be vital as we seek to foster job creation and tackle daunting dilemmas, such as communicable diseases, shortages of purified water, weather fluctuations, and the potential for worldwide food shortages.

A New Approach: "Organized Innovation"

We have proposed a new approach to innovation, which we call Organized Innovation.[9] It is a blueprint that goes beyond previous approaches to innovation to better equip leaders who are tasked with promoting innovation success. We see university leaders, government policymakers, and business executives as the organizational architects of innovation.[10] We urge leaders to go beyond simply hiring bright individuals or promoting their connectivity via social network structures. As we discuss later, we emphasize that bundling the three organizational pillars of Organized Innovation - Channeled Curiosity, Boundary–Breaking Collaboration, and Orchestrated Commercialization - are necessary to refresh our nation's innovation ecosystem.

The Organized Innovation Framework

We look to the National Science Foundation's (NSF) Engineering Research Center (ERC) program as an example from which we could learn about optimal ways to organize and manage innovation.[11] It was founded to create boundary–spanning organizations - combining science and engineering departments within universities and connecting academia with industry. Over the past 25 years, the NSF has funded nearly 50 ERCs across the country with an overall investment of roughly $1 billion. ERC funding demonstrates a terrific return on investment. The market value of ERC innovations to the U.S. economy is well into the tens of billions of dollars, and ERCs have generated over 140 new firms.[12]

Using qualitative, survey, and archival performance data, we found that institutional leaders can – to a much greater extent than generally thought possible – organize the conditions for technology breakthroughs that lead to new products, companies, and world–leading industries. Indeed, our findings showed that the success of the ERCs stems, not from the popular notion that innovation comes from the solo genius whose insight cannot be planned, but from "organized" innovation – an interdisciplinary, hybrid approach to technology commercialization. These findings led us to propose the three pillars that comprise our framework of Organized Innovation or "three C's":

- Channeled Curiosity

- Boundary–breaking Collaboration

- Orchestrated Commercialization

Channeled Curiosity refers to the integration of curiosity–driven research, strategic planning, and understanding market demand.

Boundary–breaking Collaboration refers to a dismantling of traditional research and academic discipline, organizational, and occupational silos to spur creativity and problem solving.

Orchestrated Commercialization requires coordinating the range of players involved in technology commercialization, including researchers, entrepreneurs, financial investors (e.g., angel investors and venture capitalists), and corporations.

The Seminal Role of Boundary–Breaking Collaboration
Boundary–breaking collaboration is critical as people cross various types of intellectual, academic, occupational, and organizational barriers to work together in the pursuit of innovation. The main boundaries in question are traditional academic disciplines as well as institutional boundaries, especially those between universities and between universities and private sector companies. Boundaries can also exist among engineers, scientists, entrepreneurs, and investors. Of the three aspects of Organized Innovation, boundary–breaking collaboration perhaps focuses the most on how leaders can choreograph the organizational conditions that foster innovation.

Collaboration can spark initial insights by bringing together individuals with diverse perspectives. For example, including academic researchers in discussions with corporate employees and managers is critical for accelerating development of working prototypes.

Avenues to work interdependently across boundaries are increasing as companies leverage available technology. For example, in a study of over 2,600 IBM employees, each additional email contact was worth $948 in revenue for IBM.[13] This suggests that social connectedness enhances productivity. Going beyond simply having more interpersonal connections, leaders can facilitate meaningful connections by encouraging and formally or informally rewarding mutually symbiotic cooperation among employees who contribute complementary areas of expertise.

Leaders can first promote interdependence by requiring various departments or teams to work together as the foundation for new projects. Beyond requiring collaboration, leaders should persuasively communicate the importance and value of such interdependence to ensure all parties understand and willingly participate. To make collaboration more effective, leaders must support information flow across boundaries throughout the lifespan of the project and then reward performance based on effectively incorporating feedback and expertise from all parties involved. In these efforts, leaders themselves must be able to speak the "native language" of all parties involved; in other words, they must effectively communicate and translate across boundaries. Finally, trust is necessary for information to flow across distinct boundaries, and leaders can help promote trust among various parties by acting as a supportive bridge.

Take, for example, a case that we discussed in detail in Currall et al. Professor Kim Stelson has embodied the practice of bringing together different disciplines, as well as breaking down walls between academia and industry. To this end, he spearheaded an effort to establish an ERC at the University of Minnesota focused on fluid power in 2006. The Center for Compact and Efficient Fluid Power (CCEFP), like all ERCs, relies on a range of scholarly fields and has deep ties to industry as it pursues its mission to develop the next generation of efficient fluid power technologies, which has developed, for example, an energy–efficient excavator prototype that consumes just half the fuel of a standard digging truck.

Vital to its success is the way CCEFP has broken through typical scholarly and institutional silos. Researchers associated with the center have expertise in fields ranging from biomedical engineering and mechanical engineering to machine design, robotics, and aging. The roughly thirty professors and sixty graduate students involved in the center span seven universities, fifty private sector companies, including Caterpillar, John Deere, and ExxonMobil, and at least three countries.

This type of collaboration across boundaries isn't always easy. Scholars can be leery of working with researchers in other fields. Communication across disciplines and across institutions often is difficult. Meanwhile, corporate officials can be harsh in their criticism of academic research as well as impatient with the pace of scholarship. There are also sticky questions about intellectual property.

But straddling the various boundaries is worth it. In ERCs, our empirical results revealed that researchers were more 30 times more likely to generate patents in climates that fostered boundary spanning in terms of specific research projects, broader research areas, and academic disciplines. The importance of boundary spanning is no surprise to Kim Stelson at CCEFP. He cites the industry–university ties at his center as vital to its real–world successes. "Working with industry is challenging," he says. "But in the end it means your research can have a great impact." We believe that this type of boundary–breaking collaboration is emblematic of a re–energized American innovation ecosystem that will ensure that our economy produces the high–quality, high–paying jobs that ensure our future prosperity.

About University of California, Davis

The University of California, Davis is a public research university located in Davis, California, just west of Sacramento. The campus covers 7,309 acres (2,958 ha), making it the largest within the 10–campus University of California system. UC Davis also has the third–largest enrollment in the UC System after UCLA and UC Berkeley.

In their 2001 book on United States universities, Howard and Matthew Greene classified UC Davis as a Public Ivy, a publicly funded university considered as providing a quality of education comparable to those of the Ivy League. The 2015 U.S. News & World Report college rankings named UC Davis as the 9th–best public university in the United States, 38th nationally, and 4th–best of the UC schools, following UC Berkeley, UCLA, and UC San Diego. UC Davis is one of 62 members in the Association of American Universities.

About the Author

Steve Currall is the Chancellor's Advisor and Professor of Management at the University of California, Davis. He also serves as Chief Strategic Advisor, and member of the Board of Directors and Executive Committee, of the 10–campus University of California's Global Health Institute. Additional leadership roles: over five years as Dean of the Graduate School of Management at UC Davis during which time the School reached the highest ranking in its history, endowed chair holder, founding Chair of an academic department, and leadership of seven centers/institutes. A psychological scientist, Currall has conducted research and taught for over 25 years on organizational psychology topics such as innovation, emerging technologies, negotiation, and corporate governance.

Currall was lead author of a book on university–business–government collaboration entitled, *Organized Innovation: A Blueprint for Renewing America's Prosperity.* He is a Fellow of the American Association for the Advancement of Science. He has served as a member of the boards of BioHouston, Leadership in Medicine, Inc., and Nanotechnology Foundation of Texas. He has been quoted over 600 times in publications such as the *New York Times, Wall Street Journal, Washington Post, Financial Times,* and British Broadcasting Corporation television. He earned a Ph.D. from Cornell University, a M.Sc. from the London School of Economics and Political Science, and a B.A. (cum laude) from Baylor University.

Talent Pipeline Management:
An Employer–led Solution to Closing the Skills Gap
By: John R. McKernan Jr., President, U.S. Chamber of Commerce Foundation

Today, the stability of the American economy is facing a serious threat. The skills gap is impacting the ability of our companies to compete and grow in today's economy while shortcomings in our education and workforce development systems continue to widen the gap. Thus, an increasing number of students are struggling to manage their transition to employment and businesses are simultaneously desperate for new workers that can help them grow and succeed in the global economy.

Unsurprisingly, a recent survey by Adecco found that 92 percent of executives believe there is a serious gap in workforce skills and nearly half are missing out on growth opportunities as a result.[14] According to Manpower Group, 40 percent of U.S. employers are struggling to fill jobs.[15] Left unchanged, the supply of skilled workers will dwindle - leaving over 5 million jobs vacant by 2018, many of them in STEM fields.[16] Simply put, the skills gap is one of the greatest threats to American competitiveness both today and in the future.

For years, the skills gap has been discussed as an education issue and left to policymakers, educators, and administrators to fix. But as the top consumer of our education system, the private sector has a huge stake in this challenge and cannot afford to wait on the sidelines for others to find a solution. With nearly 54 percent of bachelor's degree holders 25 and under either unemployed or underemployed, the time for employers to act is now.[17]

The business community must be more involved. To that end, the U.S. Chamber of Commerce Foundation (USCCF) has launched a partnership with USA Funds to explore a new vision for demand–driven education and workforce systems - one that yields more effective employment transitions for students and a better prepared workforce for all employers.

This approach - a bold departure from prior practice - identifies how employers can lead the way by applying lessons learned from supply chain management to their education and workforce partnerships. We call it: *talent pipeline management*. Playing off of the increasingly sophisticated management of supply chains that employers are already using to source goods and services locally and globally, talent pipeline management similarly uses adaptive supply chain partnerships. It involves demand–driven relationships between the "end-use customer" (employers) and "suppliers" (education and workforce providers) to create and share value.

Moreover, the business community has the ability to lead the way. Employers control the greatest currency in today's education and workforce marketplace: *jobs*. By playing an expanded leadership role through talent supply chain partnerships, employers can exercise their investment and hiring to drive behavior among leading suppliers and achieve a more skilled workforce - benefitting individuals, institutions, and businesses.

Principles of Talent Pipeline Management

Drawing on lessons learned from supply chain management, talent pipeline management offers a promising new approach that is demand–driven and transformative for how employers engage education and workforce partners. In a white paper that was recently released by the U.S. Chamber of Commerce Foundation, we identify three foundational principles from which we build a new, employer–led education and workforce paradigm:

- Employers Drive Value Creation - Employers play a new leadership role as the end–customer in closing the skills gap for those jobs most critical to their competitiveness.

- Employers Organize and Manage Scalable Network Partnerships - Employers organize and manage flexible and responsive talent pipelines in partnership with their preferred education and workforce providers.

- Employer Measures and Incentives Drive Performance - Employers work collaboratively with their partners to develop measures and incentives designed to reinforce and improve performance across all partners.[18]

These principles applied require all of the stakeholders - employers, providers, students/workers, and policymakers - involved in managing a talent pipeline to rethink their role and how they engage with one another in the talent supply chain. Once employers begin to understand their role as the end–customers in managing talent supply chain partnerships, they can reshape the education and workforce systems as an extended chain of talent providers that prepare learners for careers in the most responsive and efficient way possible.

Case Study - Alcoa: Aligning Talent Strategy within the Company

Alcoa is a global leader in lightweight metals technology, engineering, and manufacturing and the world's third–largest producer of aluminum. Through the contributions of its Foundation - over $22M in 2013 and more than $590M since its founding in 1952 - Alcoa strengthens its ties to these communities by supporting non–profit programs that promote environmental sustainability and train the next generation of manufacturers. Yet despite the company's philanthropic and corporate efforts to build its workforce, an internal needs assessment showed that Alcoa did not have the breadth or depth of talent in place to meet its business demands. The critical implications of this issue prompted Alcoa to rethink the alignment between its talent and foundation strategies in 2014, resulting in an internal reorganization where Alcoa Foundation began reporting directly to the company's Human Resources department.

With its new structure in place, Alcoa's talent management strategies focus on meeting the company's internal skill needs while also supporting broader skill development in the communities in which it operates. An example of this dual–purpose investment is in Barberton, Ohio, where Alcoa manufactures forge aluminum wheels and where qualified entry–level talent is in short supply. Through a grant provided by the Foundation, a local non–profit partner was able to assess the core skills required for entry–level positions in manufacturing, take inventory of local providers that could equip people with these skills, and determine an effective approach to preparing entry–level talent for the workforce. The result has been a more qualified workforce for all of the areas manufacturers, including Alcoa. Alcoa has since replicated investments like that in Barberton around the globe, leading to larger pools with the right skills and stronger local talent supply chains.[19]

Join the Movement

Companies across America are already leading the way. Alcoa is a leading example of what an employer can accomplish when they organize around a talent supply chain approach and link their education and workforce investments to their business strategy. However, employers need not tackle the skills gap on their own.

About the Author

Former Maine Gov. John R. McKernan Jr. is president of the U.S. Chamber of Commerce Foundation and a senior adviser to U.S. Chamber President and Chief Operating Officer Thomas J. Donohue. McKernan provides both strategic and ongoing leadership to the U.S. Chamber of Commerce Foundation, which is dedicated to strengthening America's long–term competitiveness by addressing developments that affect our nation, our economy, and the global business environment. As senior adviser, he counsels Donohue on a broad range of issues impacting the business community.

McKernan also serves as chairman and Chief Operating Officer of consulting and investment firms McKernan Enterprises, Inc. and Nottingham Equity, Inc. in Portland, Maine. Until August 2012, he was chairman of the board of directors of Education Management Corporation where he served as Chief Operating Officer from 2003 to 2007 and still serves as a director. Education Management has more than 130,000 students as of October 2012, 20,000 employees, and $2.8 billion in revenue. It is among the largest providers of postsecondary education in North America based on student enrollment and revenue. McKernan serves on the boards of directors of BorgWarner, Inc., Houghton Mifflin Harcourt, and the American Action Forum, a Washington, D.C., policy institute.

He is also chairman of the board of directors of the Foundation for Maine's Community Colleges. He served his native state of Maine for two terms in the U.S. Congress from 1983 to 1987 and then as governor for two, four–year terms from 1987 to 1995. During his two terms as governor, McKernan was chairman of the Education Commission of the States and the National Education Goals Panel and was recognized as an Outstanding Governor by the American Society for Training and Development. He is the author of *Making the Grade*, a book on youth apprenticeship. McKernan has a B.A. from Dartmouth College and a J.D. from the University of Maine School of Law. He and his wife, former U.S. Senator Olympia J. Snowe (R–Maine), reside in Falmouth, Maine, and in Washington, D.C.

Scaling the Number of STEM Professionals
By: Steven M. Rothstein, Chief Executive Officer, Citizen Schools

The United States has a long, proud history of excellence in STEM. Today more than ever before, America's economic growth depends upon continued success in these fields. However, the country's STEM talent pipeline is currently insufficient and lacks the diversity necessary to meet the challenges of the 21st century. For our economy to reach its full potential we have to invest in the STEM talent pipeline, especially with students from underrepresented groups.

At US2020, an operating division of Citizen Schools, we work to dramatically scale the number of STEM professionals mentoring and teaching students through hands–on projects, with a focus on serving underrepresented youth. We partner with companies, schools, non–profits, government agencies, and communities across the country in an effort to reveal the promise and the possibility of STEM.

Research has shown that student interest in STEM has been found to be more strongly predictive of the pursuit of a STEM degree than academic achievement. Yet a Lemelson–MIT survey found that the majority of teenagers may be discouraged from pursuing STEM careers because they do not know anyone who works in these fields and they do not understand what people in these fields do. A 2012 study by The Girl Scout Research Institute found that although the majority of girls are interested in STEM–related subjects, they are far less likely to choose a STEM career; this disparity is, in part, due to gender stereotypes and negative STEM associations. Minority girls in particular have had less exposure to STEM and less adult support for pursuing STEM fields.

Quality mentorship is uniquely positioned to address the barriers to pursuing STEM careers the lack of exposure to STEM and the lack of connections to STEM professionals. Research has shown that having adult role models, specifically mentors, provides academic and emotional benefits for students, particularly at–risk youth. Additional studies concluded that students engaged with STEM professionals have more confidence in their STEM capabilities and more knowledge of STEM careers.

US2020's education partners provide mentorship opportunities for students to engage with STEM professionals through hands–on activities and projects. Particularly within the sciences, multiple studies have shown that hands–on activities lead to greater student interest in science, and greater motivation to do science. Perhaps most importantly, students' interest persisted long after participation in the hands–on activities had ended.

Citizen Schools has engaged STEM professionals in hands–on, multisession apprenticeships with middle school students in low income communities for the past 20 years. In 2011–2012, Citizen Schools conducted a study and found that after participating in STEM apprenticeships, 80 percent of 8th grade students expressed interest in STEM fields and careers – more than double the national average of 33 percent.

At US2020, in conjunction with our many partners, we believe that if we can scale the number of STEM mentors engaging with students in high quality, multi–session, experiential learning opportunities, we can significantly increase inspiration and achievement in STEM education and the pursuit of STEM careers. US2020 is proud to partner with best–in–class organizations in this effort, including Girl Scouts, Citizen Schools, Boys and Girls Clubs, MentorNet, 4–H, Spark, Project Lead the Way, Million Women Mentors (MWM), and many other organizations.

US2020 launched at the 2013 White House Science Fair, with the mission to dramatically scale the number of STEM professionals mentoring and teaching students, especially those who have been traditionally underrepresented in STEM fields. US2020 has been building a network of more than 250 organizations in 10 cities actively working together to develop local STEM Mentoring movements and is building a STEM Mentor matching website to facilitate the volunteerism of STEM professionals. Other key initiatives include the following, business and higher education can support and move all of these forward:

- **Setting an ambitious goal to rally the corporate community** – All of US2020's work is in service of their core vision: a United States with one million STEM professionals annually mentoring students in meaningful ways by the year 2020. US2020, in partnership with many others, is working to form local STEM Mentoring movements, and built a STEM Mentor matching website to facilitate the volunteerism of STEM professionals. This new announcement builds on accomplishments that include:

- **Working closely with cities** – In 2013, US2020 ran a competition asking cross–sectorial coalitions from across the country for plans to increase STEM Mentoring in their community. This competition led to the creation of public/private coalitions in 52 cities across the nation and engaged over 600 companies and civic organizations in the work of scaling STEM mentorship. From that competition emerged the US2020 City Network, a collaborative community of city partners developing movements at the local level, including: Allentown, PA; Baton Rouge, LA; Boston, MA; Chicago, IL; Indianapolis, IN; Philadelphia, PA; Research Triangle Park, NC; San Francisco, CA; Tulsa, OK; Wichita, KS. The coalitions of these 10 leading cities include over 250 companies and organizations working to connect STEM professionals with opportunities to teach and mentor students.

- **Building a cohort on the ground mobilizers** – US2020 was one of the first recipients of a cohort of AmeriCorps VISTA members as part of the Corporation for National and Community Service's (CNCS) new STEM AmeriCorps program. CNCS committed 25 AmeriCorps VISTA members to US2020, an investment of more than $550,000, and these capacity–builders are now deployed in 8 cities across the country and actively engaging more communities and volunteers in this important work. Through the work of these VISTA members, US2020 is building a blueprint for how service corps members can be a key part of sparking local STEM Mentoring movements.

- **Creating an online platform to match professionals with volunteering opportunities** – In partnership with pro–bono developer Tata Consultancy Services, US2020 is creating an online platform that matches industry professionals with mentoring programs. The platform will include the use of five core badges that US2020 is implementing in an effort to badge the STEM mentoring field.

- **Creating a media campaign to promote STEM volunteering** – Discovery Communications, US2020's communications partner, developed a Public Service Announcement that highlighted the importance of STEM mentoring and aired nationally across Discovery's portfolio of 13 U.S. networks recently.

We are excited to work with local, state and federal government agencies, groups including, non–profit agencies, educational agencies, high educational institutions, several valued corporate partners and many others to create opportunities for every children to learn about the exciting and engagement from writing computer code, learning the practical applications of algebra in cooking, carpentry and other fields, the amazement of science and the human body. By engaging mentors who in turn will engage students throughout our nation we will advance a jobs-driven economy.

About Citizen Schools
Citizen Schools is dedicated to helping all children discover and achieve their dreams. They mobilize a team to enable public middle schools in low–income communities to provide a longer learning day rich with opportunities. Their deep partnerships with schools put young adults on track to succeed by connecting the resources of communities, companies, governments, and philanthropies.

Citizen Schools is an American non–profit organization that partners with middle schools across the United States to expand the learning day for low–income children. Its stated mission is "educating children and strengthening communities". Currently, Citizen Schools serves over 4,400 students and recruits over 4,000 volunteers over 31 program sites in 17 cities across 8 states. The center pieces of the Citizen Schools model are its apprenticeship programs run by volunteers that culminate in public demonstrations called WOW!s, and partnering with some middle schools to expand learning time for students. Citizen Schools offers the AmeriCorps National Teaching Fellowship providing a 2–year leadership development program with an optional enrollment in a Master's program in out–of–school learning.

About the Author
Steven M. Rothstein started as Chief Operating Officer of Citizen Schools in September 2014. Citizen Schools is a national non–profit organization that partners with middle schools to expand the learning day for children in low–income communities. Citizen Schools mobilizes a team of AmeriCorps educators and volunteer "Citizen Teachers" to teach real–world learning projects and provide academic support in order to help all students discover and achieve their dreams. For more information visit www.citizenschools.org . US2020 is an operating division of Citizen Schools. www.us2020.org

He recently completed over 11 years as President of Perkins School for the Blind. During his tenure, Perkins grew from serving 40,000 people to roughly 900,000 people throughout the U.S. and in 67 countries around the world. Perkins started to grow hundreds of schools worldwide, completed its largest capital campaign in its 185 years of service, built more buildings on campus in 100 years and significantly expanded its teacher training, technology and educational programs. Steven graduated from Williams College and received an MBA from Northeastern University.

Crucial Principles Every Board Should Know About a Jobs-Driven Economy
By: J. Noah Brown, President and Chief Executive Officer,
Association of Community College Trustees

How Community College Boards Can Advance a Jobs–Driven Economy
Community Colleges are governed by boards of trustees, one–third of whom are either elected by voters from within their communities, with the remaining two–thirds appointed by a publicly elected official (usually a state governor). The trustees who make up any given college board may vary greatly on an individual basis; however, members of each board all share a unique connection in that they are all active and vital members of their local communities. In many cases, they are prominent business or community–service leaders who have a vested interest in the economic health of the community.

Likewise, the community and technical colleges overseen by governing boards are anchored in their local economies and workforces. The majority of nurses, first responders, and other public community–service professionals, for example, attain their degrees and certifications at community or technical colleges. And a great number of community colleges have established strong ties to businesses in their communities, forging partnerships that allow them to tailor educational programs directly to the needs of an employer, with the employer guaranteeing employment for those who complete a degree or certificate.

Board Roles and Responsibilities
Where the president, other administrators, and faculty are under the employ of the college, responsible for executing and implementing day–to–day activities, trustees are responsible to the larger community - the residents, businesses, and charitable organizations outside of the college. They are responsible for knowing community needs and trends, engaging with that community, debating and discussing college issues in public, and generally serving the public good. College boards set the policy direction of the college only after seeking out and integrating multiple perspectives when making policy decisions. In short, it is the board operating as a unit, integrating multiple perspectives, speaking with one voice, and with all members supporting the decision of the board once it is made, that has true authority over of the college on behalf of the entire community.

Overall, a board is responsible for setting and enforcing policies, selecting and evaluating the college chief executive officer - usually a president or chancellor - and advocating on behalf of the college at the local, state, and federal levels.

The Board's Role in Advancing a Jobs–Driven Economy
As suggested by the board's roles and responsibilities discussed above, a community college board has dual responsibilities to the community at large and the institutional community. While all colleges and universities are responsible to a degree for making sure students are prepared for work when they graduate, this is especially true of community and, most especially, technical colleges. Oftentimes, degree and certificate programs exist primarily to train students for existing or emerging jobs that require special skills. This is particularly true for STEM occupations and manufacturing sectors, where specific skills and competencies must be tied to specific industries and employer needs. So what, specifically, is the responsibility of the board in advancing a jobs–driven economy?

- **Know the needs of businesses in the community.** Trustees should be aware of their local economies - specifically, are any local businesses unable to find qualified employees for existing jobs? In many cases, the community college can serve a role in training students for these unfilled positions.

- **Help bring new businesses to the community.** Through networking, advocacy, and promotion, community college board members often have the opportunity to engage with businesses. Because of their direct ties with the local community, these boards also know what the community has to offer to businesses.

- **Monitor institutional performance.** Traditionally, most community college boards equated institutional performance with enrollment rates. Today, most boards are becoming more familiar with institutional performance data, and creating and enforcing policies that support the practicalities of a jobs–driven economy. It is still useful for boards to monitor enrollments in technical programs, eliminating those that perform poorly, and creating opportunities for new programs that will meet local workforce demands.

- **Focus on STEM.** Environmental, medical, and technical engineering are just a few of the fastest–growing job markets projected in coming years; without question, STEM education is the foundation of a greater number of jobs than ever before. Community college boards have a responsibility to make sure their institutions' course offerings include and prioritize STEM–related courses, and especially those that are designed to prepare students for real–world jobs.

- **Build partnerships with K–12 schools.** Whenever possible, community college boards should partner with K–12 schools to align programs - particularly match, science, and English curricula - to curb the need for remediation, which remains a primary responsibility of community colleges, and which often prevents students from persisting in higher education.

- **Consider nontraditional approaches to remediation.** While remediation remains a necessity for many students who enter community colleges, many colleges are implementing new policies designed to keep students engaged. The non–profit Complete College America is recommending changing from a pre–requisite entrance policy to a co–requisite policy - so that if a student scores poorly on a math placement test, for example, but scores well on the English language exam, that student would be able to take regular non–math courses while completing necessary developmental courses in mathematics at the same time. This approach can keep students engaged and prevent stopping out and dropping out and increase the likelihood of attaining a practically applicable credential.

- **Support legislation that strengthens workforce development.** The Association of Community College Trustees (ACCT) advocates in Washington, D.C. on behalf of community college boards throughout the country. ACCT always supports, and urges college boards to support, legislation such as the new Workforce Investment and Opportunity Act, Community College to

Career Fund, Adult Education and Family Literacy Act, Trade Adjustment Assistance Act Community College and Career Training Grant Program, and other jobs–driven legislation that supports community college students.

- **Support programs that strengthen STEM education.** College boards should also be aware of and encourage their members of Congress to support programs such as the National Science Foundation's Advanced Technological Education (ATE) program and other programs that emphasize STEM and assist community and technical colleges in meeting the needs of manufacturing and other sectors dependent upon workers with skills and competencies developed through STEM education and training.

About The Association of Community College Trustees

The Association of Community College Trustees (ACCT) is a not–for–profit educational organization of governing boards, representing more than 6,500 elected and appointed trustees who govern over 1,200 community, technical, and junior colleges in the United States and beyond. Located in Washington, D.C., ACCT is a major voice of community college trustees to the presidential administration, U.S. Congress, the Departments of Education and Labor and more.

ACCT educates community and technical college trustees through annual conferences focused on leadership development and advocacy, as well as through publications, online, face–to–face institutes and seminars, and high quality supporting services to boards.

About the Author

J. Noah Brown is a widely recognized and award–winning higher education policy and governance expert, author, and educator whose experience spans more than 30 years in the nation's capital working in the non–profit sector. Noah has served as president and chief executive officer of the Association of Community College Trustees (ACCT) since 2005, and has worked for the association since 1996. He also serves on the faculty for the Doctorate in Community College Leadership program at Ferris State University in Michigan. Noah's inaugural book, *First in the World: Community Colleges and America's Future*, won the 2013 Bellwether Book Award.

Noah has earned a reputation as a popular speaker at a wide array of events, including college commencement and convocation ceremonies, international conferences, state college association conventions and other events. He has been featured in PARADE magazine's "Intelligence Report" and has contributed writing to a number of publications, currently serving as a contributing columnist to FE News, one of the United Kingdom's foremost further–education publications, and is a regular commentator for Higher Education Talk Radio.

Noah holds a Bachelor of Arts in Philosophy from the University of Michigan, Ann Arbor, a Master of Public Policy degree from the University of Maryland, College Park, and an Honorary Associate of Arts from Atlantic Cape Community College in New Jersey.

Why "Work Smart, Not Hard" is the Worst Advice in the World
By: Mike Rowe, TV host, Writer, Narrator, Producer, Actor and Spokesman

"Not all knowledge comes from college, but skill is a matter of degree."

Work Smart NOT Hard

When people hear me say that, they immediately assume that I am anti-college. I'm not. I'm anti-debt and I've pretty much always been so. When I was 17 my high school guidance counselor tried to talk me into going on to earn a four–year degree. I had nothing against college, but the universities that Mr. Dunbar recommended were expensive, and I had no idea what I wanted to study. I thought a community college made more sense, but Mr. Dunbar said a two–year school was "beneath my potential." He pointed to a poster hanging behind his desk: On one side of the poster was a beaten–down, depressed–looking blue–collar worker; on the other side was an optimistic college graduate with his eyes on the horizon. Underneath, the text read: Work Smart NOT Hard. "Mike, look at these two guys," Mr. Dunbar said. "Which one do you want to be?" I had to read the caption twice. Work Smart NOT Hard?

Back then universities were promoting themselves aggressively, and propaganda like this was all over the place. Did it work? Well, it worked for colleges, that's for sure. Enrollments soared. But at the same time, trade schools faltered. Vocational classes began to vanish from high schools. Apprenticeship programs and community colleges became examples of "alternative education," vocational consolation prizes for those who weren't "college material."

Today student loans eclipse $1 trillion. There's high unemployment among recent college graduates, and most graduates with jobs are not even working in their field of study. And we have a skills gap. At last count, 3 million jobs are currently available that either no one can do, or no one seems to want. How crazy is that?

I think often about the people I met on Dirty Jobs. Most of them were tradesmen. Many were entrepreneurs and innovators. Some were millionaires. People are always surprised to hear that, because we no longer equate dirt with success. But we should.

I remember Bob Combs, a modest pig farmer who fabricated from scratch a massive contraption in his backyard that changed the face of modern recycling in Las Vegas by using the casino food–waste stream to feed his animals. He was offered $75 million for his operation and turned it down. He's a tradesman.

Then there was Matt Freund, a dairy farmer in Connecticut who thought his cows' manure might be more valuable than their milk, and who built an ingenious machine that makes biodegradable flowerpots out of cow crap. He now sells millions of CowPots all over the world. He's a tradesman.

Mostly, I remember hundreds of men and women who loved their jobs and worked their butts off: welders, mechanics, electricians, plumbers. I've met them in every state, and seen firsthand a pride of workmanship that simply doesn't exist in most "cleaner" industries. And I've wondered, why aren't they on a poster? Why aren't we encouraging the benefits of working smart AND hard?

The skills gap is bad news for the economy, but it also presents an opportunity. Some time ago I ran into a woman named Mary Kaye Cashman, who runs a Caterpillar dealership in Las Vegas, and she told me they had more than 20 openings for heavy–equipment technicians. That's kind of astonishing. A heavy–equipment technician with real–world experience can earn upward of six figures. And the training program is free! But still the positions go unfilled? In a state with 9.6 percent unemployment? What's going on?

Here's a theory: What if "Work Smart NOT Hard" is not just a platitude on a poster? What if it's something we actually believe? I know it's a cliché, but clichés are repeated every day by millions of people. Is it possible that a whole generation has taken the worst advice in the world?

Work Smart NOT Hard

Look again at the image on this poster, which I reproduced just the way I remember it. Those stereotypes are still with us. We're still lending billions of dollars we don't have to kids who can't pay it back in order to educate them for jobs that no longer exist. We still have 3 million jobs we can't fill. Maybe it's the legacy of a society that would rather work smart than hard.

I recently launched a modest campaign that's an attempt to get people talking about the skilled trades in a more balanced way. If you're not opposed to a little tasteful vandalism, check out my updated version of Mr. Dunbar's poster on ProfoundlyDisconnected.com the image might amuse you, but the caption is no joke - Work Smart AND Hard.

I don't know if changing one little word in one stupid slogan will reinvigorate the skilled trades. I just think it's time for a new cliché. My own trade - such as it is - started with an "alternative education," purchased for a reasonable price at a two–year school. I suspect a lot of others could benefit from a similar road. So get a poster and hang it high. And if you see Mr. Dunbar, tell him I turned out okay.

P.S. If you or someone you know are interested in the trades, check out mikeroweworks. com and see if there are scholarships currently available. However, be warned that you will need to sign the SWEAT Pledge. Yeah, I know…some people might find the notion of signing a Pledge to be silly. Others might philosophically disagree with its content. Well, if that's the case, the particular pile of free money offered by mikeroweWORKS is not for you. Remember – mikeroweWORKS is not just a Scholarship Fund – it's a PR Campaign for hard work and skilled labor. Taking The SWEAT Pledge is a simple but important part of that campaign. If you can't bring yourself to take the SWEAT Pledge, you will not qualify for any mrW Scholarship. It's non–negotiable.

"The S.W.E.A.T. Pledge"
(Skill & Work Ethic Aren't Taboo)

1. I believe that I have won the greatest lottery of all time. I am alive. I walk the Earth. I live in America. Above all things, I am grateful.

2. I believe that I am entitled to life, liberty, and the pursuit of happiness. Nothing more. I also understand that "happiness" and the "pursuit of happiness" are not the same thing.

3. I believe there is no such thing as a "bad job." I believe that all jobs are opportunities, and it's up to me to make the best of them.

4. I do not "follow my passion." I bring it with me. I believe that any job can be done with passion and enthusiasm.

5. I deplore debt, and do all I can to avoid it. I would rather live in a tent and eat beans than borrow money to pay for a lifestyle I can't afford.

6. I believe that my safety is my responsibility. I understand that being in "compliance" does not necessarily mean I'm out of danger.

7. I believe the best way to distinguish myself at work is to show up early, stay late, and cheerfully volunteer for every crappy task there is.

8. I believe the most annoying sounds in the world are whining and complaining. I will never make them. If I am unhappy in my work, I will either find a new job, or find a way to be happy.

9. I believe that my education is my responsibility, and absolutely critical to my success. I am resolved to learn as much as I can from whatever source is available to me. I will never stop learning, and understand that library cards are free.

10. . I believe that I am a product of my choices – not my circumstances. I will never blame anyone for my shortcomings or the challenges I face. And I will never accept the credit for something I didn't do.

11. I understand the world is not fair, and I'm OK with that. I do not resent the success of others.

12. I believe that all people are created equal. I also believe that all people make choices. Some choose to be lazy. Some choose to sleep in. I choose to work my butt off.

On my honor, I hereby affirm the above statements to be an accurate summation of my personal worldview. I promise to live by them.

Signed _____ Date _____

About the Author

Mike Rowe is a TV host, writer, narrator, producer, actor and spokesman. His performing career began in 1984, when he faked his way into the Baltimore Opera to get his union card and meet girls, both of which he accomplished during a performance of Rigoletto. His transition to television occurred in 1990 when - to settle a bet - he auditioned for the QVC Shopping Channel and was promptly hired after talking about a pencil for nearly eight minutes.

Thanks to QVC, Mike became practiced at the art of talking for long periods without saying anything of substance, a skill that would serve him well as a TV host. Then, through a horrible miscalculation, he pitched a three–hour special to the Discovery Channel that ended up resulting in the show "Dirty Jobs."

Over the next decade, Mike would become known as "the dirtiest man on TV." He traveled to all 50 states and completed 300 different jobs, transforming cable television into a landscape of swamps, sewers, ice roads, coalmines, oil derricks, crab boats, hillbillies, and lumberjack camps. For this, he has received both the credit and the blame.

Mike runs the mikeroweWORKS Foundation, which awards scholarships to students pursuing a career in the skilled trades. He is closely associated with the Future Farmers of America (FFA), Skills USA, and the Boy Scouts of America, who honored him as a Distinguished Eagle Scout. For reasons he cannot explain, Forbes identified Mike as one of the country's 10 Most Trustworthy Celebrities in 2010, 2011 and 2012.

In addition to his foundation, Mike's website, mikeroweWORKS.com, focuses on all the issues related to the widening skills gap, aging workforce, high unemployment and millions of unfilled jobs.

Currently, Mike is in production for his new show, "Somebody's Gotta Do It" which debuted October 8, 2014 on CNN (Wednesdays at 9 pm). From CNN's pressroom blog: Rowe's new series Somebody's Gotta Do It, brings viewers face–to–face with men and women who march to the beat of a different drum. In each episode, Rowe visits unique individuals and joins them in their respective undertakings, paying tribute to innovators, do–gooders, entrepreneurs, collectors, and fanatics–people who simply have to do it.

CHAPTER TWO

Nurturing Innovation

"An innovation has no value until an ambitious entrepreneur builds a business model around it and turns it into a product or service that customers will buy."

— Jim Clifton, Chairman and Chief Executive Officer
Gallup

From STEMconnector® Advancing a Jobs-Driven Economy National Leaders Summit, on October 7-8, 2014, Washington, DC

Innovation Excellence: The Turbocharged Engine that
Powers Sustainable Enterprise Growth
By: Dr. Heidi Kleinbach–Sauter, Senior Vice President of Global Foods R&D, PepsiCo

A decade ago, few Americans were familiar with the acronym "STEM" - other than to associate it with the stalk of a plant. Today, across government, industry, the education sector, the non–profit sector and the news media, the acronym is instantly understood. We have made remarkable progress in a short time.

Our success in putting STEM on the national agenda is a testament to the tenacity of its proponents' unwavering belief that STEM innovation must be unleashed. As Microsoft founder Bill Gates noted, "If the United States truly wants to secure its global leadership in technology innovation, we must, as a nation, commit to a strategy for innovation excellence - a set of initiatives and policies that will provide the foundation for American competitive strength in the years ahead."[20]

The first wave of STEM engagement, defined as STEM 1.0, rightly focused on strengthening the STEM education system and inculcating in young people STEM skills. The next phase, STEM 2.0, which we are entering now, marks a crucial turning point in how schools and employers are collaborating to make the transition from classroom to career seamless.

To be sure, this is easier said than done.

The highly technical "hard" STEM skills relevant for tomorrow's new economy are not easily acquired. Indeed, employers continue to struggle to fill 26 million STEM–related jobs in the U.S. with a limited supply of qualified candidates.

And while employers welcome candidates who satisfy their often-exacting requirements, new STEM hires must understand that technical proficiency in their field is merely "table stakes." The real work begins the first day of work, when new STEM hires are expected to transform their academic skills into actual products and services others are willing to pay for.

While technical STEM skills are crucial, complementing them with business–relevant skills is the key differentiator between a valued employee and invaluable one.

Accordingly, STEMconnector®'s Innovation Task Force (SITF), a thirty–five–plus member consortium working to develop new pathways to STEM careers, has identified Innovation Excellence as the engine that will propel sustainable enterprise growth.

In our culture, we celebrate inventors - from Thomas Edison in his lab, to Steve Wozniak and Steve Jobs in the garage. While these remarkable individuals can and do change the world, so too can teams inside established companies - provided they recognize that a creative spark is just the start, and must be supported by a robust innovation process that transforms an idea into a commercial offering. This evolution requires a shift from focusing on solving complex technical problems to defining and redefining the right problem before solving it - and doing this in the context of the market and business environment of the future.

Within my company, for example, we view innovation as a catalytic force that transforms the company, its portfolio, and the industry. With rigor and discipline, every day, our STEM–trained R&D colleagues drive PepsiCo's business by providing unrivaled technical skills and solutions to offer more enjoyable and nutritious foods and beverages to more people, in more places, engendering more trust worldwide. As an academy R&D organization, we use experts to drive science, technology and innovation thought leadership. And through a combination of deep consumer insight and unmatched product design, we work closely with PepsiCo business partners to deliver on today's brand and market priorities as well as the growth opportunities of tomorrow.

Of course, my R&D colleagues at PepsiCo - and across multiple industries - must constantly look ahead. From the employer's perspective, that means identifying and developing next–generation STEM talent. And the best way to accomplish that, many believe, is by closing the gap between the often binary worlds of "school" and "work."

In the past, schools concerned themselves with skills impartation. Teachers transferred learning to receptive students in a one–way intellectual transaction. Alternatively, in the workplace, students were called upon - often for the first time, and often on the first day - to lead information transactions. The roles were reversed. The new STEM employee had to "educate" peers and supervisors about the salience of his or her ideas and innovations. Thus the transition between school and the workplace, for many, was no easy feat. And while some companies offered transitional guidance for their new hires; just as many did not. The result was a "sink or swim" career environment where - despite entering the workplace with equal technical credentials - some STEM employees flourished and others stalled.

Because we want every prospective STEM practitioner to flourish in the employment marketplace, SITF, after intensive discussions with key stakeholders, is convinced that career– focused experiential learning can convert academic knowledge into value creation in the workplace.

To facilitate this in the U.S., in March 2014, SITF and PepsiCo piloted an event called "STEM Career Accelerator Day," which offered a firsthand look at how STEM translates from the classroom to the workplace.

Conducted simultaneously at corporate workplaces, on university campuses, and online, the event brought together 4,300 U.S. high school students, their parents and teachers, Arizona State University and corporations such as PepsiCo, Honeywell and Tata Consultancy Services (TCS).

Participants were introduced to the concept of "Excellence in Innovation" - specifically, the discrete scientific steps and critical employability skills (such as leadership and shepherding an idea through complex matrix structures) that propel a product from drawing board to commercialization and final purchase. Students received insights into jobs and STEM skills needed for these jobs. Along with mentoring by seasoned STEM professionals, students also participated in hands–on activities designed to bridge the gap between academic theory and commercial action.

At PepsiCo, STEM scientists and others in R&D openly discussed the innovation process for new products, and how six new products - among them Gatorade Frost Glacier Cherry, Tostitos Cantina tortilla chips and Muller Quaker Yogurt - evolved from "interesting idea" to products now tracking to achieve major annual retail sales in the U.S. Next, students were challenged to apply their STEM knowledge - and experience "Innovation Excellence" in action - by creating new food and beverage products themselves.

Our pilot proved immensely successful. Moving forward, more schools, more students and more companies will partner to expand the initiatives reach. In 2015, for example, Career Accelerator Day will be expanded to become Career Accelerator Week, with events occurring nationally over the course of a five–day period, from October 19–23. At PepsiCo, we will increase student exposure to our facilities - from the three R&D centers we opened up to students in 2014 to many more additional corporate locations in 2015 - with an aim to conduct STEM events at 20 sites by 2020.

The emergence of STEM 2.0 is creating tremendous opportunity for everyone concerned about STEM - from teachers and students to employers. But there is still much work to be done. The goals of SITF are bold and disruptive - as the best innovations are - and will require SIFT and key stakeholders to continue collaborating closely. Yet I am convinced the rewards will be worth the work: the introduction of new workplace–related skills, imparted in a "career focused experiential learning" environment, will be the key unlock to accelerating the transition of STEM 1.0 knowledge into a STEM 2.0 innovation economy - yielding handsome dividends for all.

Our commitment, as a nation, to inculcate in students a deep culture of Innovation Excellence will require actions between educators and the private sector to offer a portfolio of "career focused experiential learning" opportunities to enable a jobs-driven economy.

About PepsiCo

PepsiCo is a global food and beverage leader with net revenues of over $66 billion and a product portfolio including 22 brands that generate over $1 billion each in annual retail sales. PepsiCo's people are united by our unique commitment to sustainable growth by investing in a healthier future for people and our planet, which we also believe means a more successful future for PepsiCo. We call this commitment Performance with Purpose: PepsiCo's promise to provide a wide range of foods and beverages from treats to healthy eats; to minimize our impact on the environment; to provide a great workplace for our associates; and to respect, support and invest in the local communities where we operate.

PepsiCo is a leading partner in STEMconnector®, with whom it collaborated to start up the STEM Innovation Task Force and launched the "STEM Career Accelerator Day" in 2014, all in partnership with a large public/private consortium of stakeholders. Further, PepsiCo strives to create more STEM opportunities for the future generation of STEM talent, and founded a PepsiCo STEM council in 2014. PepsiCo is demonstrating strong support to females with its participation in the STEMconnector® Million Women Mentors (MWM) program. PepsiCo is also a Founding Partner in the Global STEM Alliance, an initiative of the New York Academy of Sciences, in partnership with governments, industry, philanthropists, schools, NGOs, and leading academic institutions around the world to address education, innovation, and workforce challenges of the 21st century.

About the Author

Dr. Heidi Kleinbach–Sauter is Senior Vice President of PepsiCo's Global Foods R&D, where she is globally responsible for PepsiCo's worldwide innovation platforms for savory snacks and overall food business.

With more than 25 years innovation and R&D experience in the CPG Foods and Beverages industry, she has a proven track record of identifying innovation opportunities, leading and commercializing a large number of food and beverage innovations in more than 10 different consumer goods categories that have delighted consumers in many parts of the world and have driven impressive business results.

Dr. Kleinbach–Sauter served as chair of STEMconnector®'s Innovation Task Force from 2013-2014 and currently serves on also serves on STEMconnector®'s Food & Ag Council. In 2012, she was named among the "Top 100 Women Leaders in STEM".

Dr. Kleinbach–Sauter earned her PhD, Master's and Bachelor's Degree in Food Science, Food Technology and Nutrition from the Universities of Hohenheim and Giessen in Germany. She has also studied Marketing Management, Consumer Behavior at the State University of New York at Albany, Product Development at the University of Tennessee at Knoxville and completed the TGMP General Manager Program at Harvard Business School.

Education at the Speed of Business
By: Stan Elliot, Director of The Missouri Innovation Campus,
University of Central Missouri

The Missouri Innovation Campus
Through the MIC, students receive their associate degree from Metropolitan Community College in Lee's Summit, Mo., soon after earning their high–school diploma, and are on track to earn a bachelor's degree from UCM in high–tech, high–demand STEM–related fields just two years later. Remarkably, students participating in the program will also complete their associate and bachelor's degrees at almost no cost to the students or their families. The MIC has three programs: information technology (IT) essentials, digital electronics and software development.

The MIC is open to students within the Lee's Summit R–7 School District as well as students who attend any of 19 sending high schools, located within the Kansas City metropolitan area's Missouri side. Currently, the school includes approximately 60 students from 10 school districts. The first cohort of students enrolled in The MIC received their high–school diplomas last spring and their associate degrees this summer. They began their remaining two years in the program at UCM in fall 2014. In addition to the program's accelerated timeframe and financial advantages, students are able to develop job–ready skills through internships with high–tech companies.

What is The Missouri Innovation Campus (MIC)?
The MIC is a collaborative effort of business partners, the Lee's Summit R–7 School District, Metropolitan Community College& the University of Central Missouri.

The goals are:

- Reduce the cost of a college degree

- Reduce the amount of time required to get a degree

- Provide a trained workforce with specific skill sets required by business and industry

- Reduce student debt and increase degree completion rates

How does The MIC programming align to the goals and outcome?
The MIC is an accelerated model where students begin their junior year of high school and go year-round for four years, saving two years of college costs and entering the workforce earlier. Upon high school graduation, they will also have completed their AAS degree or by the end of the summer semester and then complete their B.S. degree in the final two years.

The MIC program curriculum is developed collaboratively by business partners along with instructors from the Lee's Summit R–7 Summit Technology Academy, MCC, and UCM. Their process insures these competencies meet industry standards and employer demands in the workforce.

The MIC Curriculum development process has been utilized with all current MIC programs, which consist of:

- Systems Engineering Technology (Networking)

- Engineering Technology/Design & Drafting

- Software Development/Computer Science

Along with developing the MIC curriculum, MIC Business Partners also provide paid internships over the last three years of the four–year program. The partners also pay an annual per intern fee to the MIC and that funding source pays the AAS tuition for the student. The final two years are paid through a combination of internship funds, scholarships, and financial aid. MIC internships begin the summer after a student's junior year and continue through degree completion.

How can the MIC be replicated and taken to scale?
Replication of the MIC requires early identification of students interested in STEM careers and a seamless articulation of high school, community college and four–year institutions curriculum and instructional programming. Dual–credit, dual enrollment and online courses must be provided for degree acceleration. Developing internship and curriculum development opportunities with business partners in the STEM field is a prerequisite for replication as well.

Is there evidence of the MIC program success?
As the MIC program enters its third year, indicators of success would be program growth (student enrollment) and the increase of MIC Business Partners as well as student retention rates, which are above 90 percent. Student enrollment has gone from 17 in 2012–2013 to 50 for 2014–15 academic years. The number of business partners has more than doubled in each of the program years.

A jobs-driven economy may or may not depend on the institution that confers your degree, your major, GPA or even class rank. For our nation to recapture its economic competitiveness or potential, the required outcomes of college must clearly demonstrate skills, abilities, talents or competencies based in creativity and innovation, while at the same time ensuring that the college graduates are workforce ready with their degrees.

Action Items

If college costs too much; takes too long; confers degrees that do not make college graduates workforce ready; and requires students to borrow in order to access, then the requirements to compete in a job–driven economy are severely limited. And, perhaps as an enterprise, the analogy of higher education as one step away from print journalism or travel agents may be so close that it hurts. However, with the tools available now, we can turn the focus of the enterprise to learner–centered outcomes, and it is more realistic to see that the vast resources represented by America's colleges and universities can be positioned to provide and equip the talent required to drive the economic potential that we share as a nation. We see this vision clearly stated by the Lumina Foundation and others who point to a "big goal" of 60 percent of our citizens with a college degree or professional certification. This underlines the value of college and the requirements to utilize the "Prefountaine principle" of running as fast as we can and then picking up our speed. We are required to provide college that is accessible on the basis of both ability and willingness to pay. We must double our efforts to ensure that those who access college cross the finish line with a degree in four years or perhaps less. And most importantly, within a jobs–driven economy, we are required to define student success in terms of skills and competencies required in a future–focused world.

The new jobs for the economy have one prerequisite that must be inverted within the traditional model to truly provide learner–centered outcomes, especially in high-demand STEM fields where the required skills and partnership must be defined in collaboration with those that will hire our graduates. This collaboration will result in a greater sense of shared responsibilities for these outcomes. As the Gallup Organization continues to advocate, access to mentors, advisors, and coaches, coupled with internship opportunities that will create more value for our students and the outcomes required to produce the future–focused leaders, we will shape and drive the jobs-driven economy.

About University of Central Missouri

The University of Central Missouri (formerly Central Missouri State University) is a four–year public institution in Warrensburg, Missouri, United States. The university serves nearly 13,000 students from 49 states and 59 countries on its 1,561 acre campus. UCM offers 150 programs of study, including 10 pre–professional programs, 27 areas of teacher certification and 37 graduate programs. Students also have the ability to study abroad in about 60 different countries in the world through the International Center.

About the Author

Stan Elliott is the first Director of The Missouri Innovation Campus, being named to that position in July 2012. Prior moving into this position, Stan served the Lee's Summit, MO R–7 School District for 33 years in a variety of leadership roles. He taught high school biology and was science department chair, served as an assistant principal at Lee's Summit High School, and then was named principal to open Lee's Summit North High School in 1994. In 2005, Stan was appointed Assistant Superintendent of Secondary Instruction, supervising three high schools, three middle schools, the Summit Technology Academy, and the district's alternative school.

Mr. Elliott was named Missouri High School Principal of the year in 2001. He has also presented at the state, national, and international level on a variety of educational initiatives including data based decision–making, school portfolios, at–risk student programs and school improvement plans. Stan also is a consultant for the International Baccalaureate organization.

Stan received his bachelor's degree in biology and science education from Truman State University along with a master's degree in biology. He received his education specialist's degree in Secondary Administration from the University of Missouri–Kansas City.

As Director of The Missouri Innovation Campus program, Stan is responsible for curriculum and program development, business partner development, student recruitment, and the MIC student internship program.

Exciting Research Careers: The Sometimes Forgotten STEM Careers
By: Dr. Dean Evasius, Director of Scientific Assessment
and Workforce Development,
Oak Ridge Associated Universities (ORAU)

The contrast is striking. The future has never looked brighter for a variety of STEM research careers. Yet there is persistent evidence that these exciting careers are failing to attract broad segments of our population, especially among women and minorities.

The need is compelling. Research and development activities are the key drivers of innovation and global competitiveness in the 21st century, and the STEM disciplines are the core of the innovation ecosystem. The Task Force on American Innovation states this clearly in a March 2014 letter. "Our international competitors have recognized what economists have been reporting for some time: science and technology are the principal drivers of economic growth." The letter goes on to state: "To succeed in the world of the 21st century, we must also make science attractive to the best and brightest students in an increasingly diverse America. We must provide the workforce of the future with both the resources and opportunities that will enable them to make transformational discoveries and create game–changing innovations."[21]

In a 2010 report, the National Science Board addressed the need for the United States to develop the next generation of STEM innovators: "The National Science Board firmly believes that to ensure the long–term prosperity of our Nation, we must renew our collective commitment to excellence in education and the development of scientific talent. The nation needs STEM Innovators - those individuals who have developed the expertise to become leading STEM professionals and perhaps the creators of significant breakthroughs or advances in scientific and technical understanding."[22]

There is an abundance of high–level policy documents that announce the urgent need for promoting STEM research careers. While arguments based upon national imperatives are important, they are not the only evidence that STEM disciplines lead to promising career paths. The annual best jobs list published by Forbes makes its case to the individual job seeker. The list is based on a formula created by CareerCast that considers a number of factors contributing to job quality and satisfaction. The top ten jobs for 2014 are overwhelming based in the mathematical sciences and the health sciences.

Forbes list of best jobs for 2014 include:[23]

1. Mathematician
2. Tenured University Professor
3. Statistician
4. Actuary
5. Audiologist

6. Dental Hygienist
7. Software Engineer
8. Computer Systems Analyst
9. Occupational Therapist
10. Speech Pathologist

What's especially exciting is the emerging evidence that STEM career paths are a common denominator among highly achieving women. When Fortune published its 2014 list of most powerful women in business they noted an interesting finding. "Here's another lesser–known commonality about the women at the very top of the list: almost all of them majored in seriously hard sciences." The remarkable women cited by Fortune include Ginni Rometty (IBM), Ellen Kullman (DuPont), Indra Nooyi (PepsiCo), Meg Whitman (HP), and Marissa Mayer (Yahoo).

The writers at Fortune go on to observe a somewhat troubling paradox. "What's remarkable about this is that these women were choosing these fields of study decades ago. Right now, tech is the engine of our economy. And even still, we have paucity of young women and girls in STEM fields."

This illustrates the core issue we must address if we are to advance a jobs–driven economy. We need cooperative partnerships between corporations, higher education, and government agencies that ensure a diverse pipeline of STEM researchers for our nation.

The mathematical sciences, which dominate the top of the Forbes list of best jobs, exemplify our challenge. Mathematics is a critical indicator because of its fundamental role in STEM and other professions. A solid background in mathematics is widely assumed as a preparation for STEM careers, and there is also strong evidence that training in mathematics is important for admission to graduate study in business and law. The entrance examinations for these programs emphasize math skills and logical thinking. Undergraduate mathematics majors as a group consistently score at or near the top on these exams.

Despite the evidence for the importance of the mathematical sciences as a career pathway, the demographics of the mathematics pipeline remain stubbornly uneven. Women and minorities now make up nearly 70 percent of the college students in the United States, and this number will continue to rise. Women and minorities represent the key demographics for the future of all STEM fields, yet they continue to be significantly underrepresented in the mathematical sciences.

According to the American Mathematical Society, the percentage of doctorates in the mathematical sciences awarded to U.S. women has been declining over the past decade: from 35 percent in 2004 to 28 percent in 2013. The numbers for minorities are even more discouraging. Among the 857 doctorates in the mathematical sciences (including statistics) awarded to U.S. citizens in 2013, just 24 doctorates were awarded to African Americans, and only 25 were awarded to Hispanic Americans.[24]

It's illuminating to place these numbers in a global context. The 2010 U.S. Census identifies 40.3M Americans as Black or African American, and 50.4 million Americans as Hispanic. A 2009 report by the International Mathematical Union, Mathematics in Africa: Challenges and Opportunities, provides estimates for the production of mathematics doctorates in Africa.

The numbers in the table below, taken from the IMU report, suggest that the United States is producing African American doctorates at a per–capita rate that is lower than the doctoral production of Algeria, Benin, Cameroon, and Tunisia. The conclusion is clear: The United States must create more and better pathways to research careers in the mathematical sciences for women and minorities.[25]

Country	2007 Population (millions)	Math doctorates awarded in 2007
Algeria	33.3	38
Tunisia	10.3	38
Kenya	36.9	21
Cameroon	18.1	26
Benin	8.1	29

The data at the undergraduate level show a similar need for action. According to the National Science Foundation, over a nearly 40 year period from 1966 to 2003 the percentage of bachelor's degrees in the mathematical and computer sciences awarded to women remained above 30 percent, ranging from a low of 30.4 percent to a high of 39.5 percent. That percentage fell below 30 percent in 2004, and has since declined to 25.6 percent in 2010. The trend in computer science is especially dire. The number of undergraduate computer science degrees awarded to women declined 44 percent between 2002 and 2011, from 13,690 to 7,700.

Over the same period, 2002–2011, the number of bachelor's degrees awarded to African Americans in all fields increased 45 percent, from 111,330 to 161,005. Yet the number of degrees in math and statistics did not increase and the number of degrees in computer science actually declined. In 2011, just 0.5 percent of the bachelor's degrees awarded to African Americans were in mathematics or statistics.

Bachelor's Degrees Awarded African Americans 2002–2011 (National Science Foundation)[26]

Year	All Fields	Computer Science	Math and Statistics
2002	111,330	5,057	843
2003	117,902	6,083	790
2004	123,636	6,259	783
2005	127,978	5,815	855
2006	133,743	5,275	847
2007	137,556	4,588	832
2008	142,576	4,011	796
2009	145,988	3,868	842
2010	152,404	4,066	834
2011	161,005	4,418	821

The future prosperity of our nation depends on a robust supply of STEM researchers and innovators. Yet the existing pipeline for these career paths is woefully misaligned with the demographic trends of our country. There are limits to the amount of STEM talent we can import from around the globe. We urgently need the education, non–profit, and government sectors to work with corporations to create a collaborative infrastructure for developing the STEM workforce.

Here are two examples that can serve as models. Volkswagen, ORAU, Oak Ridge National Laboratory, and five Tennessee colleges and universities are working together to bridge the gap between cutting edge scientific research and automotive manufacturing. The leading incubator of high tech start–ups, Y Combinator, is partnering with ORAU's HBCU/MEI Council and the Department of Energy to help develop the next generation of minority STEM entrepreneurs.

These examples are demonstrations of the actions that we need to take: 1) encourage cooperative partnerships between corporations, higher education, and government agencies that support fundamental and applied research that is supported by and applicable to business and industry, and 2) support the new generation of entrepreneurs and businesses that will provide the next generation of transformational discoveries and create game–changing innovations.

There are plenty of successful examples of these partnerships. What we need is an infrastructure that allows them to scale and multiply. The STEM 2.0 initiative provides an excellent framework for building these partnerships. Let's get started!

About Oak Ridge Associated Universities (ORAU)

ORAU provides innovative scientific and technical solutions to advance national priorities in science, health, education and national security.

From our 114–member university consortium to our strategic partnerships with the Department of Energy and Oak Ridge National Laboratory (ORNL), we bring together university faculty and students to collaborate on major scientific initiatives that help keep America on the leading edge of science and technology.

Our nation needs a steady supply of scientists and engineers to meet future needs in critical science and technology areas. Students in STEM fields need the skills, knowledge, and experience to stay competitive in an ever–changing global marketplace. To address these national workforce and science education needs, ORAU provides a comprehensive resource for developing and administering high–quality, research–based and experience–based programs. We partner with government agencies, higher education institutions, and corporations to fill the pipeline with the next generation of science and technology leaders. Last year alone, we supported more than 8,000 students and faculty who took part in internship, scholarship, and fellowship programs that either provided further direction for their careers or encouraged them to pursue degrees in areas of critical national need.

About the Author

Dr. Dean Evasius is a Senior Vice President at ORAU, where he is the Director of Scientific Assessment and Workforce Development. He joined ORAU in August 2012. He is responsible for the leadership of ORAU's $260M portfolio of peer review and science education programs.

He previously served as Senior Advisor for Science and Head of the Office of Multidisciplinary Activities at the National Science Foundation. He also served as a Program Director in the Division of Mathematical Sciences at NSF for eight years. Prior to his time at NSF he was a research mathematician for the National Security Agency. He holds a Ph.D. in mathematics from the California Institute of Technology.

The TechShop Case Study: Inspiring STEM through Making
By: Dr. Mitzi Montoya, Vice President and
University Dean of Entrepreneurship & Innovation, Arizona State University

ASU is the first university in the world to partner with TechShop. TechShop is a membership–based do–it–yourself facility that provides the public with tools, equipment, training and a vibrant supportive community of makers. Through this partnership, ASU and TechShop collocated a facility called the Chandler Innovation Center located in Chandler, AZ. The center hosts TechShop and an ASU engineering and technology education hub that holds classes for ASU student, corporate partnership and community groups.

As a physical embodiment of the maker movement, the center provides makers with workspace and state–of–the–art prototyping tools including plasma cutters, a water jet, 3D printers, laser printers, CNC routers, and other industry–standard tools. In total, this partnership places over $1M in equipment in the hands of student and community makers.

ASU provides free memberships to any full–time ASU student and reduced memberships to faculty, staff and alumni who apply for memberships. To date, over 600 ASU students have activated memberships and student startup companies have launched prototypes for consumer products at TechShop. Over 1,500 K–12 students in the Phoenix region have participated in STEM camps, tours and workshops at TechShop. Though ASU is the first and only university to enter into a partnership with TechShop, the company is located in cities throughout the U.S. and thus, similar public–private partnership between TechShop and higher education institutions is replicated.

The ASU Teaching Innovation Fellows Program: Supporting K–12 innovation
The ASU Teaching Innovation Fellows Program supports high school educators – Fellows – by embedding innovation and applied community–based projects into their curriculum. The program provides a structure for Fellows of a variety of disciplines to learn applied project methodologies. The program is an adaptable platform to leverage content expertise from across the university. Fellows engage in a customized experience that match their academic expertise, including sustainability, computer science, engineering, biology, and more, dependent upon school and sponsor goals.

The Verizon Foundation partnered with ASU to create the inaugural cohort of Fellows – the Innovation through Design Thinking (iDT) Fellows – who are learning how to teach design–thinking, innovation, entrepreneurship and STEM skill–building in their high school classes. Students in the iDT Fellows' high school classes will collaborate with local businesses to solve real–world challenges by creating mobile apps that meet their needs.

The Teaching Innovation Fellows program was made possible through a $620K grant from the Verizon Foundation. With additional corporate sponsorship, this model can be replicated and scaled to include new cohorts that meet the programmatic needs of the sponsor and the educational goals of ASU.

The Alexandria Innovation Network: Transforming the role of museums and libraries

The Alexandria Innovation Network is a collaborative network of libraries, museums and community partners that advance and promote local innovation and entrepreneurship through open–access knowledge sharing. The partners in the network provide members of the community with broad access to continuing education in entrepreneurship, mentorship, service providers and other community–based resources for current and aspiring small–business owners. The network is a repository of open resources and a network for sharing best practices in advancing local and regional entrepreneurship and innovation.

ASU was awarded a $250K grant from the Institute of Museum and Library Services to grow the Alexandria Innovation Network. Currently, four libraries in the Phoenix region are members of the network. With additional grants through new partnerships, ASU plans on expanding the network to 40 libraries by 2016.

The Women's Entrepreneurship Initiative: Inspiring Women Business Ownership

The Women's Entrepreneurship Initiative at ASU provides a student accelerator program designed specifically for ASU student entrepreneurs whose companies are founded and led by women. Housed within the award winning Edson Student Entrepreneur Initiative, the Women's Entrepreneurship Initiative provides office space, seed money, mentorship opportunities and training specifically tailored for women entrepreneurs with scalable ideas.

Entering its tenth year, the Edson Student Entrepreneur Initiative has supported over 260 student teams and over 1,000 students. Edson is a highly responsive, individualized, and student-centered entrepreneurship program that delivers economic, social, and educational impact in real–time.

ASU was awarded over $225K in external grants from JPMorgan Chase and the U.S. Small Business Administration to create the Women's Entrepreneurship Initiative. With this grant, ASU partnered with the Think Global Institute to launch its first Phoenix–based cohort of women business owners. Think Global Institute hand selects women-owned businesses that are in revenue and provides mentorship and business development training to help business–owners scale their operations.

About Arizona State University

Arizona State University (ASU) is committed to growing an innovative enterprise within a public university system. ASU students, faculty and staff in every discipline and at every level work to identify community needs, articulate how to meet them and implement innovative solutions. ASU infuses innovative programs and initiatives throughout the university and the communities we serve to create a culture of innovation that is woven into the fabric of the university, permeating every activity.

Arizona State University has developed high impact partnerships to help support this commitment to innovation. These partnerships develop new pipelines of talent to STEM careers and entrepreneurship to help advance a jobs-driven economy. Through these partnerships, ASU is better positioned to transform the way in which a university can affect change.

About the Author

Dr. Mitzi M. Montoya is Vice President and University Dean of Entrepreneurship & Innovation at Arizona State University. She is a Professor in the Management Department of the W.P. Carey School of Business and serves on the board of the Center for Entrepreneurship. Dr. Montoya received her Ph.D. in Marketing and Statistics and a B.S. in Applied Engineering Science, both from Michigan State University.

Dr. Montoya is responsible for advancing ASU as a leader in entrepreneurship and innovation, including supporting student and faculty entrepreneurship, enhancing the entrepreneurial ecosystem, and driving innovative collaborative initiatives across ASU. Previously at ASU, Dr. Montoya served as Dean of the College of Technology & Innovation and Vice Provost of the ASU Polytechnic campus. She led the development of a new model for higher education that embedded hands–on, real–world projects in the curriculum in partnership with industry and the community. Dr. Montoya established ASU as a national leader in the growing maker movement and developed public–private partnerships to advance both higher education and the regional innovation system, including development of a public open prototyping facility that unites the community, local companies and the university. In Arizona, Dr. Montoya established the Aerospace & Defense Research Collaboratory, a state wide platform for collaboration across the aerospace and defense supply chain and research institutions, and she currently leads ASU's USAID–sponsored global training program for clean energy.

CHAPTER THREE

Partnerships That Drive Success

"CHS and the CHS Foundation have placed a high priority on building and sustaining innovative partnerships between education and industry which maximizes the potential of STEM education to help meet future workforce needs."

– William J. Nelson, Vice President, Corporate Citizenship, CHS Inc. and President, CHS Foundation

Note: *Advancing a Jobs-Driven Economy* is filled with partnership models. We encourage you to view all submissions as successful, viable, and replicable models.

Cementing the Link: Creating Real Partnerships between
Community Colleges and STEM Employers
By: Mary Wright, Program Director, Building Economic Opportunity,
Jobs for the Future

Across the country, employers struggle to find workers with the skill sets they require. Despite a 5.8 percent national unemployment rate, which translates to nearly 9 million workers, there are approximately 4.7 million unfilled jobs.[27] This "skills gap" is reported by the majority of employers regardless of industry and affects their ability to find employees who are ready to work.[28] At the same time, potential employees also lament the inability to find a job using the skills they worked to obtain, believing that these skills would lead them to viable employment.

This skill mismatch leads to an unprepared workforce, and costs the U.S. economy billions of dollars in lost revenues. As an example, The Manufacturing Institute estimates that failure to fill 600,000 jobs due to lack of qualified workers can cost the economy $67.8 billion in exports, $47.4 billion in foreign investment and $8.5 billion in lost research and development.[29] It also requires employers to skill–up their workforce. According to estimates of the American Society for Training and Development in 2012, $164 billion was spent on corporate training.[30] While the portion of these costs attributed to remedial education is difficult to estimate, General Motors estimates remedial training is 15 percent of its overall training budget.[31] This suggests that remedial education is costing U.S. businesses nearly $25 billion. Furthermore, The Conference Board's 2009 Research Report The *Ill–Prepared U.S. Workforce* finds that, of the 46 percent of firms that offer workforce readiness training, most believe that providing this training should not be their responsibility, and many believe that it is not cost-effective.

More important, however, are the costs to the nation's unprepared workforce. Nine million Americans are out of work, struggling to get the education and training needed to enter good jobs that pay family-supporting wages.

Middle skill STEM jobs offer an opportunity to address this skills gap and improve employment outcomes for the nation's under–skilled and underprepared students. While STEM is the subject of frequent and heated disputes over labor shortages at the PhD level, middle–skill STEM opportunities have not received adequate attention until a recent Brookings Institution report revealed a "hidden" STEM economy. Brookings estimates that one in five jobs in the United States are STEM jobs - 20 percent of all employment. Half of these jobs, 13 million in 2011, are available to workers with less than a baccalaureate degree, and pay a premium; at $53,000 the average wage is 10 percent higher than the average wage for all jobs with similar educational requirements.[32] Most often, individuals are prepared for these jobs through a community college. Given the disproportionately high enrollment of low–income, minority, and first–generation college–going students in community colleges, pathways to STEM jobs can be particularly effective routes to economic stability for underserved populations, and could ultimately help reduce the nation's income, wealth, and educational attainment inequalities.

Matching the students in our community colleges to middle–skill STEM jobs can go a long way toward closing the skills gap. But to do this right requires an overhaul of the existing partnerships between community colleges and employers.

Two Core Recommendations

A fundamental disconnect between employers on the demand side and postsecondary education on the supply side exacerbates unemployment and the skills gap.[33] From an employer perspective, postsecondary education fails to provide students with the skills required to perform minimum job requirements. A recent Gallup Poll suggests that only 11 percent of employers strongly agree that new college graduates have the skills necessary to succeed in the workplace.[34] However, a recent survey conducted by Inside Higher Education indicates that 96 percent of university academic officers believe that schools are effectively preparing students for success in the workplace.[35]

To address this disconnect, Jobs for the Future advocates:

- **Community colleges must get serious about a new approach to employer engagement.** More and more leading companies are partnering with colleges and universities to help provide ideas on how to revise their curricula so that students will acquire the necessary skills as a strategy to bridge the gap between supply and demand.[36] However, these partnerships require significant time and investment. All too often, employers complain that educational partners move too slowly, waste their time, and rehash the same content at meetings. JFF is working to develop a dramatically different approach to college engagement of employers through a number of initiatives, including the National Fund for Workforce Solutions and the STEM Regional Collaboratives. These initiatives are applying strict standards to employer engagement, encouraging colleges to develop tight agendas, communicate strategically and regularly, deliver content that employers need, ensure that meetings end with clear to–dos, and design follow–up meeting agendas that deliberately build on previous progress.

- **Employers must be more active partners.** Employers can flip their traditional role, and supply schools with the content to teach the skills they seek in their employees. Through the newly organized College Employer Collaborative, a partnership between JFF and CorpU, a leading provider of online education, employers and community colleges will work together to deliver the skills that employers find most important. Employers will identify the desired skills and work with educators to determine the best way to deliver this online material; colleges will embed this material into their coursework. Care will be taken to include instruction in both technical and workforce readiness or applied skills to be sure that students have both the skills to perform on the job from a technical capacity but also have the capability to grow and advance professionally.

Conclusion

Improving the pre–employment pool requires the concerted effort of both employers and educators. Employers can view this as both a workforce effort, since creating better prepared job candidates saves significant time and expense, as well as a philanthropic effort, since it helps improve the readiness of all workers. Educators need to welcome the involvement of employers in sharing what they know best - content and skills required in the work world - and focus on what they do best - integrating the material into a supportive learning environment. By collaborating, all parties win. Educators provide the training that helps learners become the employees employers want to hire.

About Jobs for the Future

Jobs for the Future works to ensure that all underprepared young people and workers have the skills and credentials needed to succeed in today's economy by creating solutions that catalyze change in our education and workforce delivery systems. Working with our partners, JFF designs and drives the adoption of innovative and scalable education and career training models and systems that lead from college readiness to career advancement.

Jobs for the Future's STEM–related initiatives include partnerships in workforce development – including The Greenforce Initiative and GreenWays – which work to teach math and engineering skills to expand green sector job opportunities for low–income individuals. In partnership with Achieving the Dream, JFF is also building STEM Regional Collaboratives that bring together college leadership, faculty and staff, local employers, P–12 school partners, community organizations and state partners to create structured middle–skill STEM pathways designed to meet high demand in local labor markets. In addition, some of our Early College High Schools have focused on preparing young people for productive careers serving their region's STEM workforce needs while reducing achievement gaps in high school completion and improving college preparedness. JFF also develops and advocates for the federal and state policies needed to support these solutions.

About the Author

Mary Wright directs Jobs for the Future initiatives that help low–skilled adults move into and through postsecondary education and on to careers that pay family–sustaining wages. Specifically, she focuses on how to better link employer demands to the outcomes of training initiatives. One project is the Credentials That Work initiative, which leverages innovations in the collection and analysis of real–time labor market information to better align investments in education and training with the needs of the economy.

She also is spearheading the College Employer Collaborative, which will take employer–created online content to community colleges to help match the employer demand for skills to the supply of educated talent. Ms. Wright has more than 20 years of experience connecting the public and private sectors in municipal finance, government affairs, and workforce development. Before joining JFF, she served as director at The Conference Board in New York City, driving its work in workforce readiness, business, and education partnerships, as well as improving the employment outcomes for people with disabilities through research and convenings.

Her non–profit board experience includes organizations that support educational opportunities for underrepresented youth, housing options for low–income families, and the arts. Ms. Wright has an MBA in public/non–profit management from Columbia University and a Bachelor's degree in urban affairs from Connecticut College.

ACC Highland: Reshaping Education for Tomorrow's Workforce
By: Dr. Richard Rhodes, President and Chief Executive Officer,
Austin Community College

ACC Highland re–envisions the future of higher education. Imagine a state–of–the–art facility, stretching 1.2 million square feet, where Austin Community College brings innovative instruction, flexible training labs, business incubator space, public–private partnerships, and non–profit resources under one roof - all to benefit students and the communities the college serves.

It's happening now in a somewhat surprising location. ACC is transforming one of the first shopping centers in the Austin, Texas area - Highland Mall - into a new regional hub for higher education.

ACC's vision calls for refurbishing the Highland Mall property into a modern education space and center for community and business partnerships. Over the long term, space not used by the college will be available for mixed–use development, with the goal of creating a premier destination for lifelong learning, living, shopping, and entertainment.

Phase I: State–of–the–Art Campus Opens
The college's first renovation at Highland Mall converted 200,000 square feet of space formerly occupied by J.C. Penney. After breaking ground in spring 2013, ACC opened phase I of Highland Campus in August 2014 with almost 4,000 students. The campus offers a variety of options:

- Transferable core curriculum classes
- Developmental education to achieve college readiness
- Continuing Education to enhance job skills

The campus includes state–of–the–art classrooms, computer labs, study areas, library and media center, student commons, and ACCelerator – the nation's largest learning lab, providing more than 600 computer stations for individualized instruction through technology.

Using Technology to Help Students Succeed
Data from the U.S. Bureau of Labor Statistics and other sources show that STEM jobs will grow faster than other jobs over the next decade and pay overall higher wages for qualified employees. Many of these jobs will require a bachelor's degree or higher, but others will not. In fact, STEM jobs requiring an associate degree are one of the fastest growing job categories in the U.S. economy. While this is good news for students and presents a viable pathway to the middle class for many people, there is a significant barrier facing students across the country. Almost all high–growth, high–wage STEM occupations require significant math skills. Unfortunately, about 40 percent of students entering community colleges are not prepared for college–level math and must enroll in pre–college–level developmental courses. Most students who begin their college

experience in developmental math struggle through several years of non–credit bearing courses and eventually drop out. This is a serious problem for students and the regional economy, with large numbers of STEM jobs unfilled.[37]

ACC is using the Highland Campus ACCelerator to revolutionize developmental education and help more students earn credentials needed to succeed in the workforce. ACCelerator offers a new course, MATD 0421 (Developmental Math) that gives students the opportunity to complete more than one course, or possibly the entire developmental mathematics curriculum, in a single semester. If students need more time, they do not begin a new semester by studying skills already mastered. They begin wherever they stopped in the last semester.

The course uses adaptive learning software, called ALEKS, to customize coursework for each student. ALEKS is an artificially intelligent, adaptive learning program that assesses students to determine current skills and create a personalized learning plan. Students also receive individual attention from faculty, tutors and academic coaches during class and open lab time. This model allows each student to more efficiently and effectively address his or her specific knowledge deficiencies, providing an accelerated route to the higher–level courses required in STEM pathways.

Initial results from the inaugural semester are promising. The course withdrawal rate is 7.5 percent, compared with 20 percent in traditional developmental courses. Of the 706 students enrolled in week 14 of the 16–week semester, 97 percent had completed the one–semester basic arithmetic course, with 64 percent continuing into the elementary algebra course. Students have provided extremely positive qualitative feedback, praising the personalized instruction and the overall high–touch, high–tech approach of the course. These results support the idea that effective integration of technology with active and collaborative learning and personalized interactions with faculty results in students who are more likely to persist to their goals.

This innovative curriculum redesign will help greater numbers of students attain necessary math skills - resulting in more individuals entering high–growth STEM fields.

Phase II: Connecting Central Texans to Jobs

The college's academic master plan calls for a variety of programming for phase II of Highland, for both credit and Continuing Education students:

- Digital and creative media cluster
- Expanded information technology programs (traditional and competency–based instruction)
- Culinary and hospitality center
- Professional incubator space
- Advanced manufacturing center
- Regional workforce innovation center
- Regional health sciences center with STEM simulator lab

With the approval of a bond package in November 2014, this work is in progress. The conversion will be transformative, with the site offering a host of new, state–of–the–art spaces for instruction, research, and collaboration. A key aspect of the college's Highland planning involves making the facilities flexible - able to adapt to different training programs as the economy evolves and new industries come to the forefront.

The Power of the Public–Private Partnership

Recognizing that ACC will not need the entire Highland space for some time, the college sought a partner organization that aligns with the community college mission to lease a four–story, 194,000–square–foot space once occupied by Dillard's. ACC currently is developing a partnership with Rackspace Hosting, a global technology company that provides managed cloud hosting services to many Fortune 100 companies.

The partnership creates new opportunities for students in a high–demand field, enhances the college's technology training, and ultimately helps ensure a pipeline of skilled workers for the region. In turn, Rackspace, one of the region's top employers, will set up its offices at ACC Highland and benefit from proximity to the college.

This public–private partnership is a key aspect of what makes ACC Highland a new model for higher education. By bringing the college's industry partners on site, students can be immersed in their field of choice from the start, with real–world experiences enhancing what happens in the classroom. This venture takes the traditional concept of the internship and grows it to encompass the entire academic and career training process. Benefits to the college and its students include Rackspace–funded scholarships, internships, Rackspace guest lecturers and adjunct instructors, continuing education for ACC faculty, and on–campus job fairs.

Collaborations of this nature are essential in STEM fields, with the rapidity at which technology evolves. Through this agreement, ACC's curriculum and offerings will remain on the leading edge of developments in the information technology sector and ensure a new generation of tech workers with the skills and training in demand by today's employers. This kind of partnership is critical to reversing the nation's STEM skills gap.

Moving Forward

The college is using a variety of funding mechanisms to bring ACC Highland to fruition. ACC funded phase I through student tuition and fees. District taxpayers approved bond funding for phase II. The renovation of the property for the Rackspace partnership will be privately funded by the partner developer.

RedLeaf Properties, which has partnered with ACC for the transformation of the Highland site, is developing plans for the mixed–use component of the project. In addition to the 1.2 million square feet of classroom space, the site is eventually expected to include:
- 800,000 square feet of office space

- 150,000 square feet of retail space

- 1,200 residential units
- 200 hotel rooms
- 20,000 students
- 6,800 employees
- 1,800 residents

The overall Highland project is the product of collaboration with business and education partners, neighborhood groups, and community leaders. ACC's component of the project is revitalizing an Austin landmark while expanding access to higher education, improving student success, and training an elite workforce for Central Texas and beyond.

About Austin Community College

The Austin Community College District (ACC) mission is to provide higher education access to all who seek it, thus transforming lives and communities. Focused on student success and offering affordable, flexible pathways to help students reach their goals, ACC is a multi–campus community college system serving the Austin metropolitan area and surrounding Central Texas region. ACC maintains 11 campuses, several centers and sites, and distance learning options serving approximately 100,000 students in academic, continuing education, and adult education programs. The college offers associate degrees and career/technical certificate programs in 100+ areas of study. ACC also provides the majority of transfer students to regional universities including The University of Texas at Austin and Texas State University.

The primary trainer and re–trainer of the local workforce, ACC maintains partnerships with local industry leaders, universities, and community–based and government organizations to ensure quality education and training. Whether enabling the dreams of individuals or responding quickly to the training needs of local business and industry, ACC is a catalyst for economic development, social equity, and personal enrichment.

About the Author

Dr. Richard Rhodes is President and Chief Operating Officer of the Austin Community College District. He joined ACC in September 2011 after serving as President of El Paso Community College for 10 years. Dr. Rhodes, a Certified Public Accountant, received his Bachelor of Business Administration in Accounting and Master of Arts in Educational Management and Development from New Mexico State University. He earned his doctorate through the Community College Leadership Program (CCLP) at The University of Texas at Austin. CCLP honored Dr. Rhodes with its Distinguished Graduate Award in 2001.

Dr. Rhodes is the Current Chair of the Texas Association of Community Colleges. He is a member of the American Association of Community Colleges' 21st Century Commission on the Future of Community Colleges and the Formula Funding Advisory Committee for the Texas Higher Education Coordinating Board. Dr. Rhodes is also a board member of the Texas Workforce Investment Council, the Texas Guaranteed

Student Loan Corporation, the Carnegie Foundation, and Educational Testing Service National Community College Advisory Council. He is active in the community serving on numerous community boards including the Greater Austin Chamber of Commerce.

Dr. Rhodes' commitment to student success is unparalleled. He works to improve pathways into higher education, strengthen awareness of the community college mission, and give students the tools to accomplish their educational, professional, and personal goals. Dr. Rhodes has enhanced the college's partnerships, working closely with regional business and industry, other institutions of higher education, and school districts within ACC's service area.

Meeting Community Needs for World Class STEM Technicians
Alamo Academies Applied STEM Pathways
By: Dr. Bruce H. Leslie, Chancellor, The Alamo Colleges

An Industry, Higher Education, and Public Education STEM Collaborative: Educating America's youth in an industry–driven, technical program of studies; producing San Antonio's pipeline of World Class STEM Technicians for FAA mechanics, Cyber security, Nursing and Certified Manufacturing workers.

The Model
The Alamo Academies is an Applied STEM dual credit pathway program in which high school juniors and seniors attend tuition–free half–day classes taught by Alamo Colleges' faculty. They complete a paid internship, earn 31–34 college credits while still in high school and earn industry–recognized certification along with their high school diploma. Currently, the four academies – aerospace, advanced manufacturing, information technology and security and nursing – partner with more than 100 leading regional employers such as Lockheed Martin, Boeing, Toyota, Rackspace, Valero, 24th Air Force, CPS Energy, the city of San Antonio and 25 ISDs in the region.

Evidence of Success – Results
The Alamo Colleges Dual Credit Academies have an exceptional record of success in increasing student participation, postsecondary attainment and improving the earning prospects by 45 percent. 86 percent of students enrolled are economically disadvantaged and 71 percent are minority students. Students graduate with a degree or industry–recognized certificate within two years. 58 percent continue in higher education and 42 percent enter well–paid STEM careers. Completion rates are almost 20 times higher than the state certificate completion rates. In any comparison, student participation and success outcomes far exceed state norms by significant margins. 729 graduates (96 percent continued higher education [community college/4–year institution], obtained jobs with the Aerospace, Advanced Technology and Manufacturing or IT Industries, or joined the Military). The Class of 2012 earned over $545,000 scholarships. Last 3 classes over $1.7 Million in Scholarships. – Gender: Males–81 percent Female–19 percent. Ethnicity: Hispanic–66 percent, Caucasian–27 percent, African–American–5 percent, Asian–2 percent. Graduates starting pay approximately $34,700: Salary: $23,900 ($11.47 x 2080 hrs.) plus ~ $10,800 benefits.

Evidence of Success – Third Party Recognition
Alamo College Dual Credit Academies received the 2012 Texas Higher Education Star Award recognizing exceptional contributions toward meeting one or more of the goals of closing the Gaps by 2015, the Texas higher education plan adopted in October 2000. The Academies earned national recognition winning the 2012 National Championship at the annual Cyber–Patriot competition, the premier national high school cyber defense competition. Graduate Annette Enriquez was invited to participate in a national press conference with President Obama. The Federal Reserve Bank of Dallas recognized the Academies as an industry–driven workforce development model that is helping fix the

broken school–to–work pipeline. U.S. Secretary of Labor Hilda Solis also recognized the successful workforce model on her visit to the program on October 24, 2012.

Impact

The San Antonio Express News (April 9th, 2011) referred to as "perhaps the biggest education success story of the past decade in San Antonio" – as it not only gives students opportunities to discover and experience exciting STEM careers and develop advanced skills while in high school, but also provides a very real college and career pathway towards long–term employment in these high–growth occupations". Since 2005, the Academies have produced 729 graduates (96 percent continued higher education [community college/4–year institution], obtained jobs with the Aerospace, Advanced Technology and Manufacturing or IT Industries, or joined the Military).

Action Items for Higher Education

Reaching out to public education and business/industry are essential to meeting local workforce needs. Alamo Colleges is aligning the Academies Model to 16 ISD High School Endorsed Pathways. Under the new HB 5 – Texas Law, all high school students will have to declare an endorsed career pathway that may allow them to participate in STEM-based career and technology programs. Therefore the Alamo Colleges Academies could grow to an estimated 5,000-student academy pipeline. In the first year of the HB–5 legislation the Academy attained maximum enrollment of 550 students.

About Alamo Colleges

The Alamo Colleges serve the Bexar County community through their programs and services that help students succeed in acquiring the knowledge and skills needed in today's world. Students are taught by highly qualified faculty with Master's and doctorate degrees dedicated to creating a learning-centered environment. Student services include counseling, computer labs, tutoring, financial services, services for the disabled, developmental instruction, veteran's services, and job placement.

The five colleges - San Antonio (est. 1925), St. Philip's (est. 1898), Palo Alto (est. 1985), Northeast Lakeview (est. 2007), and Northwest Vista (est. 1995) - offer associate degrees, certificates and licensures in occupational programs that prepare students for jobs, as well as arts and science courses that transfer to four–year colleges and universities and lead to AA and AS degrees.

Bexar County voters elect the Alamo Colleges nine–member board of trustees locally to six–year terms. The Chancellor, the district's chief executive officer, guides and implements the programs and policies of the Alamo Colleges.

About the Author

Dr. Bruce H. Leslie assumed the duties of the Alamo Colleges' Chancellor on November 1, 2006. As Chancellor, he is the Chief Executive Officer of the Alamo Colleges, overseeing five colleges, with a student enrollment of over 60,000 credit and 30,000 continuing education students each semester. Prior to assuming the Chancellorship, Leslie served as Chancellor of the Houston Community College System, Chancellor of the Connecticut Community–Technical Colleges, a state system of 12 colleges, and as President of Onondaga Community College in Syracuse, New York.

Leslie earned his bachelor's degree from Baldwin–Wallace College in Ohio, master's degree from Sam Houston State University in Huntsville, Texas and, Ph.D. in Higher Education Administration from the Community College Leadership Program at the University of Texas at Austin.

Leslie also serves on the national board of the Council for Adult and Experiential Learning (CAEL), and is President of RC–2020. His numerous awards include the Association of Community College Trustees (ACCT) Western and Eastern Region Chief Executive Officer Awards, the ACCT Charles Kennedy Equity Award, the Phi Theta Kappa Shirley B. Gordon Leadership Award, the AARP Pinnacle Award for Service to Hurricane Katrina Evacuees, and the Diversity Leadership Award from the Center for the Healing of Racism.

Successful Partnerships Need Good Chemistry
By: Dr. Jean Goodnow, President, Delta College

Science Transfer Degrees and Chemical Process Technology

Delta College has a long partnership with The Dow Chemical Company through advisory committees, business training and financial contributions. We have a strong base of students pursuing associate degrees, with the goal of transferring on to four–year universities. Delta also initiated the Chemical Process Technician Program in 2002, and it offers associate degrees in Chemical Process Technology & Manufacturing and Industrial Technology.

A recent survey in the Great Lakes Bay Region (GLBR) indicated that 71 percent of employers had difficulties hiring STEM jobs within the last year. And, 53 percent indicated that applicant availability has prevented them from developing new products or services. Clearly, a focus on STEM education is critical for the GLBR's economic development.

The region's economy is diversifying into high–wage, high–skill and high–demand jobs in advanced manufacturing (primarily in the chemical industry) and alternative energy (primarily solar). And, Delta is well situated to be a leader in preparing workers for those jobs. With donated equipment and financial support, the College has worked with Dow to offer laboratory based training, featuring equipment similar to what is seen at many chemical manufacturing sites.

Fast Start

Delta has a non–credit training division called Corporate Services (DCCS), established decades ago to offer customized training. The global not–for–profit business unit provides nimble, cost–effective solutions for clients on a national and international basis. Based upon program content evaluation and input from employers, DCCS developed a new concept – Fast Start – during the economic recession.

Michigan added more than 68,000 manufacturing jobs in the past few years, the largest increase of any state in the country. Through partnerships with Dow, Dow Corning Corporation and Hemlock Semiconductor, Delta developed the award–winning "Fast Start" training model, focused on getting laid–off employees back to work as soon as possible.[38]

Fast Start training programs partner the College, Great Lakes Bay Michigan Works!, and regional businesses. Designed for individuals who commit to a full–time, 40 hour per week classroom experience with an additional ten hours per week outside of class, they provide potential employees who have technical skills. With job placement rates as high as 89 percent, they have won national awards for excellence.

Training through DCCS meets a growing need in our community. Based on the employer survey, nearly 60 percent of employers indicated that the highest level of education needed for hard–to–fill STEM positions was either a high school diploma, a one–year certificate or a two–year degree. With more than 50 percent of the survey's businesses indicating they could not find people with the right technical skills to perform the job, Delta remains in a strong position to step up and increase its training.

Dow partners with DCCS on a Chemical Process Operator Fast Start program. This accelerated, condensed training is designed to deliver just–in–time instruction to meet the company's hiring schedule and provide sufficient numbers of qualified job candidates as defined by the company.

Applicants must have achieved the appropriate skill levels according to the Work Keys technical skills assessment. Great Lakes Bay Michigan Works! (GLBMW) supplies the candidate pipeline by recruiting the best candidates and by offering training to help individuals meet program entry requirements. GLBMW provides funding for program tuition, so that employer customers have access to the very best candidates regardless of their ability to pay for training.

STEM Explorer

The Herbert H. and Grace A. Dow Foundation was established by the founders of Dow to support the region, with goals that often align between the foundation and the company. With 38 percent of the GLBR's GDP primarily driven by two STEM intensive industries – manufacturing and health care – even area foundations are focused on strengthening manufacturing education.

In late Fall 2014, Foundation Trustees donated $4 million to Delta for an innovative and unique project that has tremendous promise. Delta officials are excited that its "STEM Explorer" project will address these issues with and strengthen STEM education with middle and high school students throughout the entire region. The grant request was written to address key facets of the GLBR, including:

- 89 percent of parents rank STEM education to be important for their children's development

- 90 percent of teachers report their students have five or less exposures to STEM jobs each year

- 62 percent of principals indicated there are no STEM elective classes offered at their schools

A 38 foot recreational vehicle will be equipped for STEM exploration at events and schools for one day rapid hands–on activities to excite interest in STEM for all age groups, and it will also support long term, deep dive project based learning targeted to seventh through twelfth grades. The vehicle will feature state-of-the-art equipment for project–based learning and hands–on activities.

With 97 percent of all STEM jobs requiring foundational math skills, most area employers are finding that acquiring math proficiencies by 7th grade is critical. Research also shows that more engaging and connected content delivery methods can increase student interest in, and enthusiasm for, STEM topics. Through an interdisciplinary approach, along with partnerships with higher education and businesses, Delta will develop curricula and project–based activities to help reach beyond the walls of the classroom.

Delta faculty will also collaborate with K–12 educators to develop instructional content and offer professional development classes for middle– and high–school teachers. Again, referencing our recently completed GLBR STEM survey, Delta and area employers are now addressing the following findings through the STEM Explorer project:

- Strong math, science and literacy skills are the core competencies required for a strong STEM workforce

- Student achievement in math and science should increase significantly in the GLB Region to assure a STEM ready workforce

- Students at or below the poverty level have lower math achievement, however, there is equal room for improvement among all students for higher achievement in math

- School administrators and teachers are not always aligned on the STEM agenda and there has been limited STEM–focused professional development

Delta's STEM Explorer will bring investigative learning directly to the students at a time when they are planning their post–secondary path. It will use project–based learning to engage students in a wide variety of STEM areas, helping them make connections between what they are learning in school and how that learning will provide them with an educational path to STEM career opportunities. Finally, Delta will benefit through increased academic collaboration and strengthened community partnerships.

Examples for Other Community Colleges

Employers are actively looking for workers with specific job skills. Fast Start programs are simple to replicate and can be developed for any industry looking for workers. Jobs are not guaranteed, but placement rates for those who complete Fast Start programs are strong. Working collaboratively with business and industry, to determine needs and how best to meet them, is the key to ensuring success.

And, several universities are purchasing and outfitting large vehicles that reach out to their communities and provide STEM education. Finding funding is the difficult part but, once this hurdle has been addressed, the project can provide unique hands–on STEM resources for students of all ages. The secret to Delta's success has not only been locating the funding, but having buy–in with faculty who are serving as key players in the development and implementation of this unique project.

Call to Action
- Higher education institutions must be willing to respond to businesses and adapt their curricula to meet their training needs.

- Higher education institutions must be willing to respond in a "just–in–time" training fashion to skill up the workforce to meet the needs of today and tomorrow.

About Delta College

Delta College serves its region by educating, enriching, and empowering a diverse community of learners to achieve their personal, professional and academic goals. The College enrolls more than 15,000 students annually.

Located in mid–Michigan, Delta College offers students 150 transfer, career and certificate programs. The college leads the way in educating for vital fields like health care, technology and alternative energy. Thirty–two percent of its students plan to transfer on to earn their bachelor's.

About the Author

Dr. Jean Goodnow has been President of Delta College, located in the Great Lakes Bay Region of Michigan, since 2005. At the national level, Dr. Goodnow serves as Chair of the Board of the League for Innovation in the Community College and on the Steering Committee of the American College & University Presidents' Climate Commitment. She is a member of the STEMconnector® Higher Education Council, which partners with industry to provide a catalyst to meet the education and training needs of the global STEM workforce. Dr. Goodnow previously served on the Board of the American Association of Community Colleges and on its Sustainability Task Force and Commission on Diversity, Inclusion & Equity.

In Michigan, Dr. Goodnow is a member of the Michigan Community College Association, serving as past Treasurer. She received Second Nature's 1st Annual Climate Leadership Award for Outstanding Individual Climate Leadership, the Shirley Gordon Phi Theta Kappa National Award and the Community College Alliance Leadership Award. Delta College's Black Faculty & Staff selected her to receive The Spirit of Dr. Martin Luther King Jr. Award, and in 2013, the Saginaw County Branch of the NAACP paid special tribute to Dr. Goodnow for her lifetime achievement in higher education and community outreach.

Empty Seats, Open Jobs, Know More

By: Rob Denson, President, Des Moines Area Community College (DMACC) and Chair, STEM Higher Education Council; Grace Swanson, Vice President of Human Capital, Accumold; and Karen Stiles, Business Connections Consultant, DMACC

The Des Moines Area Community College (DMACC) Scholars Program is a partnership between area businesses and the community college. It was formed to create an opportunity for businesses to assist in the recruitment and training of their future workforce and at the same time help raise the general awareness of and enrollment in DMACC skilled trades programs.

The program was established in response to a growing companies' need for skilled workers. The process begins with business-assisted recruitment from the general population, followed by an application and selection procedure by the company. After the candidates are selected, the business sends them to DMACC for skill training, covers tuition for technical training courses, and offers part-time employment at the company on an "earn while you learn" model. Successful completion of the DMACC program qualifies graduates for a full-time position at the area business with a competitive salary and excellent advancement potential.

In 2006, DMACC's Scholars Program was launched with Accumold, a successful global manufacturer in Ankeny, Iowa, as the "Accumold Scholars Program". DMACC will be forever grateful to Roger Hargens, President of Accumold, for the idea and inspiration to create this successful model program.

Accumold is a high-tech manufacturer of micro-sized and small injection molded plastic parts and components. For more than 25 years Accumold has produced extremely small plastic parts with very complex geometries and tight tolerances. These parts are used in a variety of market sectors from consumer electronics, medical devices to top-secret military applications.

As the world of microelectronics continues to grow Accumold is well positioned to service the high demands of this market. Through revolutionary tooling and production practices Accumold has developed a unique process to produce these products sometimes by the millions. The Micro-Molder® was invented by the founders of Accumold for the sole purpose of supporting this industry.

The Company creates these parts and components for businesses all over the world. Much of what is produced on a daily basis is shipped outside the U.S. to manufacturing facilities from Mexico to Malaysia. This "little" company in Ankeny, IA with 200 employees, and growing, has truly developed a worldwide operation through state-of-the-art facilities, dedicated, smart employees and the spirit of an innovative culture.

The Accumold Tool & Die scholarship covers the technical credits required for the DMACC Machinist Diploma (1st year) and the Die Making Diploma (2nd year). The award is estimated at over $9,000. It is important to note that prior to the Accumold

Scholars Program, DMACC's program enrollment in Manufacturing and Tool & Die had been at about 50 percent of capacity, putting it at risk of reduction due to equipment cost. When DMACC had held recruitment information sessions for these programs few if any interested persons showed up. The first information session hosted by Accumold attracted 40 interested persons and DMACC's programs have remained at full capacity ever since. This showed DMACC the power of business-driven recruitment.

Accumold Evidence of Success

- Scholars work an average of 1000 hours a year while attending classes
- Rate of pay is $11.00 per hour. Over 2 years: $22,000 plus Tuition = approximately $40,000
- After graduation, scholars make a two year commitment to work at Accumold
- Accumold has added over 18 toolmakers to their staff, 1 Robotics Scholar and 1 IT Scholar*, 1 CAD Technology Scholar* = 21 total Scholars [*Note some Scholars have gone on for a second degree.]
- Salary ranges depend on their position in the Tool Room after graduation.
- Currently in the Accumold Tool Room, 40 percent of the employees came through the DMACC Scholars Program.
- 80 percent of Scholars participating in the program are still employed at Accumold.

Benefits for Students

- Apply real-world skills and experience to classroom instruction, benefitting other students and faculty
- Work part-time and earn wages at Accumold, reducing or eliminating student debt
- Receive support for education expenses
- Be considered for full-time employment

Benefits for Businesses

- Access to motivated students who possess a wide range of skills and potential to complete a rigorous academic and experiential curriculum
- Opportunity to observe students' skills and work habits in real-time for a possible full-time job after graduation
- Improve the pipeline of skilled workers for employment
- Reduce potential payments to recruiting firms by grooming future employees internally
- Get the word out about the opportunities the business offers

How can this initiative be replicated and scaled up?

Accumold has already expanded their Scholars Program to include additional areas of study in Automation & Robotics, CAD, IT and Industrial Maintenance.

DMACC is expanding the Accumold model and has replicated the DMACC Scholars Program, which is now open to students and businesses in multiple fields. While still in the initial stages, the Vermeer Corporation is investing in scholars in DMACC's Industrial Maintenance program; TMC Transportation and Housby Mack are investing in scholars in DMACC's Diesel Technology and Auto Collision Technology programs; and, ProRestore DKI is investing in a Building Trades scholar.

The DMACC Scholars template is being implemented to address a significant IT skill shortage that cuts across all business and organizational sectors. The new collaboration, called the "DMACC - IT Industry Partnership Board", is providing a new vision and strategy for generating more IT graduates. The Board is made up of a "who's who" of local employers including Nationwide Insurance, the Principal Financial Group, IBM, Shazam, Workiva, Alliance Technologies, GuideOne Insurance, Farmers Mutual Hail, Keyot and others. As the first and very important step of the initiative, with the guidance of the Board DMACC is reorganizing its entire IT program to better align graduates to the needs of Central Iowa employers.

Initial Components of the IT Scholars Program
- Creation of a $200,000 IT Scholarship Intern Program. With public and private support, select DMACC IT students will get paid for internships that offer on-the-job experience and a path into full-time employment.

- A new IT Apprenticeship Program in partnership with the Technology Association of Iowa and the Iowa Office of Apprenticeship will provide industry partner employees the required Related Technical Instruction (RTI) in an "Earn while you learn" structure.

- Developing a large pool of local employers eager to hire DMACC IT graduates for full-time employment at generous wage levels. These employers will have many opportunities to interact with DMACC IT students while they are still in college.

As the need for skilled workers increases, the interest in this Scholars Program expands. It's just one of the solutions that have come from DMACC's strong partnership with local business and industry.

Action Steps for Replication
- Understand the employee skill needs of the business entity.
- Align skill needs with college course competencies.
- Align course schedules with business work shifts.
- Conduct business driven and hosted Scholar information sessions, with assistance from college, to inform potential candidates as to real job opportunities and the "earn and learn" model.
- Arrange for scholarships and supplemental funding for tuition, tools and books, utilizing any available state, federal or college resources.
- Assign a staff person, in the role of a Navigator, to monitor enrollment and provide support to students as needed.

About Des Moines Area Community College

Located in Central Iowa with a mission focused on Quality, Service and Affordability, DMACC serves approximately 37,000 credit and 27,000 non–credit students each year through its ten campus sites and centers. Its 153 academic programs and certificates are centered on the needs of students and businesses, preparing students for immediate employment or transfer to any public or private college or university. DMACC has direct consulting and training relationships with all area businesses and conducts over 340 active projects annually, ranging from bonded training to short–term skill upgrades and consulting. Promoting engagement and an excellent student experience, DMACC has created a required gateway student success course, a University College Transfer Program, better ways for businesses to engage potential employees, and is also the service provider for federal workforce programs.

DMACC is governed by a nine–member Board of Trustees who are elected and serve four–year terms. DMACC is active on the STEMconnector® Innovation Task Force, the Food and Ag Council, and the Higher Education Council, and understands that a focus on STEM transcends all academic program boundaries and forms the core of learning for all great jobs. DMACC also has an active campus–wide STEM Council designed to integrate and coordinate all college STEM activities.

About the Author

The first native–born Iowan to be President of DMACC, Rob Denson has a B.S. in Political Science and Economics and a M.S. in Higher Education Administration from Iowa State University. He worked for Iowa State as an Assistant Dean for three years before moving to the University of Florida to serve as an Assistant Dean of Students.

Rob graduated from Law School at the University of Florida in 1979 and was an Associate University Attorney for three years before operating his own law practice for 16 years. He is a board–certified civil trial lawyer. In 1996, he became Assistant to the President and Dean for Institutional Advancement at Santa Fe Community College in Gainesville, Florida.

In 1998, Rob returned to Iowa as President of Northeast Iowa Community College in Calmar, Iowa. Rob came to DMACC in 2003 and loves his job. He is active on a number of community boards, including the United Way of Central Iowa, the Greater Des Moines Partnership, Iowa Ag Literacy Foundation, Iowa Economic Development and Authority, Iowa Innovation Council, Iowa Student Loan Corporation, and the Iowa Caregivers Board, among others. In addition to his DMACC position, he serves on the National Board of Gateway to College, a drop–out recovery program; the Governor's STEM Advisory Council and Executive Committee; the National STEMconnector® Innovation Task Force, and the Food and Ag Council; and, the National Leadership Council of Opportunity Nation. He also chairs the National STEMconnector® Higher Education Council.

Advancing a Jobs-Driven Economy
Building What Business Needs
By: Dr. Jim Catanzaro, Former President, Chattanooga State Community College

By 2010, Chattanooga State had a twenty–year history of offering a wide range of training and degree programs through our Corporate College, which were configured specifically to address corporate technical employee development requirements. Chattanooga State's Corporate College partners with more than 100 local companies including Tennessee Valley Authority and DuPont.

When two major German corporations, Volkswagen (VW) and Wacker, decided to expand into the local Tennessee area, an even greater opportunity was afforded to our Corporate College. Chattanooga State seized this opportunity and now VW and Wacker have invested more than $4.5 billion in the area and employ over 3,500 employees. They've also led to the arrival of 15 major suppliers employing an additional 9,000 workers. The region is now exploding economically, businesses are thriving and opportunities for well–paying jobs have sky–rocketed. Chattanooga State's Engineering Technology Division has also grown in enrollment by over 20 percent a year for the past 6 years.

There were three strategic interests that led the Chattanooga State Community College leadership team to build powerful relationships with VW and Wacker.

Our number one strategic interest was to support state and community efforts to bring Volkswagen's only North American plant to Chattanooga, and Wacker's largest chemical plant investment outside Germany to a nearby site. By demonstrating our college's proven capability to build and sustain a world–class workforce, through the backing and testimony of local VW and Wacker executives, we were able to settle concerns from both firms regarding American worker ability to perform at levels that of which were already expected by their German counterparts. In addition, the collective industry experience of my colleagues and I gave us the awareness of the workplace requirements, teamwork, professionalism, and manufacturing culture, which resonated with VW and Wacker.

Our second strategic interest was more self–serving and consisted of establishing long–term alternative funding sources for the college. In Tennessee, budgets are tight for public higher education and state support has declined over the past decade, resulting in increased tuition for families. However, through Chattanooga's new Volkswagen partnership, the college gained access to new sources of financial support, including the state's economic development department, federal grants, and corporate commitments. They also supported the college's initial task of screening over 80,000 applicants for 2,300 technical positions. Given this success, Chattanooga State is still funded as VW's only outside training partner worldwide.

Our first responsibility in this VW partnership is to prepare the workforce with skills necessary to produce VW's state–of–the–art Passat and to operate and maintain the most advanced automotive assembly plant in the world. All of this has been accomplished in the partner–built Volkswagen Academy, a 40 million dollar, 165,000 square foot facility filled with the same robots as in the plant, state–of–the–art paint booths, and other extraordinary training modules.

Wacker announced in 2012 the 2.5 billion dollar construction of a polysilicon plant in the region. They also committed to build on Chattanooga State's campus a Wacker Institute equipped with the most technologically advanced chemistry, engineering, and computer labs. Constructed in a vacated space on campus, the Institute features the largest all–glass and fully capable chemical training installation in North America. Wacker provided nearly four million dollars to construct the plant while several million dollars in federal and state support finished the job. Today, the Wacker Institute is utilized by a local STEM high school and Chattanooga State's college engineering technology labs. The institute is a prime destination for corporate, government and education visitors and winner of the coveted Bellwether Award for corporate partnerships.

The Wacker Institute experience consists entirely of credit courses, 14 are chemical engineering technology and STEM related disciplines. Courses are taken either over a fast–track six–month term or continuously over one calendar year. The good news is that Wacker Institute graduates are exceeding all company expectations at the local facilities and also at the home facilities in Germany; where they are many times more prepared than their German counterparts. Furthermore, 87 percent of those accepted into the Institute complete their course of study and virtually all are employed or promised employment upon certificate completion.

Lastly, strategic interest three. From the demanding experiences of the partnership with VW and Wacker comes a growing conviction that our colleges must expect much more of our graduates. We must go beyond subject matter competency to mastery. We must ensure the knowledge and skills demonstrated at the end of each course are to become part of our graduates' skills sets as they enter the workforce for years to come. To truly prepare a world–class workforce for any organization, public or private, as well as entrepreneurs for success beyond business start–ups, we in higher education must start with a very precise understanding of the requirements and challenges of technical and professional work in the emerging global economy. We must demonstrate that our graduates meet these requirements. But it's a tough challenge, especially since we are reaching deeper and deeper into our own applicant pools and publicly committing our institutions to substantial improvements in student persistence and graduation rates.

These three strategic interests provide a roadmap that any higher learning institution can use to build the workforce that business needs, putting these in a general context, they:

1. Support the economic development efforts of your local business community,

2. Create and provide the training that the businesses require in a way that creates a sustainable business model for both the business and your own institution, and

3. Make sure that graduates have true content mastery, not just competency.

If you can do these, your institution will be the preferred training partner for your businesses.

About Chattanooga State Community College

Chattanooga State Community College, also known as Chattanooga State, is a public, comprehensive community college located in Chattanooga, Tennessee. The college is a member of the Tennessee Board of Regents System and is accredited by the Southern Association of Colleges and Schools (SACS). Athletically, Chattanooga State is a member of Region VII of the NJCAA.

Chattanooga State offers a variety of programs and degrees including 50 career programs; three university parallel degrees (Associate of Science, Associate of Art, and Associate of Science in Teaching) with areas of emphasis in the arts, humanities, mathematics, and natural sciences; 20 technical certificate programs; corporate training; continuing education; adult education, including GED preparation; Collegiate High at Chattanooga State (formerly Middle College High School); Early College (dual enrollment); and community service programs.

About the Author

For thirty–five years Dr. Jim Catanzaro has been known nationally as a leader in the community college movement – for five years as a community college president in California, for six years in Ohio, three in Illinois, and now for over twenty–four years in Tennessee. Previously, Dr. Catanzaro was the Human Resources Director for a 7,000 employee manufacturing firm in California.

Dr. Catanzaro holds a Ph.D. degree from Claremont Graduate University in Philosophy of Religion. He studied leadership at The Wharton School and at the University of Texas at Austin. His "Second Generation" online course, Religions of the World as Practiced in America, has been selected by the Monterey Institute Hewlett Foundation Study for inclusion in the Institute's National Repository of America's best web–based courses.

Dr. Catanzaro is a frequent speaker, including national conferences. He addressed the Positive Psychology Summit in Washington, D.C. and he was the keynote presenter at the International Higher Education Conference in Melbourne, Australia. President Catanzaro edited the Chattanooga city magazine, Chattanooga on the Move, for four years.

Partnerships to STEM Pathways
By: Dr. Dena Maloney, Superintendent-President, Taft College

Taft College's partnership with business and industries including Chevron, Occidental Petroleum, Sempra Energy, Linn Energy Aera, Synagro, Nabors, Paramount Farms, Bolthouse Farms, Freeport-McMoRan, Wells Fargo and more is an on-going enterprise. Taft's industry partnership efforts have been multi-fold that include: a) education and training, b) workforce learning and economic development, and c) community engagement and development. In addition, Taft College continuously partners with local elementary, middle school, junior and high schools to increase STEM awareness and to improve preparation of K-12 students interested in STEM through targeted outreach. Moreover, Taft College has been working in partnership with California State University, Bakersfield and University of La Verne to create STEM pathways to improve the STEM pipeline close curriculum gaps and align student learning outcomes with degree completion and workforce preparedness.

Education and Training
As a community college, it's Taft College's mission to prepare individuals to be workforce ready and to attain higher education. Taft College has deliberately and intentionally sought the expertise, skills and knowledge of industry in exploring and developing curriculum that reflects what occurs in the workplace. This included sitting alongside industry personnel to review curriculum topics and to incorporate subject-matter elements that reflect the workforce needs of industry. The outcome and impact of such deliberate partnership was the culmination in the development of two education programs at Taft College, which are:
- Associate in Science Degree and five certificate options in Energy Technology
- Associate in Science Degree in Engineering

External/Workplace Learning
A key element in TC's efforts to prepare individuals to be workforce and transfer education ready includes:
- hands-on practical experience in the classroom through the use of equipment, materials, and software as used in industry,
- participation in onsite observation and learning experiences in industry,
- instructors with the experience, education, and skills from industry who teach the core classes in energy technology and engineering programs, and
- participation in paid internships with various places of business.

The outcome and impact has been that students are receiving real work experiences in the classroom and on the field provided by subject-expert instructors and industry. Similarly, internships have provided students with opportunities to gain first-hand workplace learning experiences. These internships have resulted in approximately nine direct hires to industry over the past two summers. Additionally, students are being promoted within their companies are a result of gaining an education and training at Taft College.

Community Engagement and Development

As part of this on-going partnership with industry are TC's efforts to engage industry and the community. Taft College does so by providing STEM Outreach interactive activities to our K-12 schools and partners. These have included working alongside our K-12 schools to provide students with STEM exploration programs to generate interest and excitement about pursuing science, technology, engineering, and mathematics as careers and education fields. In Spring of 2014, Taft College hosted over 170 high school seniors from our service area with a STEMvitational event that included classroom demonstrations and hands-on activities by Taft College STEM faculty. Furthermore, in the summer of 2014, the college provided two one week Mad Science Camps for junior high students that also included hands-on lessons based on the scientific method. With these activities plus many others that the college provided in the Spring and Summer of 2014, TC served close to 1,000 K-12 students in their STEM Outreach programs.

Another key community and industry engagement effort TC pursued was hosting the 1st Petroleum Summit at Taft College in October 2013. This summit brought in industry, business, political, and community leaders to converse about workforce development, propose strategies for the future in energy, and to celebrate the economic impact petroleum has provided to our community. The success of this event resulted in the creation of the Taft College Foundation Petroleum Partners Circle where it continues to bring in industry and community partners to discuss and promote efforts to advance workforce development in energy. The second petroleum summit will in 2015.

All of these efforts can be replicated, scaled and/or enhanced. All of these efforts are made possible by the commitment and support from industry and community partners through their expertise, time, and financial resources.

The success of these efforts is seen and will continue to be seen through our students. Students' lives are being changed. Students are being taught, students are gaining life experiences, and students are being hired. Moreover, efforts and programs gave TC administrators, faculty and staff opportunities to work together as a team and most importantly implement programs and services that are intentional, measurable and create impacts to the success of the students, businesses and the community.

About Taft College

Located in western Kern County northwest of Taft, CA, Taft College (TC) prides itself as a small and comprehensive institution with a wide range of educational programs and support services to students. Taft College offers 44 Associate Degrees and 40 Certificates in transfer education and career-technical education programs. Last year, Taft College served over 2,600 Full Time Equivalent students seeking to advance their education and achieve their goals. Students at Taft College have access to innovative, caring faculty members and the support programs needed to promote student achievement.

Taft College is a leader in offering state-of-the-art curriculum in high-demand fields including Energy Technology, Dental Hygiene and more. The college offers various guaranteed transfer programs and students are focused on success --- whether they plan to continue their education at a four-year college, or enter the workforce in a new career. In 2013-14, Taft College launched a major project to update its comprehensive Educational Master Plan, which will set the course for Taft College for the next ten years. The development of an Education Master Plan is an important component in the college's overall planning process. An Education Master Plan begins with an analysis of data about the college and the communities it serves. Data are used to project growth potential for current and future academic and student support programs. The planning document will help inform decision making over the next 10 years, with periodic updates as part of the planning cycle.

About the Author

Dr. Dena Maloney began her career in higher education as the Director of Contract Education in the Santa Clarita Community College District. In 2001, Dr. Maloney became Dean of Economic Development at College of the Canyons. In 2007, Dr. Maloney was named Founding Dean of the Canyon County Campus, a start-up campus that quickly grew to over 5,000 students.

In May 2012, Dr. Maloney became the Superintendent-President of the West Kern Community College District and Taft College. She leads a staff of nearly 225 faculty, classified and management personnel and is responsible for all aspects of the college district including instruction, student services, facilities, technology, finance, advocacy and community relations.

Dr. Maloney earned a Bachelor of Arts degree in Political Science from Loyola Marymount University, a Master of Arts in Government from Georgetown University, and a Doctorate in Education from the University of La Verne.

CHAPTER FOUR

Industry Models

"We are excited about the role that partnerships between the educational pipeline and industry leaders can bring to ensure the learning opportunities that will set a framework and an interest in STEM fields for all students. We must: 1) Advance partnerships that will brings students and industry leaders together, 2) Prepare all students to be successful in STEM fields, 3) Expose students to innovation required to feed 9 billion people that will be on this planet by the year 2050."

- Dr. Sherri Brown, Vice President, Global Science Strategy, Monsanto, and Chair STEMconnector®'s STEM Food and Ag Council 2015

Note: Though industry models are contained throughout *Advancing a Jobs-Driven Economy,* this chapter focuses specifically on **Agriculture** with Tuskegee University, National FFA Organization; **Biotechnology** with Madison Area Technical College; and **Petroleum** with Chicago State University.

Important Milestones for STEM Food and Agriculture Education
By: Dr. Walter A. Hill, Provost, Tuskegee University and
Dr. Olga Bolden–Tiller, Associate Professor, Agricultural Science, Tuskegee University

Tuskegee University was founded in 1881 and, from its inception, agriculture was integral to the development of the institution and to the people and communities it served. George Washington Carver joined Booker T. Washington at Tuskegee University in 1896, and in 1897 the Tuskegee Agricultural Experiment Station was funded by the Alabama Legislature. Carver and the Experiment Station facilitated science based agriculture provided to socially disadvantaged farmers and rural communities. The four–wheeled demonstration wagon initiated in 1897 evolved to the 'Jesup Wagon' which took knowledge and skills about food and agriculture into rural communities and homes. The work so impressed USDA's Seaman Knapp that in 1906 Thomas Campbell was named the first "demonstration agent" in the United States, an important forerunner to the USDA Cooperative Extension System, which was formally initiated in 1914. Because of its pioneering work and unique research and outreach programs, Tuskegee University is recognized and supported by the State of Alabama and the U.S. Congress as an 1890 Land- Grant institution.

Today more than 50 percent of Tuskegee University's students are in STEM and related fields – including animal and veterinary sciences, environmental, natural resource and plant sciences; food and nutrition sciences; biology, chemistry and physics, and mathematics; electrical, mechanical, chemical and aerospace sciences engineering; materials science and engineering, integrated biosciences, veterinary medicine, science education, mathematics education, agribusiness, agricultural economics, computer sciences, and information sciences. Collectively, the programs have led to Tuskegee University being recognized as a leader in producing minority graduates in STEM areas, and the institution was recently recognized by "Diverse: Issues in Higher Education" for its efforts, including #1 in producing minority graduates in the Agriculture, Agriculture Operations and Related Sciences degree field; #2 for graduates in Natural Resources and Conservation field; #7 and #10 for Architecture and Related Services and Engineering degrees, respectively. The institution also claimed the #12 spot for M.S. degrees in Engineering; #2 in Physical Sciences, and #1 for professional doctoral degrees in Veterinary Medicine.

Sponsors of students and programs in STEM Food and Agriculture areas at Tuskegee University include a wide variety of private and public partners, such as Monsanto, DuPont, Proctor and Gamble, PepsiCo, Dow Chemical, Ag Credit Bank, Nationwide, Walmart, Coca–Cola, USDA, NSF, NIH, EPA, NPS, DOI, DOT, DOD, DOE, USAID, and many others.

K–12 STEM pipeline programs at Tuskegee University are diverse and include AgriTrek (agricultural sciences), SciTrek (natural sciences), AgDiscovery (agricultural sciences), FasTrac (engineering), VetStep (vet sciences), Youth Community Gardens, Calf and Goat shows, Summer Youth College (Nutrition; 7–9), ESTEAM (K–6), Tuskegee Tiger 4–H Camp (9–19), Smart Camp (STEM; 1–8), SHAFE (Sustainable Health and Fitness; K–12). These activities collectively serve to inspire the interest of elementary, high school and college students (who serve as mentors to K–12 students) in agriculture and STEM disciplines. A partnership of Tuskegee University with Walmart, W. P. Rawls, PuraVida, C.H. Robinson, Alabama Legislature, USDA – NRCS, RD, and FSA has helped to develop a Small Farmers Agricultural Cooperative that is selling fresh fruits and vegetables on an increasingly commercial scale, bringing profitability and sustainability to small farmers in persistent poverty counties. A partnership of Tuskegee University with eight USDA agencies will soon cut the ribbon on the new "Carver Integrative Sustainability Center" which will focus on profitability, policy and resource delivery to small farmers and communities for economic development in "Strike Force" (Persistent Poverty) Counties and serve as a springboard for other such projects.

A partnership with Monsanto and USDA is building a new plant sciences lab on the campus that will serve to expand research and student learning in plant biotechnology, genetics and breeding at Tuskegee University. Carver has been quoted as saying "Ye shall know science and science shall make you free." This statement remains foundational at Tuskegee University.

Numerous campus events occurred during 2014 that commemorated the 150th birth year of George Washington Carver. Among them was the inaugural "George Washington Carver Lecture Series" on October 30, 2014, co–sponsored by PepsiCo, Kellogg, and ConAgra Foods among others, which brought together noted speakers to honor Carver's scientific legacy by addressing "Innovations in Food and Nutrition Sciences in the 21st Century." The culminating event for the 150th birth–year celebration of George Washington Carver will be the 72nd Professional Agricultural Workers Conference, on December 7–9, 2014 which annually brings together 500 agricultural professionals, farmers, faculty, and high school and college students to share and discuss agriculture and community issues in an array of presentation and dialogue formats with sponsorship from AgCredit, Nationwide, Walmart, Monsanto, USDA and many others.

There have been many universities that have partnered with Tuskegee University, sustaining the graduate and professional school STEM Food and Agriculture pipeline. Past and current initiatives include, among others the 1890 Land Grant Universities, Iowa State University, Purdue University, University of Illinois, University of Florida, Auburn University, Mississippi State University, The Ohio State University, Earth University (Costa Rica), Sokoine University (Tanzania) and Des Moines Area Community College.

As the 150th birth–year of George Washington Carver ended, seeds were planted for the 2015 celebration of the 125th Anniversary of the founding of the 1890 Land Grant Universities. The kick–off event occurred on November 3, 2014 in Orlando, Florida during the Annual meeting of the Association of Public and Land Grant Universities (APLU). During the APLU meeting, the Council of 1890 Deans voted to join STEMconnector®'s STEM Food & Ag Council. A major celebration of the 125th Anniversary of the 1890 land grant universities is planned for Washington DC on July 13–15, 2015 and events will be hosted on all of the 1890 campuses throughout the year. An important part of this celebration will focus on strengthening the pipeline of students in STEM Food and Agriculture careers. We ask you to join us in this milestone celebration as we launch the next 125 years of excellence and service.

About Tuskegee University

Tuskegee University is an independent and state–related institution of higher education. Its programs serve a student body that is coeducational as well as racially, ethnically and religiously diverse. With a strong orientation toward disciplines which highlight the relationship between education and workforce preparation in the sciences, professions and technical areas, Tuskegee University also emphasizes the importance of the liberal arts as a foundation for successful careers in all areas. Accordingly, all academic majors stress the mastery of a required core of liberal arts courses.

Tuskegee University is located in Tuskegee, Alabama, which is 40 miles east of the Alabama State Capitol in Montgomery, Alabama, and 20 miles west of the city of Auburn, Alabama. It is also within easy driving distance to the cities of Birmingham, Alabama and Atlanta, Georgia.

Tuskegee University was the first black college to be designated as a Registered National Historic Landmark (April 2, 1966), and the only black college to be designated a National Historic Site (October 26, 1974), a district administered by the National Park Service of the U.S. Department of Interior.

About the Author

In addition to serving as Provost, Dr. Walter A. Hill is also the Vice President of Academic Affairs; Dean of the College of Agriculture, Environment and Nutrition Sciences; and Director of the 1890 Land-Grant Research and Extension at Tuskegee University. He has been a faculty member and Dean/Director for 36 and 27 years, respectively. He co–founded the Carver Integrative Sustainability Center, Black Belt Family Farm Market & Innovation Center, Alabama Land Grant Alliance, and Professional Agricultural Workers Journal. He is a Fellow of the American Society of Agronomy and a member of Phi Beta Kappa, Sigma Xi and Gamma Sigma Delta Honor Societies. Walter is chair–elect of the Agricultural Heads Section of APLU and chair of the 1890 Council of Deans. Walter received his PhD in Agronomy from the University of Illinois, Master's degrees from the University of Arizona and University of Chicago and B.S. in Chemistry from Lake Forest College.

Dr. Olga U. Bolden-Tiller serves as the Head for the Department of Agricultural and Environmental Sciences at Tuskegee University (TU). She holds a BS degree in Agricultural Sciences (Animal Sciences) from Fort Valley State University (1997) and a PhD degree in Animal Sciences (Reproductive Biology) from the University of Missouri-Columbia. She completed her postdoctoral training at the University of Texas-MD Anderson Cancer Center before joining TU at the rank of Assistant Professor and later promoted to Associate Professor (2012). She has served in numerous leadership roles within the department and directs several high school and undergraduate research programs. In addition to her administrative and teaching duties, her research interests entail elucidating the molecular mechanisms of testicular function in rodents and ruminants. Collectively, she has served as a research mentor for numerous high school, graduate and undergraduate students, is the author/co-author of numerous of refereed journal articles and conference proceedings and is an active member and serves in leadership roles in several professional societies. Her research and training programs are funded by USDA, HHMI, NSF and the state of Alabama. Dr. Bolden-Tiller has received several awards for research, teaching and service as well as several administrative and fellowships in leadership.

School–based Agricultural Education Integrated Model
By: Dr. W. Dwight Armstrong, Chief Executive Officer, National FFA Organization

One of the keys to the success of FFA over the past 87 years has been the integral model of school–based agricultural education. Its three components (classroom/laboratory instruction; experiential learning; and leadership development through FFA) work together to provide an excellent and well–rounded educational experience for students.

School–based agricultural education (SBAE) is an essential educational program delivered through career and technical education in every state and in five U.S. Territories. There are approximately one million agricultural education students in the nation in more than 7,665 schools who are taught by nearly 11,000 secondary, postsecondary and adult instructors. School–based agricultural education in the United States consists of three integral core components that include:

- Contextual, inquiry–based instruction and learning through an interactive classroom and laboratory.
- Experiential, service and/or work–based learning through the implementation of a supervised agricultural experience program.
- Premier leadership, personal growth and career success through engagement in FFA.

The complete integration of these three components helps ensure students' career success or continuation with higher education related to agriculture, agriscience or agribusiness following high school graduation.

Classroom/Laboratory Instruction
Contextual, inquiry–based instruction is an integral core component of school–based agricultural education delivered in a classroom, laboratory, greenhouse, or outdoor setting. Interactive classrooms, laboratory instruction and learning may include units based on natural and social sciences such as environmental science, agribusiness, natural resources, aquaculture, food science and safety, animal and plant sciences, entrepreneurship and many other career options.

Students enrolled in these courses or career pathways have the unique opportunity to apply core content concepts in an agriculturally related context. For example, when using STEM, a student learning about hydrogen and covalent bonding in chemistry is able to apply these concepts when examining the chemistry of food processing. By enhancing their core content knowledge base with the agriculture, food and natural resources career cluster, students gain real world hands-on experiences that enhance career and college readiness.

Experiential Learning
Experiential, service and work–based learning through a supervised agriculture program allows students to practice the application of their knowledge and skills. Implementation of a supervised agricultural experience program (SAE) is under the direct supervision of the agriculture teacher and typically involves employers or parents.

There are a variety of experiential, service and work–based learning opportunities from which students and young adults may choose to implement. These may include entrepreneurship (owning and managing their own businesses), internships, working at agricultural businesses or completing independent research projects that enhance their STEM skills. Experiential, service and work–based learning develops and enhances leadership, employability and life–long career skills. The interaction of the student, teacher, business manager, alumni and parents helps ensure the learning is relevant to each individual student's career cluster and/or career pathway. School–based agricultural education prepares students for careers and college far beyond the traditional classroom.

FFA

Premier leadership, personal growth and career success through FFA form another integral core component of the comprehensive school–based agricultural education delivery model. The National FFA Organization (FFA) is a Career and Technical Student Organization (CTSO) that enhances comprehensive school–based agricultural education programs. CTSO programs and activities provide student opportunities for leadership, personal growth and career success. Through engagement in FFA, students have opportunities to develop leadership, communication, employability, career readiness and personal development skills that will help them succeed in the future.

All students are encouraged to participate in activities that highlight and enhance the success of their interactive classroom and experiential, service and work–based experiences. These may include public speaking, career development events, career planning, career progress, agricultural sales and marketing, food science, biotechnology, agricultural issues, meat science, livestock evaluation, veterinarian science and experiential, service and work–based recognition. Many students also have an opportunity to give back through service–learning and community enhancement initiatives.

Connections to Postsecondary Opportunities

Critical to the delivery and success of school–based agricultural education is the presence of highly qualified, highly motivated local agricultural education instructors in middle and high schools across the United States. In most states, these teachers hold at minimum a bachelor's of science degree in agriculture and related sciences, plus education coursework that helps them meet teacher certification requirements in their respective states. Historically, U.S. land–grant universities have played critical roles in preparing agricultural science instructors for service in local agricultural education programs. Today, with a membership of more than 610,240, FFA depends heavily on local agricultural science teachers who also serve as FFA advisors. In many states, the supply and availability of qualified agricultural education instructors is a limitation to access and growth of programs.

Land–grant universities and colleges of agriculture work closely with state agricultural education/FFA leaders to serve as host sites for state FFA conventions and state level career development event competitions. For many FFA members, these are opportunities for their first visit to a college campus and to see themselves participating in postsecondary education. As these students progress through planning and preparation for career success, the connection with these universities is an important factor in deciding what majors to pursue and what postsecondary education institution to attend.

Summary

Agriculture, like many other fields, has seen an explosion of STEM that is revolutionizing how food, fiber and fuel are produced. With its membership on the STEM Food and Ag Council and the Higher Education Council, FFA is strengthening the STEM connections, resources and initiative to advance the organization's mission.

Through postsecondary partnerships with land–grant universities and two– and four–year institutions, FFA helps students achieve career success by preparing them for the next steps in education and successful careers in the food and agriculture industry. Not only does this produce talented individuals for industry, these partnerships help ensure highly qualified and motivated teachers are available to teach future generations of school–based agricultural education students.

FFA and agricultural education offer a compelling value proposition to industry through a time–tested, proven model of attracting students to the field of agriculture from rural, urban and suburban settings. FFA helps recruit students to agriculture at an age when they can still shape their educational and career paths. The program offers industry access to a deep pool of talent to fill its human resource needs. The hands–on, experiential learning in the classroom, combined with the leadership and career skill development programs of FFA, helps students discover their talents, explore careers and maximize what they gain from their time in education. These young leaders are developing skills that make them solidly college and career ready. These will be the workers, managers and leaders we must have for agriculture to grow.

About National FFA Organization

Founded in 1928 as the Future Farmers of America (FFA) brought together students, educators and industry to prepare a new generation for agriculture. Renamed FFA in 1988, the organization continues to help young leaders rise up to meet the challenges of feeding a hungry world by preparing its members to develop their unique talents and explore personal interests across a broad range of career pathways in agriculture.

FFA evolved in response to expanded opportunities in agriculture and the need for skilled and competent employees in more than 300 careers. The organization helps students prepare for careers in such areas as business, marketing, science, communications, education, horticulture, production, natural resources, forestry and many others. According to a survey of FFA members, 87 percent are interested in learning about career exploration, 81 percent about college preparation and 81 percent about technology.

The National FFA Organization just achieved an all–time high membership of 610,240 students ages 12–21 in 7,665 chapters across the United States, Puerto Rico and the U.S. Virgin Islands. More than 11,000 agricultural educators nationwide, many of whom also serve as local FFA advisors, deliver an integrated agricultural education program that combines inquiry–based classroom and laboratory instruction, real world experiential learning and interpersonal development through FFA leadership and career programs that test students' agricultural skill development and recognize achievement.

About the Author

Dr. W. Dwight Armstrong is the Chief Executive Officer of the National FFA Organization. An active FFA member in high school, he earned a B.S. degree in agriculture from Murray State University in 1971 and Master's (1973) and Ph.D. (1975) degrees from Purdue University in animal science. After serving on the faculty at North Carolina State University in the Animal Sciences Department 1975–1982, Armstrong built a career in the swine nutrition area beginning at Akey, Inc., in Lewisburg, Ohio, where he served as Director of Nutrition, Director of Sales and, finally, President. In 2000, the company was sold to Provimi, located in The Netherlands. There, Armstrong served as Chief Operating Officer of North American Nutrition Companies, Director of the Americas and Global Group Vice President. In 2008, he retired from Provimi to start his own consulting business in the animal nutrition and agribusiness areas. He joined the National FFA Organization in 2009.

Emerging Programs in Biotechnology:
Breathing Life into the National Bioeconomy
By: Dr. Thomas Tubon, Project Director, Co–PI, Human Stem Cell Technologies
Education Initiative, Madison Area Technical College

Wisconsin's taxpayers receive $12.20 for every dollar invested in the Wisconsin Technical College System (WTCS). In addition, 9.6 percent of employers say their local technical college is important to the overall success of their businesses. For over a century, Madison College has paved the way in creating innovative STEM programs that cultivate the growth of our state economy. As an example, program development in agricultural technologies has led to a partnership between Madison College and John Deere, teaching students technical theory and specialized skills needed to service equipment under realistic dealership conditions. Madison College graduates from this program are highly sought after by over 1,650 John Deere dealerships. This pioneering spirit has gained Madison College a national reputation as a leader across a broad range of high–tech STEM programs, from advanced manufacturing to electron microscopy and biotechnology.

In 1987, in response to our emerging regional bio–economy, Madison College developed one of the first Biotechnology programs in the nation designed around building the bioscience workforce. At present, direct bioscience employment in Wisconsin generates over 24,000 private sector workers, creating enough economic activity in the state to support 72,240 jobs. Over 600 bioscience companies can be found in 53 counties, and in all seven of the state's economic development regions. Activity is in all four sectors: agriculture, feedstock and chemicals, drugs and pharmaceuticals; medical devices and equipment; testing and medical labs. The total impact of direct and indirect activity for the Wisconsin bioscience sectors is nearly $7 billion in income generated.

Since its inception, our flagship Biotechnology program at Madison College has received over $4 million in National Science Foundation Advanced Technological Education (NSF ATE) awards to support workforce development in the bioscience sector. In 2014, President Obama defined the impact and role of the NSF ATE through "building strong partnerships in education and industry, government and the non–profit sector, to help prepare students for their careers. And by building our technical workforce, it contributes to our nation's security and competitiveness. In a dynamic economy, technology is constantly changing. Community and technical college faculty are key to ATE centers, training students for today's high–tech jobs and emerging technologies."

One of the most recent and rapidly growing areas of biotechnology is in stem cell science, with key scientific discoveries and industries originating in the Madison area. Reported industry revenues for stem cell–based products in the United States totaled $974,000 in 2005, and increased dramatically to $36.9 million two years later in 2007. By 2020, the projected forecast for stem cell industry revenues is expected to exceed $20 billion. The rapid growth of stem cell–based industries will undoubtedly give rise to an increasing demand for specialized education and skills in many areas of the country. In 2007, with support from the NSF and the WiCell Research Institute, Madison College started a pilot program to teach techniques in culturing human stem cells. Including Madison College, only six 2–year colleges offer career technical education in stem cell methods; all of them, except for Madison College, work primarily with non–human culturing systems.

In 2011, with precedence for prior success, we were awarded an \$851,454 grant from the NSF ATE program to create comprehensive technical education curricula in human stem cell technologies and regenerative medicine. We accomplished three objectives as a result of this initiative: (i) development of a 32–week certificate program in stem cell technologies designed to prepare individuals for the workplace, (ii) integrated industry–supported stem cell laboratory practices into AAS Degree program, and (iii) pilot instructional materials for national dissemination and program adoption. This initiative evolved in response to the lack of industry–based stem cell education opportunities both locally as well as nationally. Strategic planning was guided by the expertise of a 40–member advisory board, with representatives from the community, 4–year colleges and universities, stem cell research scientists, and industry stakeholders. We began work to create educational resources for bridging the gap between growing industry needs and the availability of qualified, highly skilled technicians. To support this initiative, Madison College constructed a 2,744 square feet state–of–the–art Biosafety Level 2 Animal Cell Culturing Education Suite (ACCES) designed to simulate the work environment. To date, three cohorts of students have completed the 32–week Stem Cell Certificate, with a 96 percent placement rate in career–track positions in the biotech industry. One hundred percent of the certificate program students and their employers report complete satisfaction with the training, skills acquired, and relevance to the work place responsibilities.

Support from industry and academic partners for the Stem Cell program is unprecedented. Since the start of the certificate program in 2011, we have received over \$150,000 in scientific equipment, cell culture media, reagents, and supplies from local biotechnology companies (Cellular Dynamics International, WiCell Research Institute, Thermo Fisher, Cell Line Genetics, and Primorigen). We have launched a campaign with community and technical colleges across the nation in the effort to scale up and create a broader impact through program adoption. In June 2014, twenty–four biotechnology department leads participated in a 1–week Stem Cell Summit at Madison College and were provided access to all course resources accompanied by hands–on training in our ACCES facility. Several institutions have already begun incorporating our curricula, and we anticipate continued and sustained efforts to make our educational materials available to others. To facilitate dissemination, we have partnered with the NSF ATE Next Generation Center for Excellence in Biotechnology and Life Sciences (Bio–Link). Bio–Link's key activities are to: (i) increase the number and diversity of well-educated technicians in the workforce, (ii) meet the ever–growing needs of a continually evolving and diversifying industry for highly educated technicians, and (iii) institutionalize community college educational practices that make high–quality education and training in the concepts, tools, skills, processes, regulatory structure, and ethics of biotechnology available to all students.

One additional major obstacle in program scale up and adoption is the high cost of specialized reagents and media that are used to culture human stem cells. Human stem cell media requires specialized recombinant factors that can cost tens of thousands of dollars – resources unavailable to most community and technical college programs. To resolve this issue, we hope to work with other academic institutions to assist in helping them to identify potential support from industry and corporate partners in their regions. We anticipate that this aspect of promoting the agenda for a jobs–driven economy is enabled by resources embedded in the STEMconnector® network and STEM Higher Education Council. To reduce program expense and increase training accessibility for our educational partners, we have also identified alternative methods for 'in–house' bio manufacturing of specialized media that allow for cost–effective substitution of commercial reagents.

The success of our academic program in human stem cell technologies at Madison College is a reflection of our commitment and support from federal funding (NSF ATE), academic collaborators, and industry partners. As we prepare to launch our campaign to make programming accessible nationwide, more industry–academic partnerships need to be created, financial support secured, and impacts measured. To this end, action points that we foresee as mission critical for the advancement of our initiative by both industry and higher education partners include:

- **Administrative support, commitment, and advocacy** - for institutions of higher education to provide resources for implementing instructional programming in Stem Cell Technologies.

- **Industry and business collaboration, sponsorship, and contributions** - to respective partnering higher education institutions that promote instruction in emerging stem cell technologies, and resources for program sustainability.

- **Creation of embedded value in the academic curricula** - by establishing industry and business commitments to create internships and pipelines to hire program graduates.

About Madison Area Technical College

Madison College (Madison Area Technical College) was founded in 1912 with the mission to train the coming generation of workers for jobs in the growing factories and businesses of the time. Over a century later, we continue this commitment to build a workforce that will allow employers who hire our graduates to compete in a global marketplace. With close to 150 career programs and certificates, as well as a robust college transfer program, we provide over 40,000 students each year with high–quality instruction, top–notch facilities, and access to nationally recognized flagship programs.

Madison College serves students in the 12 counties that define south–central Wisconsin. Campus locations include five sites within Madison, and four regional sites in the cities of Reedsburg, Watertown, Fort Atkinson, and Portage. It is among the largest of the 16 schools in the Wisconsin Technical College System (WTCS), serving 40 school districts, 224 municipalities, and 744,676 residents.

Madison College is accredited by the Higher Learning Commission (HLC). The HLC is an independent corporation and a member of the North Central Association of Colleges and Schools (NCA), which was founded in 1895. The tradition of excellence at Madison College is under the leadership of President Jack E. Daniels, III.

About the Author

Dr. Thomas Tubon is an established scientist and professor in the Biotechnology Department at Madison College. He teaches program courses in the Applied Associates Degree in Biotechnology, Post–Baccalaureate Certificates in Biotechnology, Stem Cell Technologies Certificate, and Industry Contract workshops in Human Stem Cell Technologies.

He currently serves as the Principal Investigator and Director for the National Science Foundation – Advanced Technological Education program project for developing workforce–centered programming in Emerging Stem Cell Technologies (DUE 1104210). Dr. Tubon oversees development of industry–based curricula, and strategic implementation for local, regional, and national–level program scale–up. In this role, he has facilitated the creation of a broad network of industry, community, and academic stakeholders through outreach and education initiatives empowering career pathways in STEM. In the last 36 months, Dr. Tubon's involvement in over 100 educator workshops and conferences, family and youth science events, and Career Technical Education (CTE) courses have directly engaged over 5,000 stakeholders in STEM, including aspiring youth in our underserved and underrepresented communities.

Dr. Tubon holds a Ph.D. in Molecular Genetics from Stony Brook University and Cold Spring Harbor Laboratory, and a B.S. in Molecular Biology from San Diego State University.

Petroleum: The Next Frontier
By: Dr. Wayne Watson, President, Chicago State University

American companies need highly skilled employees to fill STEM vacancies. Problems exist because many skilled employees in historically established positions would retire over the next five to ten years. Relatively new technology companies are looking for employees to help them grow. In each of these cases, jobs will go unfilled because potential employees are not prepared. Chicago State University (CSU) is successfully preparing underrepresented minority students to fill these positions. To connect students to potential career positions, CSU is aggressively developing working relationships with several companies. These partnerships allow CSU students to have quality work experiences in corporate environments and to explore company campuses, receive information about internships, resume critiques, and mock interviews.

When companies and universities work in tandem to push the frontiers of knowledge, they become a powerful engine for innovation and economic growth. Silicon Valley is a dramatic example. For over five decades, a dense web of rich and long–running collaborations in the region have given rise to new technologies at a breakneck pace, and transformed industries while modernizing the role of the university.
-Making Industry-University Partnerships Work, 2012 Science Business Innovation Board

During the past five years, CSU's partnership with the Illinois Petroleum Council (IPC) has generated an open circle of interactions. The IPC represents all sectors of Illinois' oil and natural gas industry, supporting more than 263,000 jobs and $33 billion of the state's economy as a result of operations involving pipeline construction, oil refining, marketing of transportation fuels and research in the New Albany Shale formation.

The IPC is a division of the American Petroleum Institute, commonly referred to as API, the only national trade association that represents all aspects of America's oil and natural gas industry. API's more than 600 members produce, process, and distribute most of the nation's energy. The industry also supports 9.8 million U.S. jobs and 8 percent of the U.S. economy.

CSU and IPC have partnered to expose minority students to the plethora of STEM–related job opportunities in the petroleum industry through internship opportunities and energy–focused seminars.

For example, IPC established an internship program for CSU students. The program provides young leaders with opportunities to develop their leadership skills and gain exposure to the public service sector. The interns spend one semester during their senior year working as interns in the program in Springfield, IL and Washington, DC.

IPC in partnership with CSU also partnered to raise awareness in the community at large about the petroleum industry. IPC/API recently hosted an Energy Forum in the Jones Convocation Center on the campus of CSU. The purpose of the Forum was to facilitate multilateral discussions about the political, environmental, technological and economic factors that influence the oil and natural gas industry on a day–to–day basis. The Forum also served as a platform for exploring the applicable positions used by relevant decision makers in support and nonsupport of the industry. Approximately 200 faculty, staff and students participated in the event that encompassed expert–led discussion panels, a luncheon with keynote speaker, and hands–on demonstrations led by local API labor groups.

These kind of strategic partnerships will not only increase the range of opportunities for students and faculty at CSU, but impact teaching and learning. Not only will CSU partners benefit from sharing information concerning their industry needs, but CSU will also serve as a conduit for serious discussions concerning ways to increase the number and diversity of students pursuing STEM disciplines. These discussions can range from possible improvements that ensure access to most modern technology, to strategies for developing more funding streams that are designed to increase the number of underrepresented minority students entering the STEM workforce.

Action Items to Advance a Jobs–Driven Economy

- **Ascertaining Needs** – Higher Education should work with Business to determine hiring needs and design curricula and training programs that are responsive to those needs. The partnership will ensure that students are acquiring skillsets that have a high likelihood of leading to employment.

- **Work–Based Learning** – Business should offer more internship opportunities to students as training paths to employment. The integration of classroom learning and hands–on experience enables students to quickly learn requisite skills for employment.

- **Accessibility** – Higher Education and Business should proactively seek opportunities to have dialogues regarding strategies to eliminate barriers that prevent students of color from entering the STEM workforce.

About Chicago State University

Chicago State University, serving more than 5,000 students, is a comprehensive, fully accredited, public university located on the Far South Side of Chicago. It was originally founded as a teacher's college in a leaky railroad boxcar in 1867 to meet the dire demand for a trained teaching force. The university now resides on a picturesque, 161–acre campus in an urban, residential neighborhood with a prairie grassland garden, the Emil and Patricia A. Jones Convocation Center, and a state–of–the–art academic library. Since its founding, the university has specialized in educating underserved, urban populations.

The university offers 38 undergraduate degree programs and 30 graduate programs in the following academic units: College of Arts and Sciences, College of Business, College of Education, College of Health Sciences, College of Pharmacy, plus the Division of Continuing Education and Non–traditional Programs and the Honors College. Students, faculty, staff, and the Greater CSU Community receive and offer services through various campus–based centers and institutes, thereby increasing CSU graduates' real–life competencies, ensuring that they will be able to make a difference in the lives of others upon degree completion.

About the Author

Wayne D. Watson, Ph.D., was named the 19th President of Chicago State University (CSU) in October 2009. Since the beginning of his tenure, he has worked tirelessly to provide leadership for the implementation of a reform agenda focused on streamlining operations, establishing accountability and transparency, and redefining the institution as a whole to lay the foundation for an institutional renaissance.

During his tenure, Dr. Watson has provided leadership in several strategic changes to the organizational infrastructure and operational efficiency that support the fulfillment of the University's mission. Under Dr. Watson's leadership, CSU was awarded a 10–year reaccreditation by the Higher Learning Commission (HLC) in 2013, the strongest recommendation a university can receive.

Dr. Watson came to CSU after distinguished 30–year tenure with the City Colleges of Chicago, one of the largest community college systems in the nation. Appointed Chancellor in 1998, Dr. Watson was profiled by the Chronicle of Higher Education as an 'Agent of Change' for his efforts to institute change, raise academic standards, and achieve new levels of excellence in education across the community college system. Prior to his appointment as Chancellor, Dr. Watson served as President of Kennedy–King College from 1994 to 1998 and Interim President of Harold Washington College from 1993 to 1994.

CHAPTER FIVE

An Inside Look At the Information Technology Sector

"There is no doubt that a nation that is technologically savvy will inevitably have a competitive edge. As we become more "digital" as a society, not only does STEM education lead to technology-led-innovations, but also increased competitiveness and productivity of a country."

- N. Chandrasekaran, Chief Executive Officer and Managing Director, Tata Consultancy Services (TCS)

Excerpt from *100 CEO Leaders in STEM,* a publication by STEMconnector®

Note: Though industry models are contained throughout *Advancing a Jobs-Driven Economy,* this chapter focuses specifically on **Information Technology** with Tata Consultancy Services, Apollo Education Group, ConsultEdu (Cisco) and TE Connectivity.

Digital Fluency {Plug–in} for Industry Context &
Career Readiness in a Jobs-Driven Economy

By: Balaji Ganapathy, Head of Workforce Effectiveness, Tata Consultancy Services (TCS) and Co–Chair, STEMconnector® STEM Innovation Task Force

I dream of a future when our country's youth can realize and utilize their full and true potential; our families, neighborhoods and communities become hubs for innovation and economic growth; and our nation a shining beacon of social prosperity. You would readily acknowledge the incredible opportunity that we are presented with to influence that outcome, as industry, academia, government or non–profits. We can use the power of partnerships between industry and higher education to provide much needed industry context, and create career readiness, preparing students as catalysts in a jobs-driven economy. While we can influence several variables of this equation, in my opinion there is none more fundamental and pervasive than the need to create Digital Fluency, a new set of skills and a new way to use those skills to develop solutions to real world problems in this digital era.

We live in a hyper–connected world, powered by digital technologies that have burst onto the scene over the past decade. The globalization of markets across developed and emerging economies, has led to businesses competing not just at a local, or regional level, but at a national and often international level. Digital technologies are also helping organizations meet their consumer's demands for responsiveness, knowledge, engagement, and individualized attention. On the other hand, employers throughout the United States continue struggling to find skilled workers, and without immediate action, the skills gap will grow to more than 5 million unfilled positions by 2018. There is a growing trend among businesses to partner directly with institutions of higher education, in their endeavor to be a part of the solution rather than part of the problem.

To create a workforce that reflects the ethnic fabric of local communities across the country, corporate leaders must effectively communicate future workforce needs, and invest resources to empower educators to deliver a skilled workforce that can contribute to the innovation and agility needed by the industry.

From a business perspective, I want to emphasize the need to identify and prioritize the focal point on these collaborations upfront, so that the investments are strategic in nature, measured against desired short, mid and long–term outcomes, and sustainability is built into the design of the programs. The more such initiatives are aligned with business growth forecasts and future workforce needs, the better will be utilization of resources allocated to these efforts. This was a foundational design principle adopted by STEMconnector®'s STEM Innovation Task Force (SITF) when we recently launched STEM 2.0, a cross-sector initiative to identify, define and teach new skills sets and critical capabilities that the future workforce will need to become successful STEM professionals in tomorrow's economy. Utilizing a strategic, actionable, scalable and sustainable approach to support the education ecosystem from a demand side perspective, we are looking to impact the deficit for STEM skills. These skill sets include Employability Skills, Innovation Excellence, and

Digital Fluency and additionally, the initiative will work to identify and find solutions for industry-specific capabilities in fields like advanced manufacturing, food and agriculture, and information technology.

Examining the structural challenges of our environment can help us gain a better appreciation for the issues, and therefore identify effective solution levers.

In its 2014 Education report,[39] the OECD reports that:

- Average investment in U.S. higher education is $100,000.

- 48 percent of adults with an undergraduate degree earn less than half the national median wage.

- With university level education, 31 percent earn more than twice the median wage.

The U.S. Census Bureau reports[40] that:

- 9.3 million Americans are unemployed versus 4.7 million unfilled jobs.

- Of those unemployed, 3.1 million are between 16–25 years age, 6.2 million age 25 and over.

- College graduates have one of lowest unemployment rates at 2.3 percent.

Yet, according to Complete College America,[41] too few graduate on time:

- 36 percent at 4–year flagship universities.

- 22 percent at land grant universities

- 19 percent at non-flagship universities.

- 4 percent at 2–year institutions.

- By 2020, ~13 million students will drop out of high school.

Today, 1 in 4 civilians with a bachelor's degree or higher, are employed in STEM & STEM–related occupations, with $3.2 million average work life earnings.

With the backdrop of these metrics, let us examine the topic that I opened with – the unique opportunity to capitalize on the talent of our country's youth and create a future workforce. Digital Fluency presents a green space for such industry-academia collaborations, illustrated by the current state of computer science skills in K–12 and higher education. 73 percent of new STEM jobs created from 2010 to 2020 are projected to require a foundation in computer science (CS), more than 1.4 million jobs created by 2020 will require CS and programming skills.[42] According to the U.S. Bureau of Labor Statistics (BLS), between 2013 and 2023, there will be two jobs available for every graduate with a CS degree. Against a current industry need for 130,000 CS graduates per year, for jobs that pay upwards of $64,000 at an entry level, there are only 65,000 CS graduates produced by our system. The drop–out rates for CS courses in college is at 69 percent, at least half of which can be attributed to switching majors due to a lack of foundation in mathematics and the other half leave college without attaining a degree or certificate. Then there is the K–12 system, where 9 of 10 schools don't even offer a CS course. It is a travesty that only 1.4 percent of graduates pass the CS AP exam in Maryland, with the pass rates even lower in the rest of the 49 states. Successful transformation would mean balancing this equation, using Digital Fluency as a plug–in for industry context and career readiness.[43, 44]

If industry and education can create Digital Fluency skill sets, the resulting workforce can fully participate in the jobs of the digital era, and exponentially impact economic growth. We need preparedness among our youth to participate in the economic growth and social prosperity that accompanies jobs in the new digital economy. We need the collaborations to focus on increasing student engagement and motivation, as well as provide early exposure to STEM subjects and CS to impact interest and persistence. We also need to open the tent to all demographics, so that traditional barriers for underrepresented groups, and ethnic minorities are removed. I offer here a non–exhaustive list of recommendations for industry and academia partners to consider, while embarking on collaborations:

- Promote and provide hands–on activities.

- Introduce role models or mentors that reflect student diversity.

- Provide activities that involve teamwork and collaboration.

- Choose activities that encourage problem solving and have an application to the real world.

- Encourage students to attend STEM related summer camps.

- Increase teacher and school counselor awareness of the STEM career opportunities.

- Market STEM classes to both students and parents.

- Encourage participation by holding outreach and academic events, such as competitions and fairs.

Together, let us broaden the base and provide our youth the educational foundation on STEM disciplines; increase the STEM pathway persistence from K–12 to college, and college to career; include underrepresented groups and all demographics; and impart Digital Fluency skills to unlock fulfilling careers in this digital economy.

About Tata Consultancy Services

Tata Consultancy Services is an IT services, consulting and business solutions organization that delivers real results to global businesses, ensuring a level of certainty that no other firm can match. TCS offers a consulting–led integrated portfolio of IT and IT–enabled services delivered through its unique Global Network Delivery Model™ (GNDM™), recognized as the benchmark of excellence in software development.

About the Author

As the Head of Workforce Effectiveness, Balaji oversees the functions of Human Resources Business Consulting, Diversity & Inclusion, and Corporate Social Responsibility for over 28,000 employees of Tata Consultancy Services in North America. His primary responsibilities include coaching sales and business teams for business growth, driving talent management and employee retention initiatives, architecting the corporate sustainability strategy, and chairing the Diversity & Inclusion Council.

Balaji serves as the Vice–Chair of STEMconnector®'s STEM Innovation Task Force (SITF), a high–level team of thirty–two leaders from industry, government, and non–profit sectors whose vision is to accelerate sustainable STEM careers and wealth through innovation science and excellence in tomorrow's new economy. He is also a member of the U.S. Chamber of Commerce Foundation's Education, Employment & Training Committee (EETC), and is on the Advisory Board of their Talent Pipeline Management initiative; an innovative approach to closing the skills gap. He serves as the Vice Chair of the Million Women Mentors (MWM) Leadership Council (MWM), leading the efforts on removing barriers for girls & women in STEM education & careers. Under his stewardship, TCS is using its technology innovation, thought leadership and skill based volunteering to impact the state of STEM education in North America; with a special focus on impacting women & girls, minorities and underrepresented groups.

How to Provide Knowledge and Skills Faster to Fill America's Tech Jobs
By: Mark Brenner, Chief of Staff to the Chief Operating Officer and Senior Vice
President of Corporate Communications and External Affairs
Apollo Education Group

The skills gap has become somewhat of a loose term, bandied about easily and in different forms by educators, employers and elected officials. In political speeches the skills gap has become a "national imperative" – but in some academic circles it remains a lofty concept, hard to define. Orthodoxy holds – and research and experience support – that employers in certain fields, particularly those related to technology, education, healthcare and science, are unable to fill certain available positions.

But I have the fortune of seeing the skills gap in much more practical terms. At Apollo Education Group, we're engaged in the straightforward – but very demanding – task of filling that conceptual skills gap. This involves imparting real skills to real people who can fill jobs in high demand fields. Done properly, this will be our most important function. America has been seeking to close many different iterations of skills gaps for many years, and it needs innovative educators to help make the necessary advancements.

One shortage in particular, is in the area of Information Technology. Ask any Chief Information Officer at any public or private organization - as Gary S. Beach did recently for his book The U.S. Technology Skills Gap - and you will hear that the widest gap may well exist in the information systems, technology and computer science fields.[45] Americans were falling behind even at the start of the information technology revolution in the 1970s - before microcomputers and the Internet and before that revolution of personal computing. Public and private employers kept their computers - as Tracy Kidder famously wrote - "behind a plate glass window, people in white gowns attending it, and those who wished to use it did so through intermediaries. Users were supplicants." [46]

The gap in our nation's ability to develop IT talent is well known. The shortage of workers is a widely documented phenomenon, but it's also a trend that is accelerating in the United States. The nation's information technology industry is hiring, but they simply can't find the skilled workforce needed in America. If left unresolved, America will lose companies, lose employment opportunities, and ultimately erode our competitiveness.

In information technology and related fields, eliminating that national skills gap, fulfilling demand for skilled labor by a supply of work–ready employees, requires not only a comprehensive and adaptable understanding of the needs of CIOs, but a truly adaptable and relevant educational offering endowed with the blessing of those same CIOs.

At the heart of this reality lies the recognition that the traditional path of higher education is not the most efficient – or sometimes even the most relevant. That's true in information technology, and it's true in a number of other fields. And it's that spirit that underlies the awarding of the certificate. The number of certificates awarded in this country has skyrocketed over the past decades – over 800 percent in the thirty years to 2009, according to the Survey of Income and Program Participation (SIPP) – a phenomenon best chronicled by Professor Anthony Carnevale.[47]

Scholars have also made clear that "certificates are particularly useful for hard–to–serve populations, such as minorities, low–income adults, and young people who didn't do well in high school." [48] And yet, for all the promise of certificates, scholars note that some confusion exists over what a certificate is. Notably, these qualifications are not the same as industry–based or company–specific certifications. They are qualifications earned through, often intensive, classroom time.

At Apollo Education Group, we've begun offering certificates in affiliation with University of Phoenix. Among our newest offerings is a web development boot camp. The term "boot camp" entered the vernacular of workforce development professions in early 2012 when new coding programs in New York and the San Francisco Bay Area were formed. The site Course Report was created to publish reviews and offer a directory of coding boot camps. At Apollo we started SkilledUp.com to establish a marketplace for boot camps and other online learning offerings. But the RockIT Bootcamp in Tempe, Arizona, has given us revealing insights into the IT human capital needs of local employers. [49]

The program is immersive. Twelve weeks of 12–hour days and hands–on opportunity to learn code in both front– and back–end languages. The program focuses on teaching these students the hands–on skills they need to be successful as entry–level web development professionals. These are well paying full time jobs that are vital to the success of many employers.

The instructors are professionals – the top of their games in their fields. They are the experts in information technology who are also given to teaching – imparting the latest frontier to others. Those instructors – like Brig Lamoreaux– are professional data architects, web developers and professionals in IT organizations, who are working closely with local employers – the very companies who need the talent they're developing. And the process is not simulated, it's reality, employers presenting problems and are imparting real skills.

As they teach, they're not just working to an abstract – they are imparting the specific knowledge required to take an entry–level position in real world companies. Companies that are hiring right now in the Phoenix area regularly visit the boot camp. The graduates of RockIT Bootcamp go into a market saturated with demands. At the time of printing this chapter (November 2014), more than 600 open web developer jobs had been posted in the past 90 days. So, it's no surprise that RockIT's graduates are being placed in jobs almost immediately. 15 out of the 18 men and women of RockIT bootcamp's first cohort are now employed in the space.

And RockIT is designed to land its graduates right into one of those jobs, as a first cohort graduate of the boot camp, Kris Faultner, notes: having different employers involved throughout the program helped me land a position quickly. The employer presentations, networking and mock interviews allowed us to get to know each other before the interview process".

It's an accelerator in its own right – it is selective, but not necessarily in the ways you might think. The selection process doesn't just look at math skills, for example. Many additional personal dimensions are considered – including sheer desire to make it in the industry.

Boot camps are remarkable for another reason: they prepare candidates for the soft skills of communications, resume writing and interviewing for developer and engineering jobs. Take, for example, one of the very first boot camps to start in early–2012, Dev Bootcamp. A graduate of Dev Bootcamp was not only taught how to code, but how to explain to hiring managers the extent of her new web development skills. She came to web development from political campaigns and the social sciences, where interviews consisted of what she called "just talking." [50] She says interviews in the IT field were much different:

"I have never seen a field where the interview process varies so much between companies as web development. You could have whiteboarding in one interview, another might have live coding, others want to talk about algorithms, and some may not have any coding at all; it's all over the map. Dev Bootcamp has an intense feedback process and makes you really introspective about yourself and your code. Dev Bootcamp really helped me develop my communication skills to communicate my thought process going through my code. When you pair program during class, you have to be able to communicate your thought process." (Ibid)

Our own RockIT Bootcamp offers similar life skills, and all educators must soon recognize that to prepare students for jobs in the Information Technology, learning must include both hard and soft skills.

This is an encapsulation of the very challenge – and the opportunity that faces America. There were more than 4.7 million job openings in the United States on the last day of September 2014 according to the Bureau of Labor Statistics. To move toward a fully employed labor force will require assessment of skills and training in fields of high demand and linking those to employers. Focusing on these activities will lift up individuals, companies, and America as a whole.[51]

About Apollo Education Group

Apollo Education Group, Inc. (NASDAQ: APOL) is one of the world's largest private education providers and has been in the education business since 1973. Through its subsidiaries: Apollo Global, College for Financial Planning, University of Phoenix, and Western International University, Apollo Education Group offers innovative and distinctive educational programs and services, online and on–campus, at the undergraduate, masters and doctoral levels. Its educational programs and services are offered throughout the United States and in Europe, Australia, Latin America, Africa and Asia, as well as online throughout the world.

For more information about Apollo Education Group, Inc. and its subsidiaries, call (800) 990–APOL or visit the Company's website at www.apollo.edu.

About the Author

Mark Brenner serves as Chief of Staff to the Chief Operating Officer and Senior Vice President of Corporate Communications and External Affairs of Apollo Education Group. His responsibilities include directing all activities related to external communications on behalf of Apollo Education Group and its subsidiaries. Prior to joining the organization in 2010, Mr. Brenner served as Vice Chairman of the Board and Executive Officer of College Loan Corporation. He also has held senior management positions with Fernwood Capital Management, Marshall Morgan LLC and William R. Hough & Co. Previously, Mr. Brenner served as Director of Legislative Affairs and General Counsel for the Education Finance Committee, and held staff positions with the House Education and Workforce Committee and the Senate Committee on Banking, Housing and Urban Affairs. He also served as an advisor to New York State Senate Majority Leader Ralph Mariano (R–NY).

Mr. Brenner received his Bachelor of Arts degree in Political Science from Siena College, as well as a Juris Doctor degree from Albany Law School, and currently serves on the national board of directors of Junior Achievement.

Making STEM Smart: The Internet of Things in Education
By: Dr. Michelle Selinger, Education Technology Specialist, ConsultEdu (Cisco)

The Internet of Things (IoT) is about smart objects - interconnected things in which the line between the physical object and digital information about that object is blurred. At the simplest level, IoT focuses on sensor networks - machines communicating with other machines, and the data created as a result. As things add capabilities such as context–awareness, increased processing power, and energy independence, and, as more people and new information are connected, we have a network of networks where billions, or even trillions, of connections create unprecedented opportunities, as well as new risks.

There are a lot of examples of how IoT will impact our daily lives. http://postscapes.com/internet–of–things–examples gives some clear examples, but how will IoT impact what is taught both in the use of technology and across subject areas? What benefits could adopting IoT bring to education and what will educators need to know in order to exploit IoT to benefit learners?

Today the Internet connects people to many things (media, photos, information, etc.) but now it can also connect people to physical objects. We can launch applications on our computer by just touching a physical object, and physical objects can "talk" to each other through an Internet connection, feed data between themselves, and even command each other to perform a physical act. As things link with people, things also become part of social networks. In the same manner that photos are currently tagged with the names of the people in them, objects can also be tagged with their owners and users as well as with commentaries. This in consequence, will give objects more history and more value for learning.

New Ways of Measuring Student Performance and Setting Activities
With the proliferation of mobile devices from smartphones to tablets and increasingly portable computers, we will be able to connect the right people together to accelerate learning as well as collecting and interpreting data on learners' behaviors and activity so developing new ways to measure their performance. Used well, this will make learning more personalized and targeted to individuals' learning needs, their learning styles and preferences, and their aspirations.

It is already clear that educators are no longer able to know about, or easily tap into, all the available knowledge in their domain; they increasingly have to rely on others to help find, assimilate and distribute the ever–growing collective wisdom. If education institutions can no longer rely solely on the core competences and knowledge of their teachers, they will need to make use of IoT to capture intelligence faster and from many external sources.

The Potential of IoT
A fundamental skill set will be cross–domain understanding and how things interact in order for users to experience the benefits from IoT. It will be important for educators to understand how people connect to the Internet to further their learning, and how they develop their understanding and application of their knowledge as a result. Time

to mastery is going to be key since whatever we know today will be added to tomorrow, and those that thrive will know how best to keep themselves updated and ahead of the pack. Finding the right people with whom to learn and who to learn from is going to be crucial. As each individual becomes a node on the network, people will want, and need to know how, to connect to the work of leading experts in a field of study and with peers with the same passions and interests. They will share ideas, discuss research and latest developments in a domain of study and develop increasingly connected communities of practice. The experts in a specific area will be sought to teach classes anywhere in the world and sharing teaching via streamed or live video will become the norm.

People experience the world through their five senses and the IoT now becomes a proxy for sensing, understanding and managing our world. Humans are notoriously bad at capturing data accurately, consistently and routinely, but with IoT, things that were silent now have a "voice" and devices gather data and stream it over the Internet to a central source, where it is analyzed and processed. As the capabilities of things connected to the Internet continue to advance, they will become more intelligent by combining data into more useful information.

Having to go to the physical object to collect data in different conditions will be a thing of the past. Learners will tag physical objects to find and analyze data collected over 24 hours and feed that information into other programs for analysis. They will have 24 hour data collection, which can make research more accurate and the skills of knowing how to measure will become less important (the device will do that), but skills like collaborative problem solving and critical thinking, such as knowing which measurements are relevant for their specific analysis and how to analyze the results, can be given greater focus in a world where such skills have become increasingly important. Learners will also be able to access data from research initiatives; monitor programs on oceanography or climate change; find out how much carbon dioxide a tree is emitting, and watch animals in real time in their natural habitat through webcams. The emergence of such authentic data will not only have a huge impact on learners' interest, it will also help the environment through the need for less field trips (which will still have value to ensure learners understand the context and issues associated with collecting raw data), and bring more real time information to learners than ever before.

IoT Across the Curriculum
An educational activity to link mathematics, science and physical education will see learners using sensors to monitor their own everyday activity. By collecting data on how far they walk or run in a day, as well as their heart rate and other metabolic data, they become more aware of their own health and begin to develop an understanding of the impact their current life style will have on their future health and longevity. As a class project, human biology comes alive and leads to greater engagement. Biology classes become more interesting as learners use data to motivate each other to achieve better fitness and to maintain a balanced diet. Instead of *talking* about what is a good life style, gathering real, personal data can give clearer and more impactful messages about the need for a better lifestyle.

As well as making their own research more accurate, working with and manipulating real data, learners can also contribute the data they have collected to data banks, so becoming contributing members of expert communities in research projects on climate change, species identification, archaeology and much more. Sharing datasets with others around the world will enhance and extend their learning experience and make it more authentic through active engagement with the research community. Not only are learners in contact with researchers, they are working with them to help solve local and global problems. For example, if learners use sensors to monitor how much time they spend cycling and the routes they take, the aggregated data collected across schools in a city can be used to persuade the authorities to build more cycle ways. And as the data collected can be specific, the location of cycle ways and the order in which they need to be built are determined through authentic, crowd–sourced data.

Teachers can also create and attach RFID tags to physical objects and learners studying a foreign language will associate the object with the word in their selected language by scanning the object with an RFID reader. It will say the word for the item in both their native language and in the foreign language. Touching the item will give learners an additional sense and may help them remember the vocabulary through association with touch.

There a myriad of uses of technology in education, but much of the use is piecemeal, ad hoc and with little 'joined–up' thinking; IoT has the potential to bring that all together.

About ConsultEdu

ConsultEdu Ltd is an independent consulting company based in the UK. The company helps clients to redesign learning and teaching through bespoke solutions and strategic advice, and specializing in the effective use of educational technology. By bringing a wealth of experience of successful deployments of innovative technology-enhanced education solutions from around the world in school, vocational and higher education, the company successfully engages in the design of innovative online and face-to-face learning and teaching environments. ConsultEdu has the ability to bring together a team of recognized experts with practical academic and technical experience that is grounded and adaptable, to deliver bespoke solutions that support sustainable transformation in a range of different education environments in developed, emerging and developing economies. CEO, Dr. Michelle Selinger, has a record of thought leadership and powerful next practice at the intersection of education and technology. A teacher, curriculum developer, educational consultant and strategist, Michelle has a global reputation as a leader in the impact on education theory and practice of technology, especially the Internet and networked collaboration.

About the Author

Dr. Michelle Selinger is an independent consultant focusing on all aspects of technology-enhanced learning. Prior to that Michelle led the education consultancy practice at Cisco where she brought her academic background to specialize in education transformation in all areas of formal learning and skills development and has extensive experience helping governments and educational institutions around the world in both developed and emerging economies to create strategies for technology–enabled education reform.

All Things Digital
An Interview with Earl Newsome, Corporate Chief Information Officer
TE Connectivity

TE Connectivity is on the cutting edge in terms of the need for the best and brightest engineering and technology skilled talent, which you know so well as Corporate CIO. Why is STEM education/workforce development critical to the future of our nation and the world?

The future of careers is really going to center around technology and engineering. If you think about the core element of what STEM involves, it's really about basing everything on data. The analysis and consumption of data is the basis of STEM.

It fits in with the evolution of economies, too. We've gone from the agricultural economy to the industrial economy, and now we're in the digital economy. The entire physical layer of our economy can be digitized through the introduction of digital essentials. The process will create what I call "digital exhaust," from which new experiences will be created for consumers and businesses.

STEM skills are required to take advantage of that digital exhaust and start successful and thriving businesses. Harvesting the data in digital exhaust will allow businesses to take advantage of new opportunities.

It is exciting to see the opportunities that are going to be enabled by this new digital economy. As an example, think of a sensor that will detect when a car hits a pothole. That sensor can be integrated into the car's suspension system to ensure a smoother and safer ride. The data from that sensor can also be relayed to an auto repair shop to customize fixes, and it can further be sent to the public works department of a local government so that they get real time information about where potholes are located and repair them quickly.

What steps should be taken by higher education leaders and business leaders to increase the STEM pathway to jobs?

The digital moments that are the foundation of the new economy represent the opportunities of the new economy, which means jobs for future generations. Higher education leaders and business leaders need to recognize that these opportunities are the jobs of tomorrow, and they need to build an acceptable product – a well–educated student – who is prepared to be a part of the workforce to leverage the opportunities of the digital economy.

How does that relate to employability and the digital experience? There's a huge gap in terms of the skills that students are getting and what employers need, so what is your challenge to higher education leaders about filling that gap?

What's running in my head as I hear this is, "how do we bring the power and ingenuity of Silicon Valley to –all of the U.S." We need to bring best practices and "next" practices to more people, encapsulate them and grow them so that their model is spread to workforce development efforts across the country. Let's go find those next practices and adopt them universally.

You speak of 4–Voices as critical to smart STEM investments: Customers (corporate America); Partners (higher education); students and TE. Share your views of 4–Voices and the challenge to the jobs–driven nature of partnerships.

The 4–Voices will give us a track in order to take advantage of opportunities in the digital economy. We got looped into this program... it's a great process with people and technology. We've got to speak to the 4–Voices, but higher education, municipalities, and corporate America have to do so as well.

Diversity and inclusion are top priorities for education and business. We look at Silicon Valley's problem with this, and so the question is: How does TE view the challenge and solution?

We are diverse by nature. But we have yet to unlock the real power of diversity and inclusion. If you think about the power of the Valley, they're very inclusive and tolerant – the culture values different viewpoints and new ideas. We really need to capture this inclusive culture, embodied in companies like Apple – the worlds most profitable – and grow it. Inclusion is about diversity, but it is about engagement as well. If you want to be like Apple, you'll embrace this – and you'll win in the digital future.

With higher education institutions and industry both working with very different business models, how do they align their agendas, move at the speed of business, and make necessary changes required to advance a jobs–driven economy?

The line between educational institutions and industry actually needs to go away. We're all about building a product. You build an acceptable product that meets your customer's needs, and you build acceptance of that product by taking something that you build within your four walls and selling it – hoping that someone will buy it. The most successful businesses in today's economy are about being customer–driven and customer–centric, and they tailor their products accordingly.

Education institutions need to follow this, change their approach, and build a product that is acceptable in the digital marketplace. They need to produce products who live, produce, support and be prepared for this new digital economy.

What is your Call to Action?

The definition of insanity is doing things the same way and expecting a different result. You want to get out in front of the digital economy. Ask yourself, if Steve Jobs bought and took control of this company, what would he do? Talk about being visionary: to be visionary you have to be comfortable with being perceived as misunderstood for a long period of time – as those getting out in front usually are.

At TE, we're a company that makes solutions – but we're moving to be a platform in the internet space to connect people. We want to be a contributing force in the new digital economy. After all, connectivity is essential to the internet of things. It's about connections between people and business. In the Internet age, every connection counts and "connectivity" is our middle name.

About TE Connectivity

TE Connectivity (NYSE: TEL) is a technology leader that designs and manufactures the electronic connectors, components and systems inside the products that are changing the world – making them smarter, safer, greener and more connected.

About the Author

Earl Newsome currently serves as Corporate Chief Information Officer and Vice President, Digital, for TE Connectivity. In this role, Newsome is responsible for transforming and repositioning how TE drives digital across the enterprise to deliver an extraordinary customer and employee experience. In addition, he is responsible for partnering with corporate strategy to ensure IT and technology innovation is a key component of the TE corporate strategy, helping to create a competitive advantage within the corporate functions leveraging technology, driving architecture throughout enterprise, and leading IT innovation and strategy.

Previously, Newsome served as vice president, Infrastructure and Operations at TE, where he was responsible for transitioning a long–term IT shared services strategy into a commercial offering, driving innovative thinking and implementation of new improved processes.

Prior to joining TE Connectivity in 2012, Newsome served as vice president, Global Shared Services for the Estee Lauder Companies, responsible for technology infrastructure and operations, risk and security, development, production support, architecture and service management services.

CHAPTER SIX

Building the Workforce of Tomorrow through Manufacturing

"…the most successful efforts have been driven by industry. However, there is also no one size fits all approach to the solution. A collective effort can defeat the challenge that looms over this industry."

-Jennifer McNelly, President
The Manufacturing Institute

Note: Though industry models are contained throughout *Advancing a Jobs-Driven Economy,* this chapter focuses specifically on **Manufacturing** with The Manufacturing Institute, Hope Street Group, EverFi, Business Roundtable/E3 (Engage, Educate, Employ) and Alcoa.

Manufacturing Framework for Action – We Must Lead
By: Jennifer McNelly, President, The Manufacturing Institute

Today's manufacturing is not what it used to be. It requires a highly skilled and trained workforce that is not easily obtainable in today's education and job training system. The skills and training gap is real, and it already impacts our nation's manufacturers. More importantly, the gap is growing. Manufacturers must make putting an end to this gap a priority.

Every day we try to combat the misperceptions of the manufacturing industry. We lose good, talented workers due to these outdated attitudes. Only three out of ten parents would encourage their kids to pursue manufacturing careers. And yet, 90 percent of Americans believe manufacturing is important to our standard of living and economic prosperity. Everyone wants manufacturing jobs... just for someone else.

While Americans value a strong manufacturing sector, the skills shortage threatens the growth of U.S. manufacturing, and it's costing manufacturers. According to the *2014 Manufacturing Skills and Training Study* by Accenture, manufacturers are losing up to 11 percent of potential earnings due to the lack of skilled workers.

In an effort to be more cost effective and focus on business needs, manufacturers have streamlined training. However, there is still a serious disconnect in workforce strategies used by manufacturers. The number one talent recruitment strategy used by manufacturers is word of mouth, not through education. Community colleges ranked last as a way for manufacturers to find skilled talent. This alone is one of the major contributing factors to the skills gap, more commonly known as the training gap. Schools and institutions should be the first place manufacturers are looking to supply their workforce and build a talent pipeline. Equally, education institutions must produce students ready for the world of work.

Manufacturers need a new workforce strategy. So what's the solution? A jobs–driven, demand–driven education and workforce system.

Close the Gap
The Manufacturing Institute has led the strategic effort to develop a qualified manufacturing workforce and pipeline. Through our research and initiatives, we have developed an evidence–based framework to close the skills gap. The framework consists of three goals: change the perception of careers in manufacturing, re–establish the U.S. as the global leader of manufacturing education, and advocate for education and job training policies that strengthen the U.S. manufacturing workforce.

Change the Perception of Careers in Manufacturing

The perception of manufacturing careers is vital to the success of the industry. Today's manufacturing is about advanced technologies, state-of-the-art facilities, and fast paced work environments. Manufacturing careers offer security with good salaries and opportunities to quickly move up the ladder of success.

It is crucial that manufacturing develops a diversified workforce. Focusing on developing the next generation of manufacturers will help build the manufacturing talent pipeline. Initiatives such as Dream It Do It, or Manufacturing Day are great ways for manufacturers to open their doors to students all over the country and show what the current industry is really all about.

In addition, we need to focus on underrepresented populations in the workforce, including women and veterans. Women make up 50 percent of the workforce, but only 24 percent of the manufacturing workforce. Transitioning veterans possess not only an unmatched work ethic but also rigorous technical training and experience. These untapped resources fill a critical need for manufacturers' talent pipeline.

Re–Establish the U.S. as the Global Leader of Manufacturing Education

Still, changing the image of manufacturing will take many years, and we need qualified workers now. More than 80 percent of manufacturers report they cannot find people to fill their skilled production jobs. With the advancement of technology comes the need for highly trained workers with advanced technical skills. The Manufacturing Institute is working to develop quality education through employer–driven partnerships and the use of industry standards and certifications.

For the past year, The Manufacturing Institute has worked with the nation's top manufacturers, educators, and community leaders to develop how–to guides on building a workforce ready talent pipeline in communities across the country. In partnership with the President's Advanced Manufacturing Partnership (AMP) 2.0, led by Eric Spiegel, president and Chief Operating Officer of Siemens, USA and Dr. Annette Parker, president of South Central College, the Institute created a variety of toolkits that provide step by step guides to engaging education and utilizing certifications, helping manufacturers, educators, and community leaders create a plan to develop and grow a pipeline to ensure a supply of future skilled talent.

Public–private partnership is key to this success. The Institute has found that in communities and states across the country, the most successful efforts have been driven by industry. However, there is also no one size fits all approach to the solution. A collective effort can defeat the challenge that looms over this industry.

Advocate for Education and Job Training Policies that Strengthen the U.S. Manufacturing Workforce

Yet, change isn't possible without support from policy makers.

The Manufacturing Institute has tirelessly worked in partnership with the National Association of Manufacturers (NAM) to improve the competiveness of U.S. manufacturing. The NAM's board–level Task Force on Competitiveness & the Workforce took on a yearlong effort to improve workforce preparedness and capabilities. They created a toolkit and guide to help manufacturing leaders collaborate in their local communities to determine the key competencies needed for new hires to succeed in today's advanced manufacturing operations, develop a plan for local workforce training providers to deliver the needed training, and grow a pipeline to ensure a supply of future skilled talent.

AMP 2.0 Steering Committee is part of the federal effort to support high–quality manufacturing jobs and enhance the U.S. manufacturing industry. The White House's recent report – Accelerating U.S. Advanced Manufacturing – aligns with the Manufacturing Institute's framework for closing the skills gap, including recommendations for technology development, building a National Network for Manufacturing Innovation (NNMI), aligning industry standards with education outcomes, and creating a positive image for manufacturing careers.

Manufacturers in Action

Manufacturing may be the answer to the world's problems – it saves lives, builds the global middle class, boosts global trade, and without it, the U.S. would not be the world leader it is today.

However, manufacturers must take action to tackle these pressing issues. It is up to manufacturers to connect with public leaders, educators, and individuals in their communities to build their workforce pipeline and keep manufacturing strong in their communities. By taking back the conversation and engaging with our most important supply chain, our talent, we will build our workforce and make manufacturing strong.

About The Manufacturing Institute

The Manufacturing Institute is the authority on the attraction, qualification, and development of world–class manufacturing talent. The Institute is the place where we exceed expectations and deliver results to help close the skills gap.

In partnership with some of the leading consulting firms in the country, the Institute studies the critical issues facing manufacturing and then applies that research to develop and identify solutions that are implemented by companies, schools, governments, and organizations across the country.

The Institute's strategies and actions are all done to achieve the following goals:
- Change the perception of careers in manufacturing to reflect its true status as the most advanced, high–tech industry in the country.

- Re–establish the U.S. as the global leader of manufacturing education.

- Advocate for education and job training policies that strengthen the U.S. manufacturing workforce.

About the Author

Jennifer McNelly was named President of The Manufacturing Institute, the non–profit affiliate of the National Association of Manufacturers (NAM), effective April 1, 2012.

Jennifer has extensive experience in workforce development, employer engagement, and business. She is a proven leader at the Institute as the Chief Architect of one of the organization's flagship initiatives, the NAM–Endorsed Manufacturing Skills Certification System. A set of nationally portable, industry recognized manufacturing skills certifications, the System is building the next generation of skilled manufacturing employees by influencing secondary and post–secondary education reform efforts in over 35 states, which is building the next generation of skilled manufacturing talent.

Prior to joining the Institute, Jennifer, a member of the Senior Executive Service (SES), was Administrator for the U.S. Department of Labor's Office (DOL) Office of Regional Innovation and Transformation. She also served as the Director of the Business Relations Group for the DOL Employment and Training Administration. In this capacity, she managed the President's High–Growth Job Training Initiative and the Community–Based Job Training Grants. Her strong private sector experience includes serving as the Senior Vice President of Strategic Partnerships, LLC, an international consulting firm specializing in assisting Fortune 500 corporations build strategic partnerships with government agencies in support of workforce development.

Connecting to Rebuild America's Workforce
By: Martin Scaglione, President and Chief Executive Officer, Hope Street Group

A clear gap exists between the needs of our nation's employers and the way in which young adults are currently preparing to enter into (and excel within) the American workforce. Public school educators often lack the time and resources to introduce students to a wide variety of potential career paths, yet a student is highly unlikely to choose a career that is unfamiliar. Rapid changes in technology have revolutionized a number of industries, but the perceptions of jobs in these industries, along with training options for the skills needed to excel in them, have not always followed suit.

The result of this mismatch has been a U.S. economy that fails to provide robust opportunities to American job seekers, thus disenfranchising our youth and hindering our ability to keep pace with global competitors.

One industry that perfectly illustrates the need for better alignment along the learning to work continuum is the U.S. manufacturing sector. The reality of a job in manufacturing today differs vastly from a job in the same sector twenty-five years ago; routine tasks have been replaced by machine labor, and employees instead are needed for their technical, cognitive, and interpersonal skills. Jobs in manufacturing and the skilled trades also offer impressive wages, making them highly viable career choices.

At the same time, manufacturing employers are struggling to fill their hiring needs and many current employees are gearing up for retirement. While this could present a worrisome problem for the manufacturing industry, it could also present an outstanding opportunity for those just starting a career in the field. Many Americans, however, especially young job seekers, remain largely unaware of this fact.

To address this issue, Hope Street Group recently partnered with Alcoa Foundation to complete a project to gain insight into the broader landscape of issues affecting the lack of young skilled workers entering the manufacturing field. The culmination of this project was the report *Missing Makers: How to Rebuild America's Manufacturing Workforce,* released in July 2014.

The comprehensive report, authored by Hope Street Group's Deputy Director of Jobs Initiatives, Sruti Balakrishnan, holistically frames the regional challenges faced by employers and educators in transitioning young people to skilled careers in manufacturing, and offers tactical recommendations on addressing these barriers.

The goal of the Missing Makers report was to map the decision making patterns of young job seekers as they navigate career and educational opportunities. Interviews were conducted with young learners, manufacturing employers, industry experts, and educators (including deans, principals, and counselors) to ask their ideas about manufacturing careers and to listen to the challenges they faced in meeting employment and/or education related needs.

The report finds that American youth are getting fewer opportunities to experience technical trades directly. Systemic challenges frequently prevent educators and employers from creating opportunities to expose students to manufacturing careers thus exacerbating the problem.

Those aiming to assist students in the career exploration process also expressed concern over significant time and resource barriers. Teachers generally felt they lacked the time and guidance to cover career education in the classroom. Manufacturing employers cited financial difficulties and a lack of coordination with other local employers and educators as major obstacles to success.

As a result, youth frequently develop misconceptions about manufacturing early on and are often unaware, uninterested in or unprepared for jobs available in their regions. Many also lack comprehensive knowledge of the rapid changes the U.S. manufacturing sector has undergone in recent years.

In exploring the best ways to tackle these issues, Hope Street Group found that:

- To fully advance the manufacturing field's recruiting and hiring process and transform the way skilled trades are perceived, conducting early outreach to students and empowering regional leaders is key.

- Companies should actively emphasize to parents and educators that technical training can enhance, rather than limit, career opportunities.

- Companies should provide opportunities, both in–person and virtual, for teachers and counselors to educate themselves on manufacturing career pathways. Companies should also consider creating a set of resources for teachers and guidance counselors, giving them the ability to educate thousands of students in turn.

- Manufacturing business owners, workforce advocates, and educational practitioners have the greatest ability to effect positive change in their own regions.

- Convening area stakeholders, determining the best means of collaboration, and managing projects effectively are all key to ensuring shared success.

Overall, the report suggests that manufacturing employers take a more active role in addressing this knowledge gap by playing a larger role in exposing students to manufacturing and other skilled careers through encouraging manufacturing education in the classroom, providing direct contact with technical trades, and creating online educational resources. The surveys, interviews, and in–depth research executed as part of the *Missing Makers* project made it clear that, across the board, to advance a jobs–driven economy, we need to do a much better job of working together across sectors.

Hope Street Group's overarching goal is the creation of a jobs marketplace in which all entities are working together productively, in which competencies are validated, and in which job seekers can feel aware of and empowered by the skills they have, as well as confident that they can acquire the skills they need to advance in their preferred career path. Building this type of collaborative employment ecosystem is essential across industries, but especially in STEM fields, where so often a lack of training and preparation has resulted in a dearth of qualified candidates. While innovation and enhanced technology are important, so is making sure that new information and opportunities are communicated at all stakeholders involved in education to career pathways.

This report is only the foundation: now it is time to move into action. Hope Street Group is creating specific playbooks to inform employers and educators alike on how to initiate recommended solutions in manufacturing and other industries. Sharing findings across industries is the next step, and one to which all employers, educators, and community members can contribute.

About Hope Street Group

Hope Street Group is a network–driven organization accelerating solutions for social impact in education, health, and jobs. As a nonpartisan non–profit, the organization's work is dedicated to expanding economic opportunity and prosperity for all Americans.

Hope Street Group's Jobs program is focused on addressing today's disjointed jobs landscape in order to provide Americans with the knowledge, skills, and credentials they need to succeed. The organization is currently working on two pieces of the puzzle that are integral to this aim: defining, validating, and advancing industry–endorsed competency models, and advancing the ability of individuals to signal their strengths clearly to an employer, through measured skills training and a commonly adopted language. By actively engaging individuals and organizations, including large and small employers, education institutions, civic and youth organizations, labor unions, philanthropic foundations, technology entrepreneurs, policymakers, and others, to collaborate on elevating best practices in the jobs marketplace, Hope Street Group is able to craft action plans to integrate and scale the most effective solutions.

About the Author

Martin Scaglione joined Hope Street Group in 2014 as the organization's President and Chief Executive Officer. Martin has been involved in recent years with several talent development technology companies as a Founder and Chief Operating Officer.

Martin has made it his life's work to create access to learning for those in need, including as the President and Chief Operating Officer of ACT's Workforce Development Division. While at ACT, Martin was responsible for all business functions supporting workforce–related programs for ACT, an organization recognized internationally for its expertise in measuring knowledge and skills that directly contribute to academic and workplace success. Martin was appointed ACT Division President and Chief Operating Officer in 2007. He left ACT in 2012 to join Viridis Learning.

Before joining ACT, Martin held executive roles with major consumer product manufacturers, including Maytag, Hon Industries, and Bosch–Siemens Household, where he served as Chief Operating Officer, Executive Vice President, and North American Managing Director. Martin has served on several boards, including the National Association of Manufacturer's Manufacturing Institute. Through his leadership in the workforce industry, he is widely credited for President Obama's Job Council program, "Right Skills Now," which today is widely recognized and adopted in multiple industries.

Closing the Skills Gap for New Manufacturing Workers
By: Jerry Jasinowski, Chairman of Critical Skills Initiatives, EverFi

Don't look now, but U.S. manufacturing is producing a steady stream of new jobs. The problem is that we could be producing even more jobs if there were enough qualified applicants to fill them.

Since 2010, manufacturing has added more than 650,000 jobs. This does not replace the 5.7 million manufacturing jobs we lost during the first decade of the new century, but those were largely low skill jobs that would have been lost no matter what we did. As the world evolves into one great marketplace it is simply not possible to pay generous wages for unskilled labor and remain competitive. The world is changing and we must change with it.

There are vast numbers of excellent manufacturing jobs unfilled today because employers cannot find applicants qualified to fill them. Closing that gap – putting qualified people into advanced manufacturing jobs – will strengthen manufacturing, spur economic growth, and provide excellent opportunities to a new generation of manufacturing workers. To make this happen, we must address both the demand and supply sides of the equation – identifying where the demand for manufacturing workers is today and supplying the skill sets that applicants need to acquire those jobs.

We must begin with understanding that the shift to high tech work processes and more demanding work is the dominant trend in U.S. manufacturing and a promising one. Our output today in dollar terms is roughly the same as China, which has more than four times our population and 10 times as many people working in manufacturing. The decisive element in manufacturing is productivity and by this critical measure the U.S. is far ahead of China.

Underpinned by the quality revolution launched by the late W. Edwards Deming many decades ago, and driven by unprecedented foreign competition, U.S. manufacturing has been achieving extraordinary advances in quality, efficiency and productivity. This has enabled us to reduce the costs of manufacturing by about a third over the last two decades while our international competitors have seen their costs increase.

We have embarked upon a new industrial revolution built upon advanced technology that is forging a new hybrid of manufacturing and services that does not fit into established categories. In addition to the 12 million manufacturing jobs now reported by the Bureau of Labor Statistics (BLS), you can add another 6 million jobs supported by manufacturing. And when you consider the hybridization with services, I believe the real world total is actually higher than that. McKinsey estimates that 35 percent of manufacturing employees are today engaged in services that range from logistics to design, research and development, and of course information technology.

This new environment blends mind and machine in new and exciting ways that have created a hybrid of manufacturing and services so that the traditional distinction between the two has less meaning. By any definition the new manufacturing is a rich mother lode of career opportunities. As we are creating substantial numbers of new manufacturing jobs we are finding it poses an unfamiliar challenge because we have not been developing a workforce with the skills required to handle the new high tech jobs.

A key driver of this transition has been a steady drumbeat of innovation in digital, robotics, biotech, additive manufacturing, materials and energy technologies. Clever exploitation of the Internet enables modern manufacturing to discern what consumers want, and to efficiently procure the supplies and parts needed for production much more quickly than in the past. To react quickly, you need your production facilities close by, not the other side of the world.

The technological and distribution revolution has also created incentives for more manufacturers to bring production back home – what is now called re–shoring. Higher production costs overseas – including higher wages and benefits and more attention to safety and environmental concerns, along with a shorter shelf life for many new consumer products, are making outsourcing an out of date idea. The Boston Consulting Group estimates that in 2014 up to half of all manufacturers are planning to bring at least some of their production back here.

The Deming revolution also laid the seeds for sustainable manufacturing, which means a growing number of manufacturers are committed to products and processes that have minimal impact on the environment and consumption of natural resources, including energy. The new model of continuous improvement is a closed loop that is more efficient, avoids waste and contributes to improving the environment of the community. Simply put, more manufacturers are going green.

Taken together, this progress is creating a new kind of manufacturing job that requires a more sophisticated set of skills. We are adding better jobs less susceptible to foreign competition, but the new manufacturing jobs are significantly different from the rote assembly line work of earlier generations. The new manufacturing is built upon advanced technologies and demands more advanced skills from workers. They must be able to grasp engineering concepts, work with computers, make mathematical calculations and adapt to constant change. A manufacturing worker today must have the equivalent of two years of college or the equivalent in technical training, and the bar is rising.

The National Association of Manufacturers (NAM) and the Manufacturing Institute are working with EverFi on more sophisticated training materials on STEM for K–12 schools. EverFi will use its interactive digital learning courses to introduce students to the technical skills needed to be competitive in a rapidly evolving global economy. Students with access to EverFi's immersive digital learning platform will learn about exciting, high–growth careers in manufacturing and the pathways to take advantage of them.

The Institute through its association with the 14,000-member NAM is uniquely placed to address the demand side of the equation working with real world manufacturers to determine where the best career opportunities lie. The Manufacturing Institute's Dream It Do It program is already steering many bright young people into manufacturing careers and will now be coordinating with EverFi to encourage a more intense focus on STEM related subjects at all levels of learning. All of this will be coordinated with the NAM Task Force on Competitiveness & the Workforce which is working to promote U.S. manufacturing, and the annual Manufacturing Day when more than 1,500 manufacturers open their facilities to the public to demonstrate the industry's exciting new career opportunities.

I foresee a rich mother lode of career opportunities emerging in these eight key areas:

- **Digital Technologies** – are rapidly transforming virtually every aspect of how we live and work, and nowhere is that transformation more conspicuous than on the factory floor. There are abundant opportunities for who's with skills in digital technology and software applications.

- **Energy** – serving the entire spectrum of the energy boom from natural gas to oil to solar panels and wind turbines.

- **Automobile/Trucking** – is growing at about 20 percent a year and is more reliant than ever on automation, robots and advanced materials.

- **Aerospace and Transportation** – is seeing a great increase in employment and this field is obviously highly reliant on advanced technologies.

- **Medical Care** – is emerging as one of the biggest sectors of our economy. Technical jobs handling new medical devices are providing excellent career opportunities for thousands of workers.

- **Biotechnology** – loosely defined as use of living systems and organisms to create new products or systems used to produce new products. There are wonderful things going on in biotechnology, and abundant career opportunities.

- **Additive Manufacturing** – sometimes called 3D printing, may be the most exciting new field of all using computers to make physical models of new designs in hours instead of days. Eventually it will supplant many forms of traditional manufacturing.

- **Sustainable Manufacturing** – or green manufacturing if you prefer, is emerging as a subset of its own. Manufacturing will always pose unique challenges to environmental protection, and emerging technologies will both complicate those challenges and offer innovative ways of dealing with them.

The challenge of preparing young people for jobs in modern high tech manufacturing is vital to them and their future as citizens, and to our economy where our leadership in manufacturing plays a decisive role. This new collaboration between the NAM/Institute and EverFi offers a promising response to the challenge.

About EverFi

In 2008, the EverFi founders drove an RV across the country meeting with students, teachers, principals, and superintendents from coast to coast. From inner–city Los Angeles to Native American reservations, from the suburbs of Chicago to the fields of the Mississippi Delta, a common story emerged about the tough issues that put pressure on students and families. We founded EverFi to tackle these tough issues.

Today, EverFi is the leading education technology company focused on teaching, assessing, badging, and certifying students in critical skills. We combine cutting–edge personalized technology, deep education research and data, and a dedicated implementation team that allows each teacher to feel as though they have a blended learning assistant in their classroom. Most importantly, EverFi partners with the private sector and foundations that sponsor this innovation across the country.

EverFi is headquartered in Washington, D.C. with offices in Boston, Chicago, San Francisco, and Toronto and has employees in thirty states across the United States and in Canada.

About the Author

Jerry Jasinowski is sought as a speaker and frequent guest commentator on network and financial news programs. From the early days of Meet the Press to the many current popular cable network business shows, his insights on a wide range of business topics, especially the state of U.S. manufacturing, continue to be valued.

Jerry served as chief executive of the National Association of Manufacturers (NAM) for 14 years and two more as President of the Manufacturing Institute, the NAM's resident think tank. Jerry is a current member of many significant private, public, and non–profit boards. He is a noted economist and the author of two highly regarded books on U.S. –based manufacturing and business – "Making It In America" published by Simon and Schuster in 1995 and "The Rising Tide" published by John Wiley & Sons in 1998.

Jasinowski makes frequent addresses to business organization discussing the most pressing business, economic and political issues of our time, and his weekly blog is widely circulated and also appears on Huffington Post. After retiring from the Presidency of NAM in 2004, after 14 years, Jasinowski spent the next three years as President of the Manufacturing Institute (MI), the non–profit affiliate of NAM.

Employers Know What They're Looking For!
By: Emily DeRocco, Director, National Network of Business
& Industry Associations, Business Roundtable and
Founder and Chief Executive Officer, E3 (Engage, Educate, Employ)

A Partnership Between Working and Learning
In late 2013, a new National Network of Business and Industry Associations launched in Washington, D.C., with a mission to improve economic opportunity and quality of life for Americans by better connecting the working world and the learning world. This National Network represents economic sectors that will be the source of nearly 75 percent of projected job growth by 2020 (an estimated 30 million new jobs), and includes leaders in the business, manufacturing, retail, health care, energy, construction, hospitality, transportation and information technology sectors.

Building an Unprecedented Collaboration
These leaders are united in their commitment to help individuals understand and gain the skills they need to enter into and advance in the jobs of today and tomorrow. This is an unprecedented collaboration of typically competitive industries, and it signals a commitment to support a better prepared and more fulfilled workforce. The Network is co–managed by Business Roundtable, the association of Chief Operating Officers of leading U.S. companies, and the relatively new ACT Foundation, that envisions a National Learning Economy and reaches across boundaries, sectors, and the nation to support working learners in their journeys toward successful careers and lives.

As business cycles change, workforce needs among American industries change as well, but workers who attempt to transition from one industry to another often find that their previous experience and skills may not meet the specific requirements of a new industry even though they are often very similar. This creates barriers for any transitioning worker, but can be particularly difficult for low–income individuals or those who otherwise lack the resources necessary to obtain expensive new training. In today's economy, here are two things we cannot afford: barriers that prevent workers and students from obtaining the skills and abilities employers want, and employers left with job openings they can't fill.

To Advance a Jobs–Driven Economy and Economic Opportunity
The National Network is focused on helping individuals understand and gain the skills they need to enter into and advance in the jobs of today and tomorrow. The Network's business leaders knew where to start. Employers in every sector emphasize the need for people with a strong academic foundation, particularly in reading and math, and the "people skills" like teamwork, problem solving, work ethic and integrity.

In our experience, we knew that each economic sector labels these skills differently, making it difficult for prospective employees and educators to interpret what is needed across industries and career paths. Focused on a practical, how–to approach, the National Network sought to create a "Common Employability Skills" framework that describes the foundational skills all employees need to be prepared for a job in all major economic sectors. The Network wanted a common language to define these skills.

The Network's Common Employability Skills framework can serve as the foundation from which industries can map their specific skills standards, credentials, and career paths. Network members believe that attainment of the core employability skills will make individuals eligible for careers in every sector of the economy and ready to further their educational goals.

In summary, here are the business defined "Employability Skills":

Personal Skills
- *Integrity* – Treating others with honesty, fairness, and respect
- *Initiative* – Demonstrating a willingness to work and seek out new work challenges
- *Dependability and Reliability* – Displaying responsible behaviors at work
- *Adaptability* – Displaying the capability to adapt to new, different or changing requirements
- *Professionalism* – Maintaining a professional demeanor at work

People Skills
- *Teamwork* – Demonstrating the ability to work effectively with others
- *Communication* – Maintaining open lines of communication with others
- *Respect* – Working effectively with those who have diverse backgrounds

Applied Knowledge
- *Reading* – Understanding written sentences and paragraphs in work–related documents
- *Writing* – Using standard English to clearly communicate thoughts, ideas and information in written form
- *Mathematics* – Using mathematics to solve problems
- *Science* – Knowing and applying scientific principles and methods to solve problems
- *Technology* – Using information technology and related applications to convey and retrieve information
- Critical Thinking – Using logical thought processes to analyze and draw conclusions

Workplace Skills
- *Planning and Organizing* – Planning and prioritizing work to manage time effectively and accomplish assigned tasks
- *Problem Solving* – Demonstrating the ability to apply critical–thinking skills to solve problems by generating, evaluating, and implementing solutions

- *Decision Making* – Applying critical thinking skills to solve problems encountered in the workplace
- *Business Fundamentals* – Having fundamental knowledge of the organization and the industry
- *Customer Focus* – Actively looks for ways to identify market demands and meet customer or client needs
- *Working with Tools & Technology* – Selects, uses, and maintains tools and technology to facilitate work activity

Each of these important skill sets are further defined by the competencies needed in the workplace.

The National Network released this framework as a "living document," to be vetted and tested by employers, educators, workforce developers, and other stakeholders. The business and industry organizations in the Network fully understand that there must be a continuous improvement process designed and implemented to maintain the framework's relevance, validity and value.

Throughout 2015, the Network will be determining the capability to "assess" an individual's attainment of the Common Employability Skills, including cognitive and non–cognitive skills. They also will be conducting broad outreach to seek and share input on this framework, expand the use of the framework in employer human resources practices and educational programming, and partner with organizations who will test the framework.

The National Network of Business and Industry Associations links and leverages the work of its 24 member organizations that share a common challenge: finding skilled talent to fill their jobs and developing solutions to help individuals achieve economic and life success.

About Business Roundtable

Business Roundtable (BRT) is an association of chief executive officers of leading U.S. companies working to promote sound public policy and a thriving U.S. economy. Business Roundtable's Chief Operating Officer members lead U.S. companies with $7.4 trillion in annual revenues and more than 16 million employees. BRT member companies comprise more than a third of the total value of the U.S. stock market and invest $158 billion annually in research and development – equal to 62 percent of U.S. private R&D spending. Our companies pay more than $200 billion in dividends to shareholders and generate more than $540 billion in sales for small and medium–sized businesses annually. BRT companies give more than $9 billion a year in combined charitable contributions. Established in 1972, Business Roundtable applies the expertise and experience of its Chief Operating Officer members to the major issues facing the nation. Through research and advocacy, Business Roundtable promotes policies to improve U.S. competitiveness, strengthen the economy, and spur job creation

About E3 (Engage, Educate, Employ)

The E3 Initiative is a three–tiered comprehensive systems approach founded in the belief that all youth deserve an education and job skills so they can reach for their dreams and experience a more fulfilling life. It endeavors to Engage, Educate, and Employ the 16 to 20 year–old population, to increase the likelihood of their becoming educated, resourceful, and contributing members of our communities.

The E3 Initiative maintains that adopting a single program will not solve Colorado's challenges. A broader approach, incorporating a range of services, is more likely to make a difference with this often difficult–to–engage at–risk population.

About the Author

In 2012, Emily DeRocco launched E3, a Washington, DC–based strategic consulting practice focused on linking education, workforce, and economic development assets for competitive advantage. She also serves as Director of National Network of Business & Industry Associations at Business Roundtable

DeRocco is past–President of The Manufacturing Institute, where she implemented a strategic national agenda focused on education reform and workforce development, innovation support and services, and research on behalf of U.S. manufacturers.

DeRocco also served in the President Bush administration as Assistant Secretary for Employment and Training, U.S. Department of Labor, where she managed a $10 billion investment in the nation's workforce. She created and led initiatives to align education, economic, and workforce development investments and to increase the capacity of the nation's community college system. DeRocco also brings over 10 years of private sector experience in managing a national non–profit organization.

Extending the Talent Pipeline –
Alcoa's Strategy for Win–Win Employer–Led Initiatives
By: Greg Bashore, Global Director, Talent Acquisition
and Workforce Development, Alcoa

With the July 2014 passage of the Workforce Innovation and Opportunity Act (WIOA) there is a call to action for employer–led initiatives that better inform the design of education and training programs to prepare individuals for timely employment and career advancement. The move towards employer–led initiatives requires corporations to change how they think as well as how they are structured to extend their talent pipelines into communities and evolve how they communicate their workforce needs with private–public sector partners.

STEMconnector®'s STEM Higher Education Council initiative is an excellent resource for corporations to examine how they are structured to help them develop holistic STEM education strategies that align with corporate objectives and strategy. Using Alcoa and Alcoa Foundation's experience with employer–lead initiatives, this chapter gives an overview of our lessons learned and best practices.

Manufacturing Context
Alcoa is a global leader in lightweight metals that thrives to enhance transportation, from automotive and commercial transport to air and space travel, and improve industrial and consumer electronics products. Across its global businesses, Alcoa faces talent acquisition challenges unique to manufacturing:

- A growing disconnect between the skills needed for advanced manufacturing careers and how educational institutions and training providers are preparing students;

- Poor public image with manufacturing seen as dirty and dangerous with limited career advancement; and

- Heightened competition for engineering and manufacturing talent as more baby boomers retire over the next 10 years.

Today, Alcoa is transforming its business portfolio by building out its innovative, multi–material value–add businesses and by creating a globally competitive commodity business. For Alcoa's talent acquisition, Alcoa's strategy presents challenges and opportunities for how Alcoa selects and develops its engineering and manufacturing talent in the short–term, and prepares tomorrow's workforce talent for advanced manufacturing in the long–term.

Restructuring for Talent Acquisition
In 2008, Alcoa created the talent acquisition center of excellence to coordinate specialized services for the three business groups: campus and experienced hire recruitment, capability development and performance, and leadership and high potential development. In 2010, Alcoa Foundation aligned its educational portfolio with Alcoa's talent acquisition and development priorities by adding guidelines and metrics for workforce development and STEM initiatives. Exhibit 1 shows how Alcoa Foundation's STEM and workforce development interests are translated into key themes and metrics:

EXHIBIT 1: Talent Pipeline – Strategic Themes and Metrics

Invest in educational and training endeavors where Alcoa, as a lightweight metals technology, engineering and manufacturing company, can offer our expertise and make a difference, specifically in the areas of:

Workforce Development – Provide education and training opportunities which lead to employment in engineering and manufacturing.

- # of individuals who acquire certification in a manufacturing field.
- # of individuals who gain employment or improve their employment status in a manufacturing field.
- # of individuals who acquire entry-level or advanced engineering credentials.
- # of individuals who gain employment or improve their employment status in an engineering field.
- # of individuals, organizations or communities impacted.

STEM – Support innovative education and training programs and teaching curriculums in Science, Technology, Engineering and Math to support careers in these disciplines.

- # of youth who gain transferable STEM skills or continue their education in pursuit of a career in STEM.
- # of teachers trained or assisted.
- # of schools impacted.
- # of individuals, organizations or communities impacted.

Advancing each generation. ⊕ALCOA

Additional alignment was achieved in 2013 when the Foundation and Alcoa's Human Resources, Environment, Health and Safety groups came under the same organizational umbrella. The restructuring coordinates Alcoa and the Foundation's workforce development practices and programming, especially those tied to the transportation and aerospace markets.

Communicating Talent Pipeline Priorities

To translate Alcoa's talent pipeline priorities into employer–led initiatives, Alcoa Talent Acquisition and Alcoa Foundation created a "pull" model that is driven by Alcoa's four talent pipelines:

- **Potential (K–12 grades)** – the future pipeline, with the goal of building awareness about manufacturing and engineering careers;

- **Entry–Level (10+ year pipeline)** – high school graduates, two–year degrees and skilled manufacturing certifications, and four year college degrees;

- **Mid–Level (5 year pipeline)** – skilled talent making a transition to manufacturing such as veterans; and

- **Experienced (current pipeline)** – primarily to leverage Alcoa's expertise and leadership as a complement to the Alcoa Foundation programs aligned with the other talent pipeline priorities

The first step with the "pull" model is working sessions with the Vice Presidents of Human Resources for Alcoa's three business groups: Global Primary Products, Global Rolled Product, and Engineered Products and Solutions. Through these sessions, Alcoa Foundation's STEM and workforce development partnerships are reviewed, and the Alcoa's talent pipeline priorities for key growth and profitable locations are identified.

For the selected locations, Alcoa Human Resource Managers and Alcoa Foundation designed community–based core projects using Alcoa Foundation funding to address Alcoa's talent pipeline priorities within the broader context of regional workforce development demands. These core projects extend Alcoa's talent pipeline priorities into communities, and become employer–led initiatives when Alcoa Foundation–funded workforce development initiatives are realized in partnership with other manufacturers, educators, training providers and governmental agencies.

NOTE – Per government regulations, Alcoa Foundation–funded initiatives cannot directly benefit the company. For example, the foundation cannot award a grant to a community college if Alcoa requires the school to select top students to be hired by the company.

One example of the "pull" model can be found in Barberton, Ohio, where Alcoa manufactures high–strength aluminum wheels, and where qualified entry–level talent is in short supply. With funding from Alcoa Foundation, our partner Innovate+Educate is assessing the core skills requirements for entry–level positions shared by manufacturers; taking an inventory of relevant programs offered by high schools and training providers. As a result of this research the organization then makes recommendations on how to best prepare entry–level talent. For its work, Innovate+Educate is using The Hope Street Group (HSG)'s Guide for Practitioners to design and develop a sustainable talent pipeline for entry–level talent.

Win–Win Employer–Led Initiatives

Accenture and Manufacturing Institute's 2014 study *Out of Inventory – Skills Shortage Threatens Growth for U.S. Manufacturing*, found "75 percent of manufacturers report a moderate to severe shortage in highly skilled manufacturing resources" representing 80 percent of the workforce for the companies that were surveyed. For manufacturing companies, competition for talent is taking place within finite regional labor pools, especially for people qualified in the middle–skill occupations due to persistent skills and training gaps.

With more private-public sector collaborations and competency based communication, manufacturers can have win-win employer–led initiatives realized through a human capital infrastructure of shared expertise and common language to design and execute education and training programs. Here are two examples for win–win employer–led initiatives:
- Private–Public Sector Collaboration – For the Advanced Manufacturing Partnership (AMP) 2.0 – Apprenticeship, Alcoa, the Dow Chemical Company and Siemens formed a coalition to build regional employer–led apprenticeship models, and created a "playbook" for robust apprenticeship

programs. Most of the playbook's content is contributions of lessons learned and promising practices provided by employers, educators, training providers and government agencies.

- Competency–Based Communication – Competencies are an employer's technical and non–technical requirements for positions, and represent the outcomes to be achieved through industry–approved certification programs. Alcoa Foundation is funding the Hope Street Group to develop comprehensive and evidence–based competency definitions for manufacturing jobs based on the U.S. Department of Labor O*NET. This work is the cornerstone for a national manufacturing competency validation center to inform the design of education and training programs leading to timely employment, and to update certifications for new advanced manufacturing positions.

In closing, Alcoa and Alcoa Foundation are on a journey with our private–public sector partners to identify common talent pipeline priorities and to have education and training programs in place for people to be employed in high paying manufacturing careers. Over time, Alcoa's and other manufacturing companies' commitment to win–win employer–led initiatives will increase the size of regional labor pools that provide access to underserved groups. For this journey, we thank STEMconnector® for this opportunity to share our lessons learned and promising practices, and to contribute to their STEM Higher Education Council's initiative.

About Alcoa
Alcoa is a global leader in lightweight metals technology, engineering and manufacturing, Alcoa innovates multi–material solutions that advance our world. Our technologies enhance transportation, from automotive and commercial transport to air and space travel, and improve industrial and consumer electronics products. We enable smart buildings, sustainable food and beverage packaging, high–performance defense vehicles across air, land and sea, deeper oil and gas drilling and more efficient power generation. We pioneered the aluminum industry over 125 years ago, and today, our approximately 62,000 people in 30 countries deliver value–add products made of titanium, nickel and aluminum, and produce best–in–class bauxite, alumina and primary aluminum products.

About the Author
Greg Bashore was appointed to his present position in August 2014. In this role he leads the Talent Acquisition and Workforce Development functions for Alcoa. He is currently focused on redesigning the U.S. based recruitment functions, evaluating Alcoa's global campus partnership efforts and improving the alignment between the talent needs of the business and corporate development programs.

Greg brings over 20 years of broad based HR and line experience. In addition to Alcoa, Greg has worked for KPMG, Signet Bank (now Capital One) and Progressive Companies. Greg's former Alcoa roles include Global HR Director positions in all three of Alcoa business groups. In addition, Greg held the position of Global Director of Talent Management for both Engineered Products and Solutions and Global Primary Products. He has also held several corporate roles focused on mergers and acquisitions and service delivery improvement.

Greg attended East Carolina University and graduated with a B.A. degree in Economics and obtained a M.B.A. from Virginia Commonwealth University. He is also the graduate of the Cornell University's Executive Industrial and Labor Relations Program, Villanova's Six Sigma Greenbelt Program, Case Western's Executive Development Program and Alcoa's Leadership Development Program.

Greg was born to a military family and lived in several states and countries while growing up. He and his wife, Barbara, have two children.

CHAPTER SEVEN

K–12 STEM Education: Laying the Foundation

"For any company or country to stay competitive, they need two things: talent and technology. The foundation for both is a real investment and commitment to STEM education. That must begin with a revamped and rigorous K-12 curriculum and continue with skill development and training for both those about to enter the workforce and those already at work."

-Jeffrey R. Immelt, Chairman of the Board and Chief Executive Officer
GE

Excerpt from *100 CEO Leaders in STEM,* a publication by STEMconnector®

Finding, Engaging, Graduating and Employing 24 Million Students (and Counting) Through the STEM Pipeline
By: Don Munce, President, My College Options (NRCCUA) and
Ryan Munce, Vice President, My College Options (NRCCUA)

The relationship between the development of STEM talent in the United States and the health and sustainability of our economy is greater and more important than many may have imagined or anticipated. The "pipeline" moving students through high school, into college and graduate programs, then providing them with access to research and training so that, in the end, we have a workforce ready to enter the job market, is a virtual sieve. While many students are never introduced to, or interested in, the STEM fields as career options, there is another subgroup which finds itself, though at one time interested, eventually discouraged or disinterested as they go through high school on their way to a post–secondary experience. These are students who, for any number of reasons, fall through some of the "holes" in the pipeline and are unlikely to ever return.

If we are expecting today's prospective students to populate STEM careers in the future, a careful and sensitive analysis of the data defining these students will be critical to our success. Addressing the issue must start at the beginning of the pipeline, where students are introduced to STEM related careers and their talents are encouraged and nurtured in their early school years, and continue into workplaces where they should find a collaborative and affirming community of colleagues.

The work will be difficult and sometimes painful, but if it enhances our ability to find, engage, graduate, and employ those students expected to enter and emerge from the STEM pipeline, it will be well worth it.

The journey students take from the beginning of their formal education to their profession of choice is complex. Children are asked at an early age what they may want to be when they "grow up" and answers range from culinary experts, to astronauts, to police officers. Whatever their career interests, the twists and turns of life influence, heavily, the chances of deferment, destruction or a simple detour from those dreams that many children have. When we follow the pipeline bringing children through school to becoming STEM trained professionals it is painfully clear what happens when distraction moves STEM–bound children away from STEM fields altogether. The "pipeline", a metaphor for a process which links the dreams of 13 year old children with the workforce needs of the mid-21st century, may rely too much on the momentum of the students' initiative to push them towards college and their careers once they express an interest in the STEM fields.

There is an obvious need for partnerships and collaboration across academic, social, and industrial lines as has never before been suggested or proposed. It is hoped that the work of STEMconnector® and partners such as the National Research Council for College and University Admissions will be a catalyst to support our efforts as teachers, mentors, researchers, and administrators in our commitment to creating, sustaining, fixing and transforming the high school to work pipeline for those entering STEM careers.

Of the initial group surveyed by NRCCUA in their most recent research report, nearly 28 percent, (close to one million) of the surveyed freshmen, indicated that they had some interest in one or more of the STEM fields for their career. What we found about the flow of STEM interest among them was that it was often not sustained from their freshman year of high school to their senior year as they are applying to college. At that point, it is expected that more than 57 percent will have lost interest. Clearly, the process of trying to plug the holes where student interest is dropping must begin long before the students are ready to leave high school and indicating a major on their college applications. From as early as their first day of high school, finding talented and interested students will need to be on the radar of everyone from parents to homeroom teachers to industry leaders. And once the students are identified, the process of nurturing that talent and interest must be both unrelenting and multipronged, using practices that are grassroots, data–based and data–driven, measurable, sustainable and flexible. Most importantly, at this early stage, these efforts will have to be intentional.

Better understanding the demographics of STEM interested students will allow optimal planning for outreach and program offerings. Great concern exists as regards the continuously growing gap between male and female college enrollment. Most colleges and universities are now enrolling freshman classes that are majority female. Getting young women interested in the STEM fields while they are in high school will ensure their equitable representation in colleges and, later in STEM jobs. This calls for an extraordinary level of collaboration and partnership with community members, teachers and counselors at high schools, industry leaders and college enrollment staff, among others. Providing role models, mentors, internship and summer employment opportunities are a few of the strategies being considered. The declining interest in STEM fields by African American and Hispanic students is also of great concern. This population is enrolling in college in numbers that are increasing at a very slow rate, with an expectation that they will level off in the very near future.

Similar to the initiatives suggested for female students, increasing interest among African Americans will benefit from a collaborative approach. Importantly, attention will need to be paid to growing additional interest and maintaining the interest already existing within each of these groups. A constant challenge is providing meaningful support and resources to keep participants involved in a sustainable manner, through the college process, workforce preparation, and into their future careers.

Over the past decade, concern has been growing among government agencies, national organizations and private industry over the declining state of STEM education in the United States. As the United States seeks to fuel the future workforce in the crucial areas of Science, Technology, Engineering and Mathematics, it is critical to apply the necessary focus and resources to the population that can produce the greatest results. That population is early secondary students with an existing interest in STEM fields.

What are the forces bringing these fields to their interest and, more importantly, what is happening between their freshmen and senior years to move them away from these interests?

This research has revealed a dichotomy of opportunities and concerns, many of which will shape the strength of industry and academia for years to come. While the economic outlook for STEM graduates is both strong and optimistic, the pipeline feeding students from their interest as children and following through to their progress into and out of college is one area that leads us to hope and collaborative action.

While the need for college graduates from the STEM fields is unlikely to abate this century, there is a significant gap in the pipeline that can be repaired with an aggressive data informed collaboration between students, high schools, colleges, and those organizations and industries poised to have them in the work force of the 21st century. Right now, the American economy is endangered not so much by a dearth of interest in the STEM fields, but by our unresponsiveness to that interest as it blossoms initially within the hearts and minds of 12 and 13 year olds. The good news is that we have the data and the analysis can be used by any of the partners suggested in this endeavor of advancing a jobs-driven economy.

About My College Options

My College Options (NRCUAA) is a FREE college planning service, offering assistance to students, parents, high schools, counselors, and teachers nationwide. It is designed to assist high school students in exploring a wide range of post–secondary opportunities, with special emphasis on the college search process.

About the Authors

In 2003, as a junior in college, Ryan Munce created the framework for the MyCollegeOptions.org College Planning Program. Over the last eleven years, the program has grown significantly and evolved to be the country's leading resource for students and families trying to plan and prepare for the transition from high school to college. Throughout his career, he has started business, counseled students and families, developed groundbreaking education research, built programs, and impacted the lives of millions. Ryan has served as an Enrollment Services Coordinator at the University of Missouri–Kansas City, and worked with the Center for Enrollment Leadership, where he assisted in the development of the Admissions Counselor Basic Training™ program. Ryan's primary career focus has been using technology to advance education.

Ryan received a Bachelor's Degree in Corporate Communications from Creighton University and is finalizing his Master's Degree in Higher Education Administration from the University of Missouri–Kansas City.

Don Munce became President of National Research Center for College & University Admissions (NRCCUA) in 1988. During his tenure as president, NRCCUA has grown rapidly to become a significant force in the student–recruitment and admissions–research arena. Membership among colleges and universities has grown from 200 to over 1,200 members under his leadership. Munce is an expert on topics relating to enrollment management, organizational leadership and strategic vision. His passion for the post–secondary aspirations of young people has affected students and universities across America. NRCCUA's free college planning program "My College Options" is one of the country's most successful tools providing access to higher education for students of all social and economic backgrounds. Munce's entrepreneurial approach to solving enrollment management challenges has helped NRCCUA achieve its current leadership position in higher education marketing and post– secondary planning.

Munce's background includes 10 years as director of admissions and financial aid at a private Midwestern college. During this ten year period, the college experienced a 99 percent increase in enrollment. He has also performed other college management roles in public relations and student services. He has served as an executive committee member of a professional organization for college admissions officers, college trustee and board member of the Non–Profit Leadership Alliance.

Leveraging Culture to Improve the Quantity, Diversity and Quality of American STEM Talent

By: Dr. Jamie M. Bracey, Director of STEM Education, Outreach and Research for Temple University's College of Engineering, and Executive Director of the Pennsylvania Mathematics, Engineering & Science Achievement (MESA)

Higher education's traditional role in producing market ready STEM talent has been to recruit, matriculate, and graduate students who have demonstrated the cognitive ability and self–efficacy (confidence) to triumph on the battlefield of competitive academics. The traditional burden has been on students to offer colleges the requisite preparation, cultural orientation and money to pay tuition; until recently higher education has enjoyed a de facto protectionism against consumer complaints because generally a college degree afforded better quality of life. That model is no longer necessarily true, nor has it been sufficient to produce a dynamically diverse and competent STEM workforce for the knowledge economy.[52] In the new normal improving the quantity, diversity and quality of American STEM talent can only occur in institutional cultures that engage, retain and motivate students to persist into their desired STEM career. The American Association of Colleges & Universities and several others are investing in helping higher education develop cultures that are more reciprocal and effective.

The heartening news is that there are many examples of institutions authentically partnering within the STEM eco–system. The tepid American economy has resulted in a generation of students who are increasingly willing to walk with their feet toward rapid certification and a job. Strategic institutions are making a tangible commitment to keep their tuition paying customers by building partnerships and infrastructure to produce blue collar (certified) and white collar (degreed) STEM talent. They are also taking a proactive role in the 25 percent of American high school students the Business and Higher Education Forum suggest are proficient but not aware of STEM career opportunities.[53] The nation's STEM talent diversity is embedded in that 25 percent tier, where many women and ethnic minorities have developed strong academic profiles but aren't the traditional population referred to engineering or computer science by high school advisors who aren't aware of the opportunities or profiles desired in the market. There is still much work to be done on that front.

The changing relationship between higher education and the STEM talent eco–system requires less accountability for who is attracted, and more accountability for the quality of talent we produce. There is limited patience for institutions that pursue the double negative of a failed mission and failure to help support the nation's competitiveness.

Temple's College of Engineering channeled the founding vision of Russell Conwell by aggressively targeting the largely minority student population in the nation's 8th largest school district, seeking Conwell's "acres of diamonds" in our own backyard. We identified the forty–year–old national Mathematics, Engineering & Science Achievement initiative (MESA USA) as the platform for serving our education consumers downstream (the K–12 pipeline) and upstream (retention to career attainment). The MESA consortium serves nearly 50,000 children per year, from elementary school through the critical early college years. MESA statewide initiatives are sponsored by: University of Arizona (Arizona MESA), University of California (California MESA), Chicago State University (Illinois MESA), Johns Hopkins University's Applied Physics Laboratory (Maryland MESA), New Mexico MESA, Inc., Portland State University (Oregon MESA), Temple University (Pennsylvania MESA), Utah State Department of Education (Utah MESA), and the University of Washington (Washington MESA).

There are several important characteristics that distinguish the MESA USA model from other national programs, starting with the national advocacy for diversity and equity. The decades of commitment to university–school–community–industry relationships is vital to the MESA talent development process. The model was founded at UC–Berkley by engineering faculty working with inner city kids. MESA uses a national curriculum in engineering aligned with common core standards, and the approach to STEM education reflects research on the importance of belonging [54, 55] the cultural preference of minority children for very strong, trusted adult–child relationships in the learning environment[56] and the emerging importance of understanding the impact of expert culture on identity and persistence.[57, 58]

The national MESA collaboration leverages industry and near peer mentoring, has standardized teacher professional development, sponsors field trips, workshops, and is easy to adapt for either in–school or after–school formats. MESA participants experience positive outcomes, including clearer expectations for post-secondary education, particularly in engineering, and particularly among underrepresented students.[59] In Pennsylvania the MESA model has been strategically modified to respond to projected needs of the United States Navy/Navy Supply Command–Weapons Systems Support (NAVSUP–WSS). The motivation was the Navy's forecasted demand for STEM talent proficiency, its aging Boomer workforce, declining numbers of students qualified to serve as officers or civilian employees, and its pride in its origins in 18th century Philadelphia.

The partnership responded to our mutual missions, with the local command investing resources to design specialized middle/high school learning labs for specific Navy medicine, naval engines and computer science careers. We offered the traditional MESA engineering model to area schools, but offered the specialized Navy programs on Temple's campus, using elements of cognitive apprenticeship pedagogy.[60] In the model, experts articulate their thinking processes while demonstrating how to solve problems. They then coach novice students through thinking, practicing, and applying new knowledge until sufficient confidence is developed to transfer that thinking to increasingly complex problems. Training Navy experts to deliver the curriculum with certified teachers, and providing access the authentic environments (Temple's School of Medicine, the Navy's Carderock R&D power and propulsion lab, Temple's computer labs) yielded compelling results for each Navy related domain.

In the biomedical health initiative, socially and culturally relevant health disparities were addressed with a cohort of 80 percent minority males who had been referred by a consortium of community organizations. The first group demonstrated a 38 percent increase in procedural (work–related) expertise after just two weeks. Similar results occurred as another group posted a 19 percent improvement in knowledge related in power, engines and mechanical engineering after twelve weeks. The Navy sponsored computer science program was cited by the 2013 US Conference of Mayors as an exemplary STEM initiative. From 2012 to 2014, the model scaled from Philadelphia, to four cities in the northeast, to five MESA states and nine cities by summer 2014.

That expansion was guided by data that helped produce a one week summer logistics math camp, 250 early high school students (57 percent male, 43 percent female, 60 percent ethnic minorities, 69 percent attending public schools) resisted "summer melt" with a modest 6 percent improvement in algebra, the gatekeeper course to STEM in higher education. However, a key aspect of the curriculum was to have Navy officers teach apprentices Microsoft Excel, including thinking through math formulas to manage and analyze data for decision making. The results included a healthy 16 percent national improvement in applied math knowledge related to Navy logistics. The scalability also yielded 60 percent of the national cohort changing their perception of Navy STEM careers from "not interested" to seeking additional information about the opportunities as civilian engineers, doctors and programmers. The Temple–Navy replication illuminates how higher education can help scale STEM nationally, to targeted STEM workforce supply needs. Equally important is the fact that underrepresented students now understand the culture of STEM careers, and identify with them before they accept the financial burden of college.

Going Forward
As higher education seeks to increase the diversity, quantity and quality of our incoming students, we must be equally committed to retaining and further cultivating them once they become our customers.

Socio-Cultural Stem Immersion to Promote Identity & Motivation to Persist

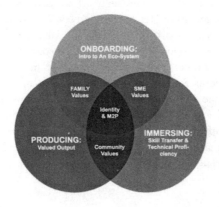

© 2012 Jamie M. Bracey, PhD

About MESA Pennsylvania

By collaborating with Temple University, MESA Pennsylvania became the ninth state program in the MESA system. MESA Pennsylvania focuses on developing public/private partnerships with industry, other academic institutions and government agencies to implement the goals of MESA and Temple's commitment to helping every student reach their full potential, regardless of background, gender or economic status, by partnering with families, districts, elected and community leaders and companies to build a solid STEM workforce necessary to compete economically in a global environment.

Temple's College of Engineering is leading the Pennsylvania MESA initiative through financial and administrative support, with Jamie Bracey, director of STEM education, outreach and research in the College of Engineering, coordinating Temple's MESA efforts. Pennsylvania MESA, in collaboration with Temple University's STEM Education, offers K-12 students access to programs designed to prepare students for academic and professional careers in mathematics, engineering, science, and technology.

Founded and headquartered at the University of California, MESA is operated at institutions around the country, including Johns Hopkins, the University of Washington, and UC-Berkley. The MESA initiative is designed to increase the number of scientists, technologists, engineers and related professionals who are able to graduate from a two- or four-year institution; and to diversify American students who achieve advanced degrees leading to research and development to create new products and to support the nation's defense. Over the past 40 years, nearly 70 percent of MESA students — many of them minorities and women — have entered STEM fields.

About the Author

Dr. Jamie Bracey serves a dual role as the Director of STEM Education, Outreach and Research for Temple University's College of Engineering, and Executive Director of the Pennsylvania Mathematics, Engineering & Science Achievement (MESA) K–12 STEM education program. She is an award winning Educational Psychologist and applied researcher who designs learning environments to accelerate student knowledge, identity formation and persistence in STEM domains. An expert in cultural competence, her published work includes articles and chapters exploring the impact of expert culture, classroom culture and social culture on minority student efficacy, identity formation, and persistence in STEM domains.

Under her leadership, Temple Engineering's Department of STEM Education has been recognized by the City of Philadelphia for its success supporting K–12 students across the nation's 8th largest school district, leading to local, state and national recognition in industry–specific engineering, computer science, and math based logistics career paths in less than three years. Dr. Bracey is an active board officer of MESA U.S.A, and serves as a national advisor to the Association of American Colleges and University's Teaching to Increase Diversity & Equity in STEM (TIDES) Initiative, working to transform institutional cultures to retain students in STEM, particularly underrepresented groups.

Engaging Students in a Jobs Discussion: Meet Them Where They Live
By: Evan Weisenfeld, Vice President of Strategic Partnerships, CollegeWeekLive

How do you best engage high school and college students in a dialog about potential careers? How do you empower the next generation of workers to best understand where job growth will be and how best to prepare to enter the workforce? Meet them where they live and feel most comfortable – on their cell phones, tablets, or laptops. That's the solution CollegeWeekLive has used to engage these same students during the college search and admissions processes.

We use video presentations with embedded chat functionality to allow teens to interact directly with admissions counselors and content experts to hear about topics such as degree programs and career paths. Students also log on to participate in major online college fairs such as STEM Day as well as invitation–only discussions with specific universities about their STEM programs.

This chat functionality continues to see tremendous success. According to MediaPost's Engage: GenY predictions for 2015, "A decade ago, it was common for teens to hang out in online chat rooms talking to random people about serendipitous topics. Eventually, social media replaced these forums, but chat rooms are experiencing a resurgence as part of the proliferation of messaging apps on teens' phones."

In addition, we've expanded those capabilities to other areas of interest to students to include studying abroad, internships, and careers. For example, CollegeWeekLive is working with Ford and Zipcar to provide insight and information to help students plan for their careers.

Here's what we share with our students:

> Ford and Zipcar put you in the driver's seat, offering an insider's look at different career choices and insights into what it's like to work for a large, global company such as Ford or a newer entrepreneurial technology and services company such as Zipcar. Match potential careers with your interests and learn what degrees and career paths can lead to working in these particular roles. Get the information you need to help steer your career in the right direction.

Ford and Zipcar have conducted two student sessions on CollegeWeekLive.com. The first was by Zipcar as a general overview on picking a major and how that relates to a future career. The second was by Ford on how to embark on an engineering career in the automotive industry. As part of their long–term commitment to help students find their future career path, both Ford and Zipcar have enthusiastically signed on for additional events. This program is a great example where companies can do well by doing good.

Outcomes and Impact

CollegeWeekLive supports more than 500,000 high school students each year with information and resources to help them prepare for college and a rewarding career. We produce more than one hundred expert presentations on a variety of topics. Our career related presentations have included experts from NASA, the U.S. Department of Labor Bureau of Labor Statistics, PricewaterhouseCoopers, and others.

Students have indicated repeatedly that they want the ability to consume information at times that are convenient to them, in the channels where they're most comfortable. Typically, 30–40 students participate in the live event, while hundreds more watch it on demand. In fact, the on–demand availability has become a key aspect of this career information. In our most recent sessions with Zipcar and Ford, live participation involved a small audience but increased by over eight times when made available on–demand.

According to MediaPost, "Generation Y has led many movements since coming of age, and for marketers, one of the most powerful movements Gen Y leads is the evolution of the uber–consumer. Through technological adoption, cultural shifts, embedded social networks, and the overall size of the demographic, this "uber–sumer" is wresting control from brands to dictate the how, when, and where of the marketplace. The rapid pace of innovation in today's world means that brands are often playing catch–up with these tech–savvy and ultra–connected consumers, and brands are often caught unaware of business– and industry–altering changes."

CollegeWeekLive is enabling a true dialogue between brands and students where student–led conversations are growing in importance and influence and companies such as Ford and Zipcar are benefiting.

Companies looking to engage busy high school and college students will benefit from understanding that students have grown accustomed to living life on their own schedules and having content available on demand (Netflix, Spotify, Pandora, DVRs, YouTube, etc.) According to MediaPost, "The insatiable 'I need it right now' consumer culture, amplified by Millennials, is continuously fed by innovation's ability to deliver a better and faster response...Millennials are enjoying the luxury of watching their content when, where, and how they want, giving them more control of their own schedules."

Scaling the Opportunity

Organizations can benefit from a similar approach to that of Ford and Zipcar by implementing their own jobs outreach programs. By establishing a connection to students early in their lives, companies can build affinity and be in the consideration set when students are thinking about their own careers. CollegeWeekLive is building a library of relevant information by hosting live presentations that encourage Q&A and a direct dialogue, and makes these presentations available on demand. There are very few limitations to scale this approach of making relevant information available to the desired target audiences.

Action Items to Advance a Jobs–Driven Economy

- **Take some risks.** It's clear that what we as a society are doing today to educate students on potential careers isn't working given the number of projected open positions and the data on where students plan to major and work for their careers. In order to effect real change, we will need to take some risks and try new things. According to MediaPost, "If we've learned anything over the past year, it's that innovations come fast and furious, disrupting whole industries in the blink of an eye. Tech–savvy Millennials embrace these innovations and drag brands along for the ride. Some brands are up to it, some are not, and some brands don't even realize that the uber–sumer has arrived." The key is to experiment with a variety of different programs, measuring what's working, and then roll the winners out on a national basis. But don't forget that what works changes over time so always test by taking additional risks and trying something new.

- **Expand your reach.** Meet students where they live and breathe online and on mobile devices. But do it in a way that meets the needs of the students. Getting them to engage in your proprietary mobile app will require a huge investment. But getting students to like you or follow you on social media won't be much easier. According to MediaPost, "Millennials -marketers' most sought after audience - are surprisingly more concerned about data security and privacy than other generations, and they are willing to switch brands quickly if they feel their privacy is compromised." The key is developing partnerships with organizations that have direct access to the students and can give you access and an endorsement by association. This will also provide the added benefit that students will be more likely to share personal data with you. It's a win–win–win scenario.

About CollegeWeekLive

CollegeWeekLive is the leading channel where students and colleges meet online. More than 1,500,000 students from 192 countries rely on CollegeWeekLive to help navigate college admissions. CollegeWeekLive helps organizations connect to high school and college students to improve the application experience, the transition from high school to college, the student experience in college, and the transition to a career. Students turn to CollegeWeekLive to gain insights from leading experts, whether they are narrowing their choice of schools or making life decisions.

About the Author

Evan Weisenfeld is Vice President of Strategic Partnerships at CollegeWeekLive, the go–to source for brands that are looking to capture the mindshare of students around the world. CollegeWeekLive's unique digital channel offers companies an opportunity to strengthen their brand and connect with a highly engaged and targeted audience.

Evan has more than 25 years' of experience in sales and marketing with extensive experience in the loyalty marketing industry. Prior to CollegeWeekLive, Evan spent more than six years at Upromise, a college savings program, and served as Vice President of Partner Management and SVP of Partner Development responsible for business development, partner relationships, and marketing programs for McDonald's, ExxonMobil, Rewards Network, Avis, Budget, American Airlines, Pep Boys, Century 21, Coldwell Banker, ERA, ServiceMaster, TruGreen ChemLawn, Terminix, and America Online.

In addition, Evan has extensive Strategic Consulting, Internet Consulting, Marketing, and Sales/Business Development experience working for companies such as Cheapflights Media, Zentropy Partners (now MRM Worldwide), Andersen Consulting (now Accenture), and Fidelity Investments. He holds a B.A. from the University of California, San Diego and resides in Medfield, MA.

UCCS STEM: Partnerships at the center of success
By: Dr. Pamela Shockley–Zalabak, Chancellor and Professor of Communication,
University of Colorado, Colorado Springs

For more than a decade, the University of Colorado, Colorado Springs has focused on developing a highly rigorous effort to recruit low–income, first–generation college students from underrepresented populations.

But the focus must not be only on recruitment. Any measure of success must be on the graduation of young people from these important and growing population groups. UCCS uses a scaffolding approach where students can pull themselves toward their goals but with clear pathways and steps to make graduation – and entry into a STEM–related career – possible.

Through its Southern Colorado Higher Education Initiative Community Connections Program, UCCS utilizes existing CU programs and southern Colorado–specific efforts in partnership with other educational institutions, community leaders, and a private technology industry.

Pre–Collegiate Development Program
For more than 30 years, the University of Colorado has operated a Pre–Collegiate Development Program to prepare and encourage middle and high school students to attend college. The program helps students who aspire to be the first in their family to complete college to develop study skills, provides leadership development activities, on–campus visits and learning experiences, and assistance with college applications both for the student and family.

Students who complete the Pre–Collegiate Program have a 96 percent college enrollment rate compared with a 44 percent college enrollment rate of peers who do not have access to such a program. Each University of Colorado campus operates distinctive programs under the Pre–Collegiate Development Program banner. At UCCS, the program focuses on the southern half of Colorado, a historically underserved area of the state with a long history of agricultural and mining industries and low college participation rates. UCCS is the only research university in the region. The UCCS Pre–Collegiate Program recruits students from first–generation college families and traditionally underrepresented groups in grades seven through ten from Colorado Springs and southeastern Colorado. Strong relationships with community colleges, public and private school systems and community support organizations generate leads for students who would benefit from such a program.[61]

Students enrolled in the program participate in hands–on activities to increase academic abilities, improve personal identity and leadership skills and improve college readiness. Students receive rigorous academic preparation in their sophomore, junior and senior years of high school including intensive math and writing development and the opportunity to earn college credit. This development is done in context of college–level academic courses including the UCCS Gateway Program Seminars (first–year student courses) and the student's potential interest areas. Pre–Collegiate also includes assistance with preparation for entrance exams as well as applications for admission, financial aid and scholarships.

Center for Science, Technology, Engineering and Math Education (CSTEME)

The Center for Science, Technology, Engineering and Math Education at UCCS offers STEM programming and academic support to all students in the Pre–Collegiate Development Program centered on engineering and basic sciences. For seven years, CSTEME has offered year–round enrichment events for middle and high school students. These events engage students with inquiry–based hands–on activities. More than 3,000 middle and high school students have participated.

As part of the CSTEME efforts, academically under–prepared but promising students in the Pre–Collegiate Development Program are targeted with STEM–focused activities. CSTEME is also focused on program evaluation, student outcomes, STEM–specific funding opportunities and partnerships.

SoColo Reach

Using high–definition CISCO provided TelePresence technology, UCCS has expanded its reach to sparsely populated, geographically expansive southern Colorado. The technology allows UCCS to offer Gateway Program Seminars and major–specific dual–enrollment college courses to high school students statewide. The courses are offered through the university's Department of Extended Studies, and students are eligible to receive college credit.

Partners

Building relationships with other public institutions as well as private enterprises is a key to the university's success. UCCS partnerships include:

Southern Colorado Higher Education Consortium

Formed in 2009 and fueled by a $750,000 Fund for the Improvement of Postsecondary Education grant from the U.S. Department of Education, a group of southern Colorado colleges and universities work cooperatively to increase the number of southern Colorado residents who attend college. The ten two and four–year college members of the Southern Colorado Education Consortium work to expand efforts to encourage current middle and high school students to continue their education past high school.

Anschutz Foundation

The Denver–based Anschutz Foundation, the UCCS Center for Science, Technology, Engineering and Mathematics and the Fountain–Fort Carson Public School District worked cooperatively to expand STEM programs for students and support for teachers to implement a STEM curriculum in the district's middle and high schools. These efforts, in part, led to the district receiving a Department of Defense Educational Association grant to further support (and replicate) STEM efforts.[62]

Specific goals for the three–year project include:

- Support and train teams of three to give STEM–focused teachers per building to serve as site coordinators and oversee use of UCCS–developed curricula by other teachers in the building.

- Maintain a level of four to six STEM–focused classes per academic year for each middle and high school teacher and one STEM–focused program for elementary teachers.

Preliminary results of student performance are encouraging. The model positively affected middle school student quarterly test scores and significantly improved student interest in pursuing more STEM courses in high school and college.

Cisco Systems

In 2011, UCCS and technology giant Cisco announced a partnership to deliver education via Telepresence, the company's high–definition Internet–based camera and monitory system. UCCS became the first university to deliver for–credit college courses using the technology when two courses, one in nursing and one in robotics, were delivered to rural Colorado students. [63]

Goal

UCCS hopes to connect 334 high schools, many in sparsely populated communities, via the CISCO Telepresence System and the Pre–Collegiate Development Program. The focus will continue to be on STEM fields and those fields that are in particularly high demand such as engineering, nursing and teacher education. Through the partnership with the Southern Colorado Higher Education Consortium, a shared curricula is possible. It is possible to replicate portions of the UCCS efforts. The technology infrastructure is based on CISCO Telepresence equipment that is proven and available. Telepresence technology requires a strong Internet connection and a hub institution to manage technology that may not exist at all locations.

Outcomes

In 2014, UCCS was designated by the U.S. Department of Education as a minority serving institution. This designation will assist the campus in achieving its mission of serving as a regional university by making it eligible for additional federal and private support.
Graduation rates for low–income, first–generation and ethnic minority students are equal to overall institutional graduation rates.

Among the Pre–Collegiate Development Program students who enroll at UCCS, 38 percent self–identify as a member of an ethnic minority group. Of the 2011–13 student cohort, 96 percent persisted in their undergraduate studies and 51 percent declared a STEM major. This is approximately three times the national average.

Last year, 607 (27 percent) of 2,214 UCCS graduates earned a STEM degree. Of these, students 75 percent were undergraduates and 25 percent earned advanced degrees. The majority of these students were Colorado residents and 19 percent of undergraduates and 14 percent of graduate students were ethnic minorities.

Going Forward

Our experience suggests two and four–year institutions should come together for regional partnerships in order to deliver state–of–the–art, engaging curriculum for our K–12 systems. These higher education partnerships will depend on partnerships with industry using technology that makes connections efficient, effective, and engaging for learners. When we enlarge the K–12 pipeline we then enhance collaborative partnerships between two and four–year institutions for all types of STEM offerings. A results–driven approach is critical and, at UCCS, we believe the results will speak for themselves.

About the University of Colorado, Colorado Springs

The University of Colorado, Colorado Springs is located on approximately 500 acres at the foot of the Austin Bluffs in northeast Colorado Springs.

The campus provides a spectacular view of the Front Range of the Rocky Mountains including Pikes Peak, a 14,100 foot mountain that inspired Katharine Lee Bates to write "America the Beautiful" in 1893.

Founded in 1965 and a member of the four–campus University of Colorado System, UCCS enrolled 11,132 students in state–supported programs for fall 2014, a new record. An additional 2,000 students participate in extended studies programs including online and weekend courses.

At UCCS, 33 percent of all students are members of an ethnic minority group (35 percent of the freshman class). The majority of students (52 percent) are female.

Almost 90 percent of UCCS students are from Colorado, though students from all 50 states and 44 countries are represented. More than 1,500 military veterans, active military and family members attend the university, as do 25 U.S. Olympic–hopeful athletes.

The current funds budget for Fiscal Year 2015–16 is $210 million. UCCS students, faculty and staff generate direct and indirect output of $606 million annually to the El Paso County community.

About the Author

Dr. Pamela Shockley–Zalabak is Chancellor (2002–present) and professor of communication. The author of eight books and more than 100 articles & productions on organizational communication, Dr. Shockley's research interests center on building organizational trust. Her latest book, "Building the High Trust Organization" was published in 2010.

In addition to her duties as Chancellor, Shockley–Zalabak continues to teach in the UCCS Communication Department. Prior to assuming Chancellor responsibilities, Dr. Shockley was Vice Chancellor for student success and the founding chair of the UCCS Communication Department. Dr. Shockley is the recipient of the University of Colorado Thomas Jefferson Award, President's Award for Outstanding Service, Chancellor's Award for Distinguished Faculty, Colorado Speech Communication Association Distinguished Member Award, 2003 Colorado Springs Chamber of Commerce ATHENA Women in Business Award, 2005 Student Government Association Student Choice for Instructor of the Year Award, 2008 Colorado Springs Business Journal Women of Influence Award, and the 2011 Leadership Pikes Peak Makepeace Community Trustee Award.

An Oklahoma native, Shockley–Zalabak earned bachelors and master's degrees in communication from Oklahoma State University, Stillwater. She earned her Ph.D. from the University of Colorado, Boulder, in organizational communication.

Partnering with Corporate America in Science and Engineering Festivals
By: Dr. John Lehman, Associate Vice President for Enrollment, Marketing, and Communications, Michigan Technological University

Attraction and Opportunity Gap

Much has been written about America's need to develop a stronger workforce of STEM experts.[64, 65, 66] Currently, only 5 percent of U.S. workers are employed in STEM jobs, yet STEM jobs are responsible for more than 50 percent of our sustained economic expansion (Adkins 2012; DOL 2012).[67] This chapter focuses on precollege students (grades 4–12) because students' introduction to STEM content during these years greatly influences whether or not they pursue a STEM degree and career pathway.[68] Informal learning is often connected to a high level of self–motivation because of the degree of learner control and personal relevance. However, if students do not have an initial attraction to STEM, few choose to attend extracurricular events; therefore, informal learning opportunities are missed opportunities for many students currently underrepresented in STEM.[69] High impact festivals can play an important role in attracting the attention of all students through a large variety of "WOW!" factor activities.[70]

Ambivalent attitudes towards and misperceptions about STEM are largely forged during pre–college years.[71, 72] Too often students' preconceived notions lead to self–selection out of the informal learning opportunities available to them. Pre-existing attitudes and ambivalence toward STEM greatly limit participation of students who would most benefit from the intellectual flexibility and hands–on learning activities STEM informal programs offer.[73, 74] Without an intervention that increases student interest in STEM, the gap between those who choose to participate in STEM and those who do not (largely rural and/or underrepresented minorities) will only widen.[75] To address this "attraction gap" those of us seeking to increase the "pipeline" of STEM invested students must do more to create high–impact, hands–on activities aimed at introducing students to meaningful STEM applications.[76, 77, 78, 79]

There is a pervasive assumption in the U.S. that STEM intelligence is a fixed entity one either is born with or not. This type of assumption is reinforced when test scores are used as indicators of whether students "have it or not."[80] However, research shows that when the fixed intelligence message is replaced with a more malleable view and more informal learning opportunities are offered, the achievement gap virtually disappears. Positive, high-energy communication of this message is key in helping participants realize that STEM learning is a life–long discovery process of fun and engaging "opportunities." Once students see there is no set "end" or "grade" to define STEM achievement, tenacity to figure things out increases, especially for female,[81, 82] low income students,[83] and underrepresented racial minority students.[84] Informal learning opportunities are a place to emphasize discovery and creativity in a risk–free environment. Our experience shows how all students, when given a personal and social context for learning, have fun in figuring out possible solutions to real–world applications, through tacit and explicit understanding of STEM concepts.

Mind Trekkers

Michigan Technological University, working with our corporate partners, recognizes this value in science and engineering festivals. Five years ago Michigan Tech launched the Mind Trekkers traveling science and engineering festival (SEF) road show. The Michigan Tech Mind Trekkers program designs activities, trains undergraduate students as facilitators, and implements science and engineering festivals for precollege students (grades 4–12). Held nationally, and usually connected with a school, town, community college, and corporate partners, a Mind Trekker fair involves setting up a carnival tent where Michigan Tech undergraduates demonstrate and educate informally on various STEM career fields, using hands–on highly interactive displays and activities. Most of these activities last no more than a minute or two. Since its inception, Mind Trekkers has reached over 1.1 million precollege students at 60 events since 2010.

The program director bases the Mind Trekkers goals of the program on two hypotheses, the first being sustainable implementation of high–quality, high–impact Mind Trekkers events that will increase the number of students attracted to future STEM informal learning opportunities. The second hypothesis is that initial interaction at the Mind Trekkers event, continued interaction in the social media community, and peer and near–peer encouragement will "prime the pump" and engage more 4th–12th graders in informal STEM learning opportunities after a fair; this will ultimately increase the number and diversity of students who plan to enter the STEM education to workforce pipeline.

Replication and Scaling Up

As Mind Trekkers has grown and evolved since 2010, it has become apparent that this model of soliciting and training undergraduate and graduate volunteers to deliver high impact informal science education can help provide talent, supporting corporate desires to offer STEM–based educational outreach. Mind Trekkers has successfully partnered with community colleges and corporate entities to help provide them with outreach outlets. Mind Trekkers thrives best when it is replicated, and thus works from an open source model. Working with a community college's students, Mind Trekkers can exponentially increase the number of students able, willing, and trained to provide science education festival (SEF) experiences.

A good example of this concept is Michigan Technological University's work with AT&T. AT&T recognized the potential of the Mind Trekkers SEFs concept and sponsored four rural SEF's in spring of 2011. The SEF's focused on three main components.

- Undergraduate/graduate students in STEM fields conducted STEM activities (30 seconds to 3 minutes per interaction). Participants were encouraged to "try out" many different activities that defied traditional logic and encouraged discussion with the near–peer mentor (facilitator) to inquire and hypothesize openly regarding the science behind the mystery.

- STEM professionals from the local community provided students with insights into careers nestled in their community that both provided a good financial living and intellectually engaged their new–found aptitudes.

- Representatives from post–secondary educational and career tech institutions in their regions provided a wide variety of informational formats to communicate different STEM academic pathways. Participants engaged in conversations about how to academically prepare for a STEM college degree program and financial support options. In addition, a list of personal support contacts to be utilized as they begin their post–secondary education journey was provided.

Impact

Like many of the Mind Trekker events, surveys were mailed to the teachers of Mind Trekkers attendees and returned approximately three weeks after the events. The results showed a positive increase in STEM interest, and in particular proved:

- Undergraduate facilitators work! In fact, facilitators were so enthusiastic about the project the student organization, Mind Trekkers, was formed and over 300 students joined in the first 6 months.

AT&T SEF Participant Survey Results

- 82.7 percent increased interest in pursuing a STEM degreee

- 54.6 percent increased interest in engineering

- 70 percent increased interest in technology

- 39.8 percent increased interest in mathematics

- Rural K–12 schools and students enthusiastically support the idea of the SEFs as a way to explore topics and experience activities not otherwise available in their communities. Rural schools were eager to serve as a hub that provided access to students, helped facilitate advertising and evaluation material, and follow–up with what was learned at the SEF in the classroom. By engaging schools, entire grades and classrooms were involved, which made reaching students who would have self–selected out of attending possible.

- Schools were willing to support costs of busing students to events located in their region and were eager to sponsor follow–up ISL events.

- Partnerships with other universities and community colleges in each region improved access to local K–12 schools, local STEM businesses, and provided increased opportunities for program replication and sustained follow up with students.

- Students and STEM faculty at other institutions showed an interest in replicating the event in their region but need access to activity guides, training in logistics, and related support.

- Interest in starting community college Mind Trekkers was high. Many facilitators were approached about the feasibility of starting Mind Trekkers high school student organizations. Michigan Tech has enabled this sort of cascade mentoring and scaling.

In April 2012 Mind Trekkers conducted a Science and Engineering Festival in Sheboygan, Wisconsin, which hosted over 1,200 4th – 12th grade students. Sponsored by the Kohler Co., Mercury Marine, and 10 other corporate supporters, the event included the normal Mind Trekker event activities, but the focus of corporate displays was on innovations within their industries. Participants experienced innovations ranging from a 'soundless' outboard marine engine to a non–powered toilet that could flush multiple objects that would clog most traditional toilets by using just gravity activated water pressure.

Sheboygan Mind Trekkers Science and Engineering Festival

Level of interest in Science

Before:	Extremely – 38 percent	After:	Extremely – 67 percent
	Moderately – 52 percent		Moderately – 33 percent
	None – 10 percent		None– 0 percent

Level of Interest in Technology

Before:	Extremely – 45 percent	After:	Extremely – 51 percent
	Moderately – 44 percent		Moderately – 44 percent
	None – 11 percent		None – 4 percent

Level of Interest in Engineering

Before:	Extremely – 35 percent	After:	Extremely – 49 percent
	Moderately – 41 percent		Moderately – 44 percent
	None – 24 percent		None – 8 percent

Level of Interest in Mathematics

Before:	Extremely – 26 percent	After:	Extremely – 35 percent
	Moderately – 52 percent		Moderately – 45 percent
	None – 22 percent		None – 20 percent

Action Items

The mission of the Mind Trekkers SEF's is to build capacity for informal STEM learning in communities through training undergraduate students to serve as lead SEF facilitators and Mind Trekker (MT) near–peer mentors. Partnerships with corporations and other organizations, many of which are facilitated by STEMconnector® are key to reaching that goal. These activities, and others like it are premised on two main action items and are STEM–based

- **Close the Attraction and Opportunity Gap**
  STEM 2.0's success is reliant on the idea that we must replace a fixed intelligence message with a more malleable view that all students can succeed in STEM. Weaving in more informal learning opportunities into our educational infrastructure can help eliminate the attraction and opportunity gaps. Positive, high–energy communication of this message is key in helping participants realize that STEM learning is a life–long discovery process of fun and engaging "opportunities."

- **Get Organized with Networks of Networks like STEMconnector®**
  Doing this is not complicated. STEM outreach and engagement cannot afford to engage in zero–sum based economic thinking. A good idea by one of our partners doesn't mean there is one less good idea for others. Knowledge and best practices should be shared, replicated, and scaled up. Mind Trekkers, while benefiting Michigan Tech immensely with exposure and enrollment fodder, is working from an open access model, willing to help institutions across the country replicate its success. In turn we know we don't have all of the answers and are always willing to learn from others.

About Michigan Technological University

Michigan Technological University (mtu.edu) is a global institution that inspires students, advances knowledge, and innovates to help create a sustainable, just and prosperous world. Home to more than 7,000 undergraduate and graduate students, the institution offers 130 innovative degree programs in engineering; forest resources; computing; technology; business; economics; natural, physical, and environmental sciences; arts; humanities; and social sciences.

At Michigan Tech, students create the future. Michigan Tech graduates earn the 10th highest starting salaries in the nation among U.S. public universities, have a 92 percent undergraduate placement rate, and are recruited by nearly 400 companies visiting campus each year. More importantly, our graduates are entering the world prepared to contribute ideas, lead, and effect great change.

Michigan Tech's engineering programs are some of the highest ranked in the nation for undergraduate enrollment (Environmental Engineering 7th, Mechanical Engineering 10th, Geological and Mining Engineering 11th) as well as for degrees awarded (Environmental Engineering 5th, Geological and Mining Engineering 13th, Mechanical Engineering 15th). The American Society for Engineering Education (ASEE) ranked Michigan Tech 10th in the nation in the percentage of engineering doctoral degrees awarded to women.

About the Author

Dr. John Lehman currently serves at the Associate Vice President for Enrollment, Marketing, and Communications where he leads seven diverse areas with over eighty staff members in the departments of Admissions, Career Services, Financial Aid, International Programs and Services, the Center for Pre–College Outreach, Student Affairs Information Systems, and University Marketing and Communications.

Lehman served as the Assistant Vice President for Enrollment Services from 2005 – 2013, and before that, he worked with the university's precollege outreach department, Youth Programs, beginning in 1996. Lehman is also a Lead Facilitator with the LeaderShape Institute and an Associate Consultant with Noel Levitz. He earned a BA from Adrian College, an MA from Eastern Michigan University, and a Ph.D. in Education from Colorado State University. He lives in Houghton with his wife, Jodi and their daughter, Maddy.

Students as Innovators in STEM
By: Scott Ganske, Education Director, Youth Service America (YSA)

"STEMester of Service engages a teacher and students in addressing a critical community problem through the application of learning in STEM content. As a company, IBM has a strong commitment to both education and community engagement. We have been impressed with the STEMester of Service program, and would strongly recommend this program as an exciting opportunity to help expose America's young students to future STEM learning and careers." Diane Melley, VP, Global Citizenship Services Initiatives at IBM Corporation."

YSA's STEMester of Service™ program is designed so K–12 students can use STEM to address the issues in their community, in partnership with colleges, universities, and the business community. Framed within the classroom curriculum and incorporating the teacher's own required academic content standards and goals, *STEMester of Service* asks students to identify and address a significant community issue, applying acquired STEM skills and knowledge in the process. The program introduces opportunities for student acquisition of specific career and workforce readiness skills and knowledge. Through this program, teachers commit to a "semester" of at least 14 weeks of ongoing service and learning activities, focused on addressing a significant issue in their community. Teachers build their own specific STEM–focused curricular goals around YSA's student service engagement framework. STEMester of Service was built upon a service–learning model designed to guide teachers and students through "IPARD/C" - five distinct stages of development and implementation: Investigation, Preparation and Planning, Action, Reflection, and Demonstration/Celebration. Students work sequentially through each of these stages, transforming their research and ideas into action. Teachers and other adults provide guidance, introducing curricular knowledge, applicable skills, and college and career and workforce readiness attributes along the way.

In the IPARD/C model, students:

- **Investigate** – identify and research a local, national, or global STEM issue they would like to address and select a strategy to address the need;

- **Prepare and Plan** – develop a strategy for change, including service and learning goals and an action plan;

- **Act** – implement the action plan to make a difference and measure the impact of their efforts;

- **Reflect** – think critically and analytically about how the service and learning relate to them, their fellow students, their community, and their future; and

- **Demonstrate/Celebrate** – showcase their results, celebrate their outcomes, and make plans to sustain their project.

K–12 and Higher Education Partnerships

K–12 and Higher Education partnerships play a critical role in an effective STEMester of Service. For example, students at First Creek Middle School in Tacoma, Washington partnered with the University of Washington – Tacoma (UWT) after they identified a watershed located on the edge of school property. Environmental chemistry undergraduate students collaborated with the middle school students; together they learned about the relationship between human activity, storm water, and the health of the watershed through the creation of a First Creek watershed water management and clean–up team. Watershed restoration efforts focused on water quality testing, removal of invasive plants, and planting and monitoring nearly 1,500 native trees and shrubs. The program, which took place both during and after school, started in September and went through June. UWT students brought water testing equipment from their campus and taught the middle school students how to use the equipment to monitor and track the watershed water–quality. The middle school and college students collected water and soil samples from the area, which were then used in the college students' and professors' research projects to determine the actual level of contamination in the stream. Through all of these activities, the college students encouraged students to get and stay involved in science, and they built students' ability to write, use technology, and interact with adults, while learning more about careers in STEM fields.

Business Partnerships

The STEMester program incorporates college and career readiness skills, with the specific intent of introducing students to future opportunities in STEM careers. Diane Melley, VP, Global Citizenship Services Initiatives at IBM Corporation, shared about IBM's experience with the program:

> *During the STEMester of Service, 54 IBM engineers worked with these classes and four others as virtual e–mentors, hoping to help students learn about, and transfer their enthusiasm into STEM–based careers. The students teamed up with the IBM employees in a series of activities designed to improve their 21st Century learning skills – critical thinking and problem–solving, creativity and innovation, collaboration, and communication – all critical to post–secondary college, career and life success.*

Evaluation

According to an independent evaluation by RMC Research, STEMester of Service students showed statistically significant and higher gains in academic engagement, 21st century skills, and STEM than did comparison students. STEMester of Service students have restored watersheds in Washington State; designed desert xeriscapes in Arizona; planted miles of street trees in New York City; developed a model to discourage the alarming growth of invasive zebra mussels in Lake Michigan; grew raised bed gardens in urban desert areas of Washington, DC; replanted wetlands in Louisiana; built greenhouses and pollinator gardens in Georgia; constructed solar ovens and wind turbines in Colorado; and developed the only battery recycling program in Hawaii.

Three Activation Onramps

The STEMester of Service framework is easy to implement and YSA provides free resources for teachers. In some cases, educators do not have the time or experience to facilitate a full STEMester of Service. The activation onramps below provide different options:

STEMester of Service	Classrooms with a Cause	Global Youth Service Day
STEMester of Service is an extended service and learning framework to engage students in meaningful service and learning activities. In order to address problems of local, national, or global importance and their root causes, teachers engage students in a semester connecting service activities with intentional learning goals and academic standards.	*Classrooms with a Cause* provides a curricular framework for students to reflect on what they have learned in the classroom, and then apply their knowledge in STEM to address a cause – an issue important to them and to their community. The Classrooms with a Cause curriculum includes a facilitator guide and customizable student guide.	*Global Youth Service Day* (GYSD) is the largest service event in the world, and the only campaign that celebrates and mobilizes the millions of young people who strengthen their communities through service. GYSD is celebrated in more than 100 countries across six continents. GYSD provides an opportunity to introduce a STEM and service into the classroom for the first time as well as an opportunity to demonstrate and celebrate existing activities.
Advanced Level	*Intermediate Level*	*Introductory Level*
Length: One semester to one school–year	*Length:* 4–6 weeks to one semester	*Length:* One day to one quarter
Ideal Implementation Time: Spring Semester, using MLK Day and Global Youth Service Day as milestones.	*Ideal Implementation Time:* Last two months of school year after testing.	*Ideal Implementation Time:* Mid–April
www.YSA.org/semester	www.YSA.org/classrooms	www.GYSD.org

About Youth Service America

At YSA, we believe in youth changing the world. With half the world's population under the age of 25, YSA and its partners leverage the creativity, passion, and fresh perspective of young people, activating them to be the problem–solvers of today.

As the global leader in the youth service movement, YSA mobilizes a diverse and powerful network of partners to create a worldwide culture of young people committed to a lifetime of service, learning, leadership, and achievement. Through large–scale public awareness campaigns, grant initiatives, training programs, and recognition platforms, YSA helps young people find their voice, take action, and make an impact on vital community issues. Visit www.YSA.org to learn more.

About the Author

As YSA's Education Director, Scott Ganske oversees three national and international service–learning programs that emphasize academic achievement, 21st Century Skills, and STEM education. He also facilitates workshops at local, state, national, and international conferences. Prior to his arrival at YSA, Scott was an Education Consultant at Service Learning Texas (SLT), where he managed a portfolio of Learn and Serve America programs, and provided support, coaching, and mentoring to school districts, education centers, and organizations. Scott has eight years of teaching experience in Arizona and Texas and also co–founded a non–profit organization that matched community volunteers with at–risk students in Title I schools. He holds a Master's degree in Public Administration and a B.A. in Education, both from Arizona State University.

Northwest Educational Council for Student Success
By: Dr. Kenneth Ender, President, Harper College

The Northwest Educational Council for Student Success (NECSS) is a partnership between William Rainey Harper College and its three high school districts. This formal partnership, approved by the four Boards provides the seamless transition of high school graduates to post–secondary education. NECSS operates under four strategic directions:

- Create a culture of innovation, accountability and transparency.

- Develop programs with educational partners that inspire postsecondary education and career readiness as a life goal.

- Increase completion and achievement of all students with a focus on underperforming student groups.

- Engage in partnerships to develop programs in existing and emerging career areas that enable students to succeed in a global economy.

The NECSS partnership includes a formal organizational structure that promotes the collaboration of faculty and staff from all twelve high schools and the college. As an organization we have aligned curriculum, identified funding and leveraged partner resources for innovative projects, and created "stackable" career and academic pathways that incorporate industry–relevant and postsecondary credentials that lead to a sustainable income.

One of the early initiatives of NECSS was the Math Remediation Reduction Project. In 2010, only 45 percent of recent high school graduates in Harper College's district were placing into college level math. Research shows students who start college by taking remedial courses are far less likely to earn a degree or certificate than students who begin in credit classes. To address these findings, members of NECSS established joint responsibility for increasing the percentage of recent high school graduates who begin college ready in math. The effort resulted in the Math Remediation Reduction Project, a data based, three–tiered program which includes:

- Testing high school juniors using the COMPASS test

- Having high school seniors take math their senior year (Illinois only requires three years of math)

- Curriculum alignment

The high school students in Harper's district are assessed for college readiness in their junior year. Based on the results of this assessment, students choose one of three mathematics pathways during the senior year of high school. Students who are college ready and who are interested in a STEM or business path enroll in pre–calculus or AP calculus.

Students who are college–ready and who are interested in a liberal arts path enroll in a dual credit Quantitative Literacy course. This choice allows them to complete their college general education mathematics requirement without breaking their sequential study of mathematics. Data revealed to us that students who did not take math their senior year, often placed into developmental mathematics when entering college. They were required to spend time and money often repeating topics already learned but forgotten over a year away from the study of math. The dual credit option gives high school seniors an opportunity to complete math requirements needed for a college degree and gives them a head start toward earning transferrable college credits. The dual credit math course provides a viable option for high school students who may have otherwise opted out of a fourth year of math.

Students placing below college level math are encouraged to take math, specifically Algebra 3, during their senior year. The high schools' Algebra 3 courses are taught by high school teachers in their buildings but using curriculum that has been aligned with Harper's highest level of developmental math, Intermediate Algebra. Algebra 3 students, who meet the threshold of our jointly developed (high school and college faculty) final exam, are deemed college ready in math and do not need to reassess if attending Harper College. We are confident that those attending other colleges score higher on institutional placements tests because of this fourth year of mathematics.

The results of the Math Remediation Reduction Project have been overwhelmingly positive. A project study determined the single biggest predictor of high school graduates who begin college–ready in math is whether they take math as a senior. As a result, the number of high school seniors enrolling in a math class increased to 98 percent. Additionally, in the last four years, the percentage of recent high school graduates beginning in college math has increased by 21 percent.

Another initiative that was fostered through NECSS involves a group of local manufacturers known as the Golden Corridor Advanced Manufacturing Partnership (GCAMP). It is a diverse group of employers, educational institutions, training providers, local government, and other stakeholders. They share the goal of ensuring the region along I – 90 in the northwest suburbs of Chicago continues to be a leader in manufacturing with more than 85,000 workers in the industry. The group, active since 2009, has been instrumental in making employment connections, marketing events, and raising awareness of the opportunities within advanced manufacturing. They provide a thorough understanding of the leading manufacturing industries, manufacturing jobs, and the training, education, and other workforce development resources already present. With this information, the GCAMP has targeted their efforts, strengthened existing linkages between education, training providers, and employers, and created new and innovative strategies to fill gaps (Manufacturing in the Golden Corridor, 2014).

The NECSS Career Committee, which is comprised of career and technical program administrators from three area high school districts and Harper College, meets monthly to keep informed of projects, initiatives, and requests for assistance and advice in career programming. The Golden Corridor has worked tirelessly with the Career Committee to provide learning opportunities for high school and college students. These include site visits, guest speakers in classrooms and at information sessions, internship opportunities, and employment leads for program completers entering the job market.

One of the most important services GCAMP provides to NECSS is networking and connecting educators to industry partners who advocate improving the image of manufacturing as a desirable career path. Over 100 industry partners have committed to assist educators because of the work of GCAMP. The partnership has created a positive effect on the interest in manufacturing in the high schools and Harper College. Five high schools in Harper College's service area now offer advanced manufacturing classes that are accepted by Harper College as "dual credit" meaning students can count the credit in high school and earn college credit. This permits them to move into the next manufacturing course in the program sequence when they enroll in college saving them both time and money.

Going Forward

It is imperative that colleges continue to partner with business and industry. For instance, Harper College and the Fabricators and Manufacturers Association (FMA) have been collaborating for several years to increase awareness of training and employment opportunities for local students and incumbent workers in the fabrication and manufacturing industries. Recently this partnership was solidified with a generous contribution to fund equipment acquisition, professional development for faculty, and scholarships for students. The equipment will lead to new certificates in metal fabrication, laser cutting, and robotic welding that will draw students from the greater Chicago area and generate a highly trained workforce to meet industry demands.

Colleges and K–12 districts must continue to forge collaborative relationships to ensure the transition from high school to college to the workforce is seamless. Through curriculum alignment and dual credit opportunities these partnerships have the potential to increase the rates of post–secondary certificate or degree completion while reducing the time and money necessary to complete.

About Harper College

William Rainey Harper College, located in Palatine, Illinois, is a comprehensive community college dedicated to providing excellent education at an affordable cost, promoting personal growth, enriching the local community, and meeting the challenges of a global society.

Harper has several ongoing initiatives to serve transfer and career students in STEM fields. Transfer students interested in engineering, pharmacy or undergraduate research have several distinctive opportunities. The Harper Pathway to University of Illinois at Urbana–Champaign (UIUC) offers qualifying students guaranteed admission to the UIUC College of Engineering after completing two years of core coursework at Harper. Recently Harper formed a similar program with Roosevelt University, the Pharmacy

Partners Program. Qualified students intending to pursue a doctorate in pharmacy will be able to matriculate from Harper directly to Roosevelt's PharmD program. The chemistry research experience, established through NSF grants, engages students in individual research projects and has resulted in scholarships and internships for participating students. Harper College has two academic divisions offering applied science programs in STEM fields: Health Careers and Career and Technical programs.

About the Author

Dr. Kenneth Ender is President of William Rainey Harper College, a large community college located outside of Chicago, Illinois. Through partnerships and alliances, Dr. Ender has positioned Harper as a leading 21st–century community college by increasing graduation, transfer and certificate completion rates, aligning Harper's curriculum with high schools, training students for new economy jobs, and implementing new accountability and transparency standards. Since coming to Harper in 2009, Harper has experienced record graduation rates and a dramatic increase in the number of students who come to Harper college–ready. The College has also formed new alliances with businesses to fill the shortage of skilled workers in key industries.

Before coming to Harper, Dr. Ender served as President of Cumberland County College in New Jersey for eleven years. Previously, Dr. Ender held a variety of positions in higher education, including Vice President for Academic Affairs at Richland Community College, Interim District Dean at Cuyahoga Community College, Associate Vice President for Administrative Services at Cleveland State University, Director of Student Activities at Virginia Commonwealth University and Director of Student Advising at University of Georgia.

CHAPTER EIGHT

Connecting Teachers and Students to STEM Opportunities

"As we think about what it will take for all students to have access to an excellent STEM education, providing opportunities for students to engage in authentic STEM experiences will be crucial. The opportunity to engage with hands-on STEM projects and professionals in the field shows students what is possible – and helps bring their classroom content to life. Teachers from pre-K through higher education, and STEM professionals, must work together to open up the wonderful world of STEM for all of our students so they have the critical thinking and problem-solving skills they will need for their future."

- Melissa Moritz, Vice President STEM and Education Initiative
Teach For America

Everyone in the Pool
By: David Bergeron, Vice President for Postsecondary Education Policy,
Center for American Progress

As a nation, we are at a turning point. An increasing share of our nation's workforce needs to hold a degree or a certificate in a STEM field. A 2013 Brookings Institution study concluded that fully 20 percent of all jobs require a high level of knowledge in a STEM field.[85] But how do we learn science and math? Like learning to swim, which we learn by swimming, we learn science by doing science and math by doing math. If we are going to meet the needs of our nation's STEM workforce, we need to all get off the deck and into the pool.

The Brookings Institution study did have one surprising finding: half of the STEM jobs require less than a bachelor's degree.[86] This should be good news as it should be relatively easy to get students through at least two years of study in STEM after graduating from high school. But it isn't. Data from the National Center for Education Statistics' Beginning Postsecondary Students survey suggest that students that began in STEM fields with a degree goal of obtaining an associate's degree or certificate were far less likely to stay in a STEM field or complete than did students with a degree goal of a bachelor's degree or higher. Just 26 percent of associate's degree students and 16 percent of certificate students who entered a STEM program completed it.[87]

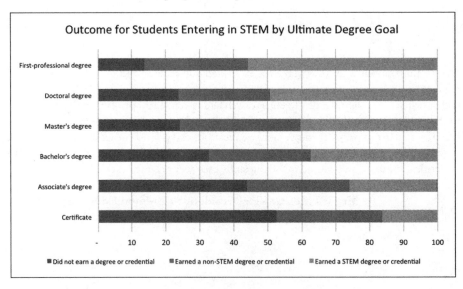

Source: U.S. Department of Education, National Center for Education Statistics, 2003–04
Beginning Postsecondary Students (BPS) Longitudinal Study,
Second Follow–up (BPS:04/09)

Fortunately, interest in studying STEM at the postsecondary level remains high. In a recent study by ACT, half of the high school graduates in 2014 that took the ACT exam expressed an interest in STEM. But this same study concluded that many of the students interested in STEM did not take steps to pursue a STEM degree or certificate at the postsecondary level and that more needed to be done to guide and nurture students so they have an opportunity to experience success and gain long–term interest in STEM fields. Critically, the study goes on to observe that achievement levels in math and science remain alarmingly low.[88]

Data from the same Beginning Postsecondary Students study found that low income students and African American and Hispanic students were less likely to be retained in postsecondary education with a STEM major than were more affluent or White or Asian students.[89] Programs, like the University of Maryland, Baltimore's (UMB) Continuing Umbrella of Research Experiences, or CURE program, can help fix the leaks in the STEM pipeline by engaging college faculty to work with young people to address the lack of preparation and orientation toward STEM among students from low–income families or from communities of color.[90] Beginning in the 2015–16 school year, UMB will work with at least 25 middle school students to provide career development activities including Saturday programs at UMB involving hands–on basic science laboratory activities. The initiative is similar to the federally funded Upward Bound Math-Science, or UBMS, program that awards grants to institutions of higher education to provide an intensive math and science precollege experience to low–income, first generation prospective college students. An evaluation of this program found that UBMS improved high school grades in math and science and overall, increased the likelihood of taking chemistry and physics in high school; increased the likelihood of enrolling in more selective four–year institutions; increased the likelihood of majoring in math and science; and increased the likelihood of completing a four–year degree in math and science.[91]

But remember, we learn to swim by swimming. We need everyone to be in partnership and no one can stand on the sideline. Institutions of higher education aren't solely responsible for creating the problems of the STEM pipeline and certainly can't solve all of them either.

Among the organizations that need to engage as active partners are the agencies that accredit postsecondary programs in STEM fields. Among this group, ABET, which accredits programs in applied science, computing, engineering, and engineering technology, has been working with institutions with accredited programs and through member societies to promote quality and innovation in STEM education. But specialized accreditors can do more to partner with institutions of higher education and elementary and secondary schools to promote STEM. Most immediately, specialized accreditors should identify and document promising practices and assist institutions in conducting rigorous evaluations of these practices. Accrediting agencies are uniquely positioned to identify promising practice because they are already routinely visiting the programs they accredit to ensure that they are delivering high–quality educational experiences for students and could use the opportunity to highlight exemplary practices that other institutions should consider emulating.

Specialized accreditors also have access to an established network of volunteers that could be asked to help promote STEM education in their local communities. In addition, given the need to reinforce the interest in STEM, this volunteer network needs to be activated to spend time with students on STEM related projects to promote a greater depth of learning.

Professional societies, like the American Society of Engineering Education (ASEE) and the American Physics Society, can similarly activate a network that can effectively demonstrate STEM concepts to young people. ASEE has been working with educators at the elementary and secondary level to develop ways to demonstrate exciting engineering concepts to young people. The work being done by the ASEE with educators is particularly critical given that very few young adults are expressing an interest in teaching STEM subjects. The ACT study cited earlier points out that interest in teaching in STEM subject areas is extremely low. Of the more than 1.8 million 2014 graduates taking the ACT, only 4,424 students expressed an interest in teaching math and only 1,115 expressed an interest in teaching science.[92]

The number of high school graduates expressing an interest in teaching science highlights the need for employers to get engaged in promoting STEM teaching. One example is the efforts that some STEM employers make to provide summer learning opportunities for prospective and current elementary and secondary school teachers but more should be done in this regard. For example, STEM employers can create opportunities for classroom teachers to work on research projects over the summer and during the academic year that help them stay current in the practice of science. From this exposure, teachers will be better equipped not just to do science but to describe to students what science looks like day–to–day in the workplace and how the results of science improve our lives.

One important way that science improves our lives is through economic growth. Economic growth occurs naturally where there is demand for new products and services and where sustainable innovation occurs to meet that demand. A scientifically and mathematically literate workforce is a necessary condition for innovation. But it isn't sufficient. For innovation to be sustainable and lead to economic growth, we need another element: inclusion of diversity. Everyone in the pool.

About Center for American Progress

The Center for American Progress (CAP) is an independent nonpartisan educational institute dedicated to improving the lives of Americans through progressive ideas and action. As progressives, we believe America is a land of boundless opportunity, where people can better themselves, their children, their families, and their communities through education, hard work, and the freedom to climb the ladder of economic mobility. We believe an open and effective government can champion the common good over narrow self–interest, harness the strength of our diversity, and secure the rights and safety of its people. And we believe our nation must always be a beacon of hope and strength to the rest of the world. Progressives are idealistic enough to believe change is possible and practical enough to make it happen.

Building on the achievements of progressive pioneers such as Teddy Roosevelt and Martin Luther King, our work addresses 21st century challenges such as energy, national security, economic growth and opportunity, immigration, education, and health care. We develop new policy ideas, critique the policy that stems from conservative values, challenge the media to cover the issues that truly matter, and shape the national debate.

About the Author

David A. Bergeron is the Vice President for Postsecondary Education Policy at the Center for American Progress (CAP). David is spearheading CAP's postsecondary agenda built on the belief that high–quality and affordable postsecondary education is key to rebuilding the middle class and advancing national competitiveness. Since joining CAP, David has written and spoken extensively on a variety of higher education issues.

Prior to joining CAP, David served as the acting assistant secretary for postsecondary education at the U.S. Department of Education from July 2012 through March 2013. In this position, David acted as the education secretary's chief advisor on higher education issues and administered more than 60 programs that provide nearly $3 billion annually to institutions of higher education and community–based organizations.

David also served as the deputy assistant secretary for policy, planning, and innovation for the Office of Postsecondary Education from 2009 to 2013. In this capacity, David was responsible for the program budget for the federal postsecondary education programs administered by the Office of Postsecondary Education and Federal Student Aid, which generate more than $160 billion in financial aid to more than 25 million students enrolled at public and private postsecondary institutions. David is also responsible for legislative, regulatory, and other policies affecting the department's postsecondary education programs including federal Student Aid. Prior to becoming deputy assistant secretary, David served in a variety of other roles in the Department of Education.

Burgeoning STEM Partnerships at a Liberal Arts College

By: Mark Peltz, Associate Dean and Director of Career Development, Grinnell College

Grinnell College has a rich history of producing graduates who embark on rewarding careers in the sciences, technology, engineering, and mathematics. Historically, one of the most popular post–graduate pathways for many talented students, particularly those in STEM–related majors, has been to continue their studies in graduate or professional school. In fact, Grinnell College ranks seventh nationally in the production of graduates who ultimately go on to earn a Ph.D., placing it ahead of Harvard, Princeton, and Yale. Even so, many students in STEM–related majors have a desire - and others a financial need - to enter the job market upon completion of their undergraduate degree.

Led by Grinnell College's Center for Careers, Life, and Service (CLS), the college began exploring opportunities in the fall of 2013 with various business partners to address three distinct but complementary goals. The first goal was to help students who have not yet chosen a major field of study to explore potential career pathways in STEM–related and other career fields. Second, current students expressed an interest in exploring STEM–related career pathways that could be pursued immediately upon graduation. This sentiment was echoed in conversations with alumni who indicated that they, too, may have benefited from such opportunities. And third, the college has been increasingly focused on developing stronger partnerships with various communities throughout Iowa, particularly Des Moines and the Iowa City/Cedar Rapids corridor, to attract more Iowa high school graduates to Grinnell and, more recently, to cultivate internship and job opportunities for its students.

Since the fall of 2013, the college has been cultivating multiple partnerships with select business partners and trade associations to address these goals. Three of these partnerships, all of which have yielded promising results, are highlighted here.

A typical entering class at Grinnell includes students from all 50 states and more than 40 countries. Even some among the 10 percent of students who are Iowa residents are surprised to learn that a leading biotechnology company focused on human and animal health is located just 50 minutes from campus. The research and development division of this company employs many scientists with backgrounds in biology, biochemistry, chemistry, horticulture, agronomy, animal science, and other related fields. After visiting one another's campuses and laboratories, Grinnell became a core recruiting school for the company's robust internship program. Lunch with faculty, a presentation to students (some of whom had not yet chosen a major field of study), and a round of initial interviews yielded the first summer intern from Grinnell College. While this outcome may seem small, it is worth noting that no other Grinnell student or alum had previously been employed by this biotechnology firm.

A similar, but notably distinct, partnership has been cultivated with a Des Moines–based Fortune 500 insurance and financial services company with more than $100 billion in assets. What distinguishes this partnership is the direct involvement of Grinnell College alumni.

In partnership with Grinnell's Department of Mathematics, the CLS hosted alumni and other company representatives on campus to help students develop a more sophisticated understanding of the opportunities that exist for them to apply their interests and skills in mathematics, statistics, computation, and modeling in the private sector. As a result of this partnership, some of these alumni agreed to host first and second year students as part of the college's job shadow program and also to help connect the college with the company's internship program. As a result, two Grinnell College students were selected to participate in this company's summer internship program in 2014.

Finally, the growing start–up environment found in central Iowa (Des Moines and Ames) and the Cedar Rapids/Iowa City corridor has created opportunities for collaboration and partnership between higher education institutions and a diverse array of technology firms. Specifically, the college has worked with representatives from the Technology Association of Iowa to ensure students from Grinnell can participate in the "Experience Iowa Technology" events they host in Des Moines and Iowa City. These showcases introduce students who are interested in tech–related careers to executives, founders, community builders, programmers, and others at early to late stage technology firms that have come to define the "Silicon Prairie" in Iowa. These events also serve as an efficient recruitment strategy for the technology firms, since students from area colleges and universities travel many miles to visit these companies. Based on feedback from Grinnell students who have participated in these events, the CLS has made it a priority to recruit students and to cover the transportation costs to ensure Grinnell students are able to participate. Student participants have yielded networking connections, internships, and full time job offers as a result of these events.

The extent to which these partnerships are scalable and replicable is contingent upon the characteristics (e.g., geographic location, enrollment, and curricula) needs and goals of the parties involved. At a cursory level, these kinds of partnerships are applicable to community colleges, research universities, and residential liberal arts colleges like Grinnell. Although these partnerships are still in their early stages, each has successfully addressed one or more of the three goals outlined earlier in this chapter.

Call to Action
- **Representatives from STEM related organizations should actively investigate and recruit the undergraduate talent at residential liberal arts colleges**. Although these institutions are frequently small in scale (often enrolling 2,000 or fewer students) and educate only 3 percent of all students in the U.S. higher education system, they attract incredibly talented students and provide them unparalleled opportunities to develop, refine, and apply their analytical, problem–solving, and communication skills. Many liberal arts colleges encourage students to work closely with faculty, become proficient with various technologies, explore problems from interdisciplinary perspectives, and complete undergraduate research, internship, and international study experiences prior to graduation. To boot, many residential liberal arts colleges have become hubs of creativity and innovation. Business leaders should encourage their employees to participate in job shadow

programs and other initiatives with these institutions and implore their human resource departments to identify and connect with regional consortia, like the Liberal Arts Career Network and the Selective Liberal Arts Consortium, to recruit these talented students.

- **Finally, residential liberal arts colleges have a considerable stake in and are a significant contributor to STEM education.** Even so, the partnerships documented in this book are grossly imbalanced. Reading about partnerships between advanced manufacturing companies and community colleges is unsurprising. So, too, is learning about partnerships between technical institutes and major telecommunications and technology companies. These partnerships are certainly of considerable importance and are central to these institutions in realizing their respective missions. But are liberal arts colleges simply not engaged in these kinds of partnerships? If not, why? Residential liberal arts colleges offer a very distinctive educational experience, and the opportunity to partner with leaders and innovators from STEM related organizations will only enhance our students' readiness for the twenty-first century marketplace. Grinnell College has witnessed the benefits of these partnerships and we would encourage our liberal arts colleagues to do the same.

About Grinnell College

Founded in 1846, Grinnell College is a highly selective, residential, nonsectarian liberal arts college of 1,600 students with a long history of curricular innovation. The college is in Grinnell, Iowa, a small town with close ties to both the college and to the prairie it surrounds.

Grinnell confers Bachelor of Arts degrees in 25 fields across the humanities, sciences, and social sciences. Annually, approximately 35 percent of Grinnell's graduates complete majors in STEM fields. The academic environment is rigorous and collaborative, combining hands–on, inquiry–based learning; small, discussion–based classes; and exceptionally close student mentoring. The college strives to develop analytical and imaginative thinkers who are prepared to become leaders and world citizens.

Grinnell's students are diverse, with 10 percent from Iowa, 11 percent international (from more than 50 countries), and more than 20 percent U.S. students of color. Grinnell admits academically qualified students regardless of their financial circumstances; it also meets 100 percent of domestic students' institutionally determined need. The result is a student body that is multicultural, socioeconomically diverse, and smart: mid–50–percent SAT scores were 610–710 math and 600–720 verbal; 88 percent of these students were in the top 25 percent of their high school class.

About the Author

Dr. Mark Peltz is the Daniel and Patricia Jipp Finkleman Dean in Grinnell College's Center for Careers, Life, and Service. Reporting directly to the college's president, Dr. Peltz oversees a comprehensive, integrated program focused on preparing students for the professional, civic, and personal commitments they will make as graduates of Grinnell College. Prior to joining Grinnell in April 2011, Dr. Peltz served as Assistant Dean and Director of the Career Center at Luther College and as Associate Director of Graduate Business Career Services at the University of Florida Warrington College of Business. Dr. Peltz holds a B.A. from the University of Northern Iowa, an M.S. from Miami University (Ohio), and a Ph.D. from Iowa State University.

Teacher Training Revolution

By: Dr. Philip Schmidt, Vice President for Compliance and Accreditation and Dean of the Teachers College, Western Governors University

What is Western Governors University's Position in STEM Education?

Western Governors University (WGU) is an online university driven by a mission to improve quality and expand access to post–secondary educational opportunities by providing a means for individuals to learn independent of time and place and to earn competency–based degrees and other credentials that are credible to both academic institutions and employers. WGU's mission has remained one of helping hardworking adults meet their educational goals and improve their career opportunities.

Truly a university without boundaries, Western Governors University is a non–profit online university founded and supported by 19 U.S. governors. To fulfill the mission, the founding governors insisted that WGU be affordable, flexible, and student–focused. Hence, WGU strives to serve as many students as possible - including minorities, first–generation college students, those with modest incomes, and others whose lives or geographic locations do not allow them to attend traditional, campus–based colleges.

WGU has flourished into a national university, serving more than 50,000 students from all 50 states, yet remains non–bureaucratic, entrepreneurial, and innovative. It continues to receive praise from employers for its academic model for the emphasis on graduating highly competent professionals. The university continues to open doors for adult learners who need flexibility to achieve their education and career goals.

WGU's partnership in STEM Education is truly a partnership with all fifty states. We are able to recommend mathematics and science candidates for the appropriate STEM licensure in all states and we work continuously to ensure that our curricula are aligned with the STEM standards in all states. As a result, WGU is now the nation's leading provider of STEM teachers, both at the undergraduate and graduate levels. In fact, more than 15 percent of the nation's STEM teaching master's degrees are earned at WGU. Given that several of the STEM teaching programs at WGU are less than 8 years old, this is truly remarkable. Finally, the BA Mathematics degree program was ranked by the NCTQ as the #1 secondary education program in the United States.

How does WGU define success for its work?

WGU's founders - the Western Governors Association - defined the University's mission to be "to improve quality and expand access to post–secondary educational opportunities by providing a means for individuals to learn independent of time and place and to earn competency–based degrees and other credentials that are credible to both academic institutions and employers." WGU believes in and is committed to achieving this stated mission. Fulfilling that mission is the focus of all University operations, both day–to–day and long–term, and its measure of success. The following benchmarks exemplify what the University considers to be minimum standard of mission fulfillment:

- The University will ensure that all academic programs undergo continuous formal review to ensure their relevance and currency; that appropriate program changes are made resulting from this review; and that, for all assessments, a minimum of 80 percent of students engaging the assessments achieve a passing score within two tries on different forms of the assessment.

- The University will take the appropriate steps to ensure that the percentage of underserved students is at least 67 percent. Currently, this percentage is approximately 79 percent.

- The University will ensure that the following are always in place, without exception: all programs are entirely online (with the exception of preclinical and clinical experiences), competency–based, and cost–effective; all assessments are delivered regardless of time and place. At present, the vast majority of students complete assessments online using secure online proctoring; the goal is 100 percent. The University also provides digital textbooks wherever possible to reduce cost to students and has very nearly achieved the goal of digitizing 98 percent of texts. Finally, WGU's very competitive tuition rate, which is $2890 per six–month term, has remained unchanged for the past 5 years, with no change anticipated for at least the next 2 years.

- The University will ensure that all programs subject to functional accreditation are accredited and that all teacher education licensure programs, including the STEM programs, are nationally recognized by Specialized Professional Associations. WGU is regionally accredited by the Northwest Commission on Colleges and Universities (NWCCU); Teachers College programs are accredited by the National Council for the Accreditation of Teacher Education (NCATE/CAEP); bachelor's and master's nursing degree programs are accredited by the Commission on Collegiate Nursing Education (CCNE); and the health informatics program is accredited by the Commission on Accreditation for Health Informatics and Information Management Education (CAHIIM).

- The University will further ensure that data show that employers verify that WGU degrees are credible. In particular, the University's goals in this area are that at least 90 percent of current employers of WGU graduates would be likely to hire future WGU graduates, rate WGU graduates' performance as good or excellent, and indicate that WGU graduates meet or exceed their expectations. The 2012 Harris Survey of graduate success indicates that 98 percent of employer's rate performance of WGU graduates as good or excellent and that they meet or exceed expectations, and 92 percent say they are extremely likely to hire another WGU graduate.

What is WGU's Commitment to STEM Teacher Education?

By 2018, Western Governors University will graduate an additional 4,000 middle and high school STEM teachers, with half of those graduates coming from initial licensure programs, and at least 70 percent of them coming from underserved populations. Qualified teachers are desperately needed throughout the United States, particularly in rural and urban communities and in STEM subjects. Western Governors University

(WGU) is a recognized leader in online, competency–based education and, in alignment with the university mission, is dedicated to improving quality and expanding access to higher education STEM programs.

WGU is uniquely positioned to successfully fulfill this commitment. WGU's academic model is well suited to handle the increased enrollments while maintaining high academic standards. WGU is the first online, competency–based university, and as such, does not award degrees based on credit hours or "seat time." Instead, all WGU degrees are based entirely on the demonstration of competence through a variety of assessments that measure the knowledge, skills, abilities, and dispositions necessary of a successful professional. This model allows for a flexible degree plan that can be accelerated by students who enter the program with significant competence, and it requires all graduates to have mastered all subject matter in their degree programs necessary for them to become highly qualified to teach the challenging subjects of math and science.

WGU and its mathematics and science programs have a proven record of tremendous growth. Since the first program launched in 1999, WGU has grown into a national university serving more than 50,000 students in all 50 states, and the WGU STEM programs have grown to more than 800 graduates annually. WGU has strong success with underserved students whose needs are not being met by more traditional forms of higher education. More than 70 percent of the student population meets the definition of underserved, and WGU has, as one of its Core Themes for the Northwest Commission for Colleges and Universities (our regional accrediting body), a continuation of our emphasis on providing programs for underserved populations. As we continue to grow we are committed to continue our focus on providing a successful pathway for underserved students to obtain their degree and become effective STEM teachers.

With Whom Does WGU Partner to Create a More Comprehensive Response to the Need for STEM Teachers?

WGU recognizes the importance of creating a workforce with the STEM background necessary to help our nation find solutions to some of our most challenging problems. We understand and value our responsibility in contributing to the goal of creating a K–12 system capable of training the next generation of STEM professionals. We also understand and value the contributions from other STEM institutes and the importance of collaborating in order to provide a more coherent and unified approach to meeting these challenges

WGU has forged partnerships with regional community colleges for the purpose of providing a pathway for two–year graduates to more seamlessly transition into, and graduate from, four–year STEM programs. We currently have signed articulation agreements with several hundred community colleges across the nation, including statewide community college agreements in Oregon, Colorado, Florida, and Louisiana.

WGU has developed partnerships with a number of states in order to launch WGU–State universities. These state universities allow us to market our programs in a way that best serves the students in each individual state. Currently, WGU has successfully launched

WGU–State universities in Indiana, Washington, Texas, Tennessee, and Missouri. WGU has also built strong partnerships with individual institutions such as the American Museum of Natural History and Carnegie Mellon's Open Learning Initiative.

Moving Forward

It is only when universities, the K–12 sector, and states come together to solve the problem of poor performing STEM programs that we will see the progress toward which we strive. Schools can only be successful if they are filled with effective teachers, and these teachers will only come from programs that are themselves effective. And each state needs to ensure that teacher preparation programs are permitted to operate in the state only if they can prove that their graduates have the kind of positive impact on learning that our students need and deserve. This is particularly important for the STEM areas. It is with this in mind that we must take seriously all data pertaining to the work we do at WGU, be it NCTQ rankings, WGU internal assessment data, or data associated with CAEP and other compliance reporting. This is not a time to argue about who should analyze schools. It is, instead, a time to take a hard look at schools in the United States and decide that dramatic change is needed.

About Western Governors University

WGU currently has an enrollment of approximately 50,000 students, divided among four colleges: the Teachers College, the College of Business, the IT College, and the College of Health Professions. The University recommends students for teaching licenses in all fifty states and the Nursing pre–licensure program operates in five states. WGU is accredited by the Northwest Council for Colleges and Universities, the National Council for the Accreditation of Teachers Education, the Collegiate Council on Nursing Education, and CAHIIM (for Health Informatics). WGU is one of only four universities nationally to be top–ranked by the NCTQ for two or more programs and is a part of the 100Kin10 collaborative, having been nominated by the Broad Institute. As part of that collaborative, we have pledged to confer at least 4,000 STEM teaching degrees by the close of 2018.

The principal mission of Western Governors University is to improve quality and expand access to post–secondary educational opportunities by providing a means for individuals to learn independent of time and place, and to earn competency–based degrees and other credentials that are credible to both academic institutions and employers. STEM teaching has always been a significant part of the mission of WGU and continues to be an area of excellent for the Teachers College. An Eduventures report issued this year indicates that WGU is the leading producer of STEM teachers in the United States among all colleges and universities.

About the Author

Dr. Philip Schmidt is the Vice President for Compliance and Accreditation and Dean of the Teachers College at Western Governors University (WGU). He has been a part of the WGU Teachers College for more than 12 years. Dr. Schmidt's background includes work in both mathematics and mathematics education. His MA degree (in mathematics) and his PhD degree (in mathematics and education) were earned at Syracuse University.

Over the past 30 years, Dr. Schmidt's interests have included developmental mathematics, the teaching of mathematics to precocious children, and online and competency–based pedagogies and instruction. At WGU, he was part of the team that provided the initial structure for the curriculum in the Teachers College, with an emphasis on STEM teacher preparation. The result is that WGU is now the largest producer of STEM teachers in the United States. Most recently the NCTQ ranked WGU's BA in Mathematics degree program the #1 secondary education program in the United States.

CHAPTER NINE

Career Focused Experiential Learning

"At Washington State University Tri-Cities, we have embraced a polytechnic philosophy: Learn by doing. Preparing our students, through capstones, experiential learning, co-ops and internship opportunities, which solidify their learning. There are opportunities for our students to intern with Pacific Northwest National Laboratory, and other fortune 100 companies in the research district. Most of our students are placed successfully at jobs within these industries. Our students are job ready when they graduate from Washington State University Tri-Cities."

**- Dr. H. Keith Moo-Young, Chancellor,
Washington State University – Tri Cities**

Employability Skills & Experiential Learning Are Critical For STEM Careers

By: Al Bunshaft, President and Chief Operating Officer of Dassault Systèmes Americas

Employers in the United States continue to face significant challenges in securing talented and skilled professionals in the STEM fields. Our company, Dassault Systèmes, is no exception. We actively recruit a broad range of STEM talent to fill highly technical positions across our business. While locating specialized technical talent is a definite challenge across a wide range of industries, other factors also contribute to the success and productivity of STEM employees in the professional work environment.

Working at a high-tech company like ours requires a multi–dimensional person equipped with the knowledge, skills, and abilities of the 21st century workplace. In addition to foundational skills in mathematics and science, and specialized expertise in a field like software engineering, employees must exhibit an understanding and proficiency in what many have termed *employability skills*. Employability skills are a discipline–independent set of competencies and behaviors that all employers expect from their employees. At the most basic level, employability skills include teamwork, communication, reliability, flexibility, and the ability to understand and adapt to new ideas. While employability skills are sometimes termed as "soft skills" or "life skills," that terminology undermines their importance. These skills are directly linked to the success of employees in the work environment.

Defining employability skills and exploring solutions aimed at addressing the STEM gap have been priorities of the STEM Innovation Task Force (SITF); a group that Dassault Systèmes has been an active member of for the past two years. The SITF is an executive–level working group comprised of 36 organizations from the industry, education, government, and non–profit sectors. The primary focus of the SITF has been the STEM 2.0 initiative, which is aimed at identifying, defining, and inculcating in students several capability platforms necessary for success in tomorrow's STEM careers. The SITF has prioritized employability skills, innovation excellence, and digital fluency as being critical to the success of recent graduates and the current workforce, all from an employer or demand–side perspective. When a STEM professional has mastered these capabilities in addition to the skills and knowledge gained from a traditional STEM degree, value to employers grows tremendously. This applies to all entry–level STEM professionals, whether high–school/vocational school graduates, community college or college/ university graduates.

Building upon the massive momentum and political will gained over the last few years, the broader STEM movement should consider a couple of important factors moving into 2015 and beyond. A specific focus should be placed on what skills and knowledge private–sector employers are looking for in their employees. The private sector in the U.S. drives economic growth and prosperity, and employs the largest number of Americans. Directly connecting the talent demands of employers to what the education system is producing will be critical for the future. Many educators at different levels, particularly in higher education, have developed excellent programs that make this connection. In particular, programs that integrate experiential learning and project and/or problem–based learning with a career focus should be scaled and replicated. As employers, we have seen that new employees with rich, experiential learning projects in their backgrounds are better prepared for the workplace and are productive more quickly.

Dassault Systèmes recognizes the importance of developing employability skills and exposing students to experiential learning opportunities. Franklin W. Olin College of Engineering in Needham, Massachusetts is the embodiment of these two essential pillars of a modern STEM education. For the past several years now, Dassault Systèmes has participated in and sponsored Olin's SCOPE (Senior Capstone Program in Engineering), a unique industry–university partnership. SCOPE matches a team of Olin seniors with a major company through a consulting project, which presents the students with a real–world challenge that the company needs to solve. This provides students with an opportunity to work on a cross–functional team (i.e. employability skills). The cross–disciplinary student team then works closely with the Research and Development team at Dassault Systèmes at various key points regarding the selected project. Our current project for the 2014–2015 school year involves students evaluating mobile device interfaces and alternatives for our 3D design software.

Olin College stands out as an example in the higher education environment, however employability skills and experiential learning are important across the entire education spectrum. As part of our STEM 2.0 work–plan, the STEM Innovation Task Force has interviewed several of the most successful organizations implementing programs focused on developing employability skills. As examples, SkillsUSA and the National FFA Organization are two exemplary organizations that focus on teaching these critical skills to our primary school–age youth. Programming takes place at the local level and includes leadership development as well as career and technical education.

As the STEM Innovation Task Force looks ahead to 2015 and beyond, we will continue our research work to validate the premise that STEM 2.0 capabilities (employability skills, innovation excellence, and digital fluency) complemented by experiential learning programs are essential skills for STEM professionals. Regarding the employability skill set, it has been observed that some skills are growing rapidly in their importance. We will work to highlight these emerging employability skills, driven by both a more diverse and global workplace, and also the increasingly interdisciplinary nature of innovation. One of our other planned actions is to inventory existing learning programs for each capability area. We will identify a range of programs that address the development of these skills across different levels of learning. The goal of this inventory is to identify successful programs that can be replicated in other contexts or that should be scaled to a national or international level. In early 2015 we will publish a white paper detailing our research findings on employability skills. It will outline an action–plan for increasing the focus on employability skills in the national STEM discussion and educational agenda. We encourage readers of this publication working to develop next–generation STEM professionals to integrate these STEM 2.0 capabilities and experiential learning into existing programs, curriculum, and training.

Advancing a Jobs-Driven Economy

Many of the best programs that convey employability skills utilize experiential learning methods and are supported by, or instantiated by, public–private partnerships. There are many examples including the Maker Movement, FIRST Robotics, and the programs cited earlier in this article. These collaborations and partnerships that build sustainable connections between educators and employers are essential to solving the growing STEM worker shortfall. Only by working together across constituencies will we make tangible progress in reducing this shortfall in our country.

About Dassault Systèmes

Dassault Systèmes, the 3DEXPERIENCE Company, provides business and people with virtual universes to imagine sustainable innovations. Its world–leading solutions transform the way products are designed, produced, and supported. Dassault Systèmes' collaborative solutions foster social innovation, expanding possibilities for the virtual world to improve the real world. The group brings value to over 190,000 customers of all sizes, in all industries, in more than 140 countries. For more information, visit www.3ds.com. DS Government Solutions is a wholly–owned subsidiary of Dassault Systèmes Americas Corporation and is dedicated to serving and supporting the United States Government with all Dassault Systèmes capabilities.

About the Author

Al Bunshaft is the President and Chief Operating Officer of DS Government Solutions, responsible for the sales, service and support of all Dassault Systèmes products to the United States Government. He is also responsible for many of the company's relationships with key stakeholders across a broad range of institutions.

As Managing Director of Dassault Systèmes Americas from 2010 until 2013, he helped build the foundation for future company growth by leading the company's American organization of more than 3,000 employees. A common thread in Mr. Bunshaft's career has been his expertise in visualization and computer graphics.

Bunshaft is Dassault Systèmes' leading voice in STEM initiatives and was named one of the top 100 Chief Operating Officer leaders in STEM in the U.S. He is a member of the STEM subcommittee of the Clinton Global Initiative – America, and is a board member of the Massachusetts High Technology Council. Bunshaft is an advisory board member at the Department of Information and Computer Science of The State University of New York at Albany. He was recently named to the Olin College of Engineering President's Council.

Bunshaft received his Bachelor of Science in Computer Science and Mathematics from University at Albany, State University of New York and has a Master of Science in Computer Engineering from Rensselaer Polytechnic Institute (RPI).

Looking For a Cost Effective Approach to
Bring Company Ideas to Reality? Try Students!

By: Dr. Phillip Cornwell, Vice President for Academic Affairs and a Professor of Mechanical Engineering, Rose–Hulman Institute of Technology

The focus of this discussion will be Rose–Hulman Ventures. We will present the operational model, discuss the types of clients and projects, and highlight Precision Planting as an example of the great clients we have at Rose–Hulman Ventures.

Rose–Hulman Ventures is a program at Rose–Hulman where students work as paid interns on engineering projects supplied by commercial clients. Based upon the needs of the client, multi–disciplinary student intern teams are assembled for each project and are led by full–time experienced engineers. Most project engagements are on a fee–for–service basis with an average project cost of about $45,000. Since the program was started in 1999, it has employed more than 980 student interns working with 170 client companies.

The infrastructure in place to support the program includes a staff of 14 individuals and a 35,000 square foot facility as shown in the figure to the right. The majority of the staff members are technical project managers. These project managers are degreed engineers with industrial experience and are not members of the university faculty. They hire and manage the  student interns, help develop the proposals that are presented to potential clients, ensure that the needs of the client companies are met, and educate the interns with respect to both technical matters and also the norms of professional practice. Rose–Hulman Ventures is equipped with an electronics shop, a machine shop, IT infrastructure, and an assortment of rapid prototyping equipment (e.g. waterjet cutter, polyjet rapid prototype and laser welder).

Operational Model

Most Rose–Hulman Ventures projects are on a fee–for–service basis, that is, the industrial client pays for time and materials. The direct labor hours applied to a project are tracked and billed against four different labor categories: student interns, technical staff, project managers and faculty members. The student interns work on the projects for pay and do not receive academic credit. Student interns typically work approximately 10 hours/week when classes are in session and 40 hours/week during the summer. Student interns are expected to dress and behave professionally and to maintain a schedule that is negotiated at the start of each academic term.

Since the student interns are working for pay as opposed to credit, it is possible to de–couple the start and end of projects from the traditional academic calendar. This offers the advantage of being able to quickly respond to the needs of the client and has helped attract clients that would not have been able to adjust the timing of their needs to the academic calendar.

Before any project work is started, an R&D agreement is negotiated and signed. Some of the important elements addressed in the agreement are compensation, intellectual property, confidentiality, indemnification and limitation of liability. One of the distinctive characteristics of the program is that no attempt is made by the university to extract revenue from the intellectual property that is created as part of the projects. In general, any intellectual property that is created during the execution of the project is assigned to the client company. This characteristic has proven to be a differentiator and has helped to attract clients to the program.

Clients and Projects

Rose–Hulman Ventures consults for a diverse mix of customers, from entrepreneurial start–ups to established companies with global operations. Clients come from diverse industry sectors including automotive and transportation; consumer and commercial products; e–commerce; energy; industrial controls; industrial machines and equipment; IT and business services; laboratory equipment and logistics; medical devices; medical informatics; pharmaceuticals; plastics and flexible packaging; private equity; semiconductors; software products and platforms; and telecommunications.

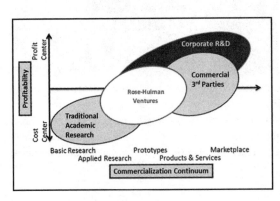

Most projects at Rose–Hulman Ventures are early stage product development and prototyping projects that do not fit neatly into the operational models of the traditional participants in research and development. The figure to the left shows three of the traditional participants in the research and development community along with where they typically exist in the continuum of R&D commercialization activities. These participants are traditional academic researchers, commercial third-party product development companies, and corporate R&D organizations. We have found a successful niche working on projects that are more applied in nature than what is pursued by traditional academic researchers, but are less defined than what is generally a comfortable fit for commercial third-party product development companies or corporate research and development organizations.

Precision Planting

A great example of a Rose–Hulman Ventures client is Precision Planting, which has been working with Rose–Hulman Ventures for over five years. Precision Planting is based in

Tremont, IL and was bought by Monsanto in 2012. Project managers and student interns at Rose–Hulman Ventures work closely with Precision Planting to develop innovative agricultural data collection tools designed to increase the yields of American farmers.

Plant spacing is crucial in determining if plants receive the water, nutrients, and sunlight necessary to grow to full maturity each growing season. Corn reacts to high density planting, changing plant size, ear size, and ear placement in order to prepare for competition. Therefore, accurate planting contributes to higher bushel yields and better profits. Precision Planting came to Rose–Hulman Ventures with a product idea in early 2012. Rose–Hulman Ventures Project Managers Zhan Chen, Barry Davignon, and Sandor Pethes conceived the original design concepts. Nine student interns worked on the project during 2012 and 2013. Three devices and an iPad platform were developed to measure approximately 300,000 cornstalks for research and development. The devices became so popular that 22 units were deployed the summer of 2013 to collect more than 1 million data points from fields across Texas, Louisiana, Kentucky, Illinois, and Iowa.

This particular project/partnership is a great example because it shows the unique value Rose–Hulman Ventures offers to clients compared to other university partnership models. Monsanto/Precision Planting has world class core competencies in agribusiness technology, but they did not have the manpower in house to accomplish this project. Rose–Hulman Ventures was able to complement their core competency with expertise in software development and device design. Precision Planting intends to continue collaborating with Rose–Hulman Ventures on fast–turn exploratory projects that cannot be included within their slower–moving internal resource planning. Rose–Hulman Ventures is able to satisfy Monsanto/Precision Planting's project needs while providing outstanding, real–world educational experiences for Rose–Hulman students. This has been a true win–win partnership.

Assessment

Rose–Hulman Ventures was assessed by surveying student interns and industrial clients. One question student interns were asked was *'Overall, how satisfied have you been with your Rose–Hulman Ventures experience?'* Typically, around 95 percent of students express that they were 'very satisfied or satisfied' with their Rose–Hulman Ventures experience. When companies were surveyed, virtually all of them (over 90 percent) said that Rose–Hulman Ventures' work had an impact on their business, and over half said the impact was high or very high. These assessments confirm that Rose–Hulman Ventures solves business challenges for clients, while providing excellent educational experiences for student interns.

Action Items

- Higher education and industry need to have clear lines of communication to ensure that both are aware of the knowledge, skills, and abilities needed and so industry has a better appreciation for the education we provide to our students.
- Industry needs to commit to working with higher education in ways other than support for traditional research to help higher education provide the quality employees industry desires.

About Rose–Hulman Institute of Technology

Rose–Hulman is a private institution founded in 1874 that focuses on undergraduate science, engineering, and mathematics education. About 85 percent of the students are majoring in one of the engineering disciplines, with the remainder studying computer science, one of the other sciences, or mathematics. Rose–Hulman is dedicated to preparing our students with the world's best undergraduate science, engineering, and mathematics education in an environment infused with innovation, intellectual rigor, and individualized attention. For 16 consecutive years, U.S. News & World Report has rated Rose–Hulman as the top undergraduate engineering college in the nation whose highest degree is a bachelor's or masters.

Rose–Hulman partners with industry through a number of activities designed to provide mutual benefit to both the Institute and the industrial partner. For example, a vast majority of Rose–Hulman students have at least one experience working on an industry–sponsored project, usually in "Senior Capstone Design." In this yearlong experience, students work on teams under the supervision of a Rose–Hulman faculty member on projects provided by an industrial client. Other partnership activities include summer internships, recruiting, industrial advisory boards, and Rose–Hulman Ventures projects.

About the Author

Dr. Phillip Cornwell is the Vice President for Academic Affairs and a Professor of Mechanical Engineering at Rose–Hulman Institute of Technology. Dr. Cornwell received his B.S. degree in Mechanical Engineering from Texas Tech University in 1985 and his M.A. and Ph.D. from Princeton University in 1987 and 1989, respectively. Dr. Cornwell has been active in curricular development, and he helped develop the Sophomore Engineering Curriculum at Rose–Hulman where engineering science is taught in a unified framework.

Cornwell spent many summers working at Los Alamos National Laboratory where he was a mentor in the Los Alamos Dynamics Summer School and performed research in the areas of structural health monitoring and energy harvesting. Dr. Cornwell is a recipient of the Society of Automotive Engineers' Ralph R. Teetor Educational Award, and he has received the two highest awards at Rose–Hulman: the Dean's Outstanding Teacher award and the Board of Trustees' Outstanding Scholar Award. Dr. Cornwell was one of the professors featured in the Princeton Review's book called *The Best 300 Professors*.

Creating Opportunities to Inspire the Scientists of Tomorrow through the Amgen Scholars Program
By: Scott Heimlich, Vice President, Amgen Foundation

A highly–skilled scientific workforce is a critical driver of today's 21ˢᵗ century economy and the advancement of knowledge. As a society, we face enormous challenges – including the fight against serious illness – that require collaborative approaches among sectors, expertise across multiple disciplines, and a deep capacity for innovation. To create and sustain such a workforce for tomorrow – as well as to deepen understanding and appreciation of science and its critical role – the Amgen Foundation is deeply committed to advancing science education at the K–12 and higher education levels. Our most significant initiative is a $50 million, 12–year commitment to a large number of higher education institutions to support the Amgen Scholars Program.

Launched in 2006, Amgen Scholars provides hundreds of undergraduates each year with access to incredible research opportunities at premier educational institutions. Participants from across the globe, many of whom have limited access to research faculty and the highest–quality laboratories at their home institutions, are able to spend the summer undertaking real scientific research projects under the guidance of faculty mentors at MIT, Stanford, Berkeley, Harvard, Caltech, Cambridge, Tokyo and 10 other top institutions. Unique to the Japan program, students globally are eligible to participate while students in the U.S. and Europe may apply in their respective region. The program truly recruits for science by opening the doors of these elite institutions to aspiring scientists everywhere, and serves as a springboard in the academic life of many undergraduates. This significant investment has already made it possible for nearly 2,500 students from more than 500 colleges and universities to participate, the vast majority of whom are now pursuing advanced degrees and careers in STEM fields.

Many Amgen Scholars now in scientific careers – whether in academia, industry or government – look back on the hands–on research opportunity as critical, but gained from the program something more through their interactions outside the lab. Beyond the research experience, Amgen Scholars is purposely designed as a cohort experience at each of the 17 host institutions, which pays heed to the powerful influence of one's peers as students delve into science and explore their future paths and careers. Thus, every host institution supports 20 undergraduates from across a large geographic region each summer, not only supporting them in a research experience but providing a meaningful array of activities outside the lab – from seminars to writing workshops to social dinners – to create the strongest possible experience and impact. As one 2014 Amgen Scholar stated,

...the summer I spent in Los Angeles has been the best summer of my life. With new friendships, mentors, and laboratory skills, I'm well equipped to do whatever I desire in the field of biomedicine.

Given the multi–year Amgen Foundation commitment, one key factor propelling the success of this large–scale initiative is a real commitment to collaborate and utilize anonymous participant data to drive continuous improvement across all host institutions. With an independent evaluator on board since the launch of the initiative, a design that allows for flexibility in how the program runs at each institution, and consistent survey instruments across the international program, the structure allows not only for rich feedback from participants, but also for comparative performance across institutions on a wide range of metrics. This allows for identification of institutions implementing best practices, such as those that best match students to particular faculty and labs or best engage students outside the lab. These practices are then highlighted at Leadership Meetings convened by the Foundation to ensure program leadership at other institutions can learn how to implement these 'best in class' elements– allowing for all programs to get stronger and enhance their impact in the coming year.

Another integral component of the initiative is the symposium and the engagement of staff from industry in particular. All Amgen Scholars – whether in the U.S., Europe, or Japan – have the opportunity to participate in a two–day symposium in their region to hear from leading scientists, network with their peers, and learn about biotechnology as it applies to medicine. While students spend 8–10 weeks in a research lab at one of the host institutions, the symposium – which engages many Amgen executives and staff in addition to other scientists – is a cornerstone experience of the summer program that truly exemplifies the partnership between educational institutions and the Amgen Foundation to inspire and prepare the next generation of scientists. Past symposia include talks ranging from *The Impact of Biotechnology on Drug Discovery and Development to My Life as a Scientist,* to roundtables and poster sessions that allow for students to share their research projects with scientists and their peers. As one Scholar stated, "[the symposium] got me really excited about science. I walked away from that weekend really excited about pursuing a PhD in the sciences."

Such initiatives and collaborations between sectors should be designed for everyone's benefit. The Amgen Foundation, with its commitment to develop the next generation of scientists, can look to the program's results – with over 90 percent of alumni who have completed their undergraduate studies now pursuing advanced scientific degrees and careers across the world. See the Alumni section at AmgenScholars.com for further detail. The host institutions who run the program not only invest significant time and expertise in supporting students who participate at their institution, but many of these participants are now eager to pursue advanced degrees and research opportunities back at that institution after completing their bachelor's degrees. And the student participant, who experiences both the challenges and possibilities of a career advancing science, is often now more eager to explore careers that will ultimately contribute to the scientific workforce needed across the public and private sectors.

Lastly, the Amgen Scholars Program is one of many initiatives in the Amgen Foundation's larger science education portfolio. The Foundation firmly recognizes how integral investments are at the K–12 level as well – for both students and teachers –

and have a myriad of substantive, evidence–based approaches to do so, including many with other higher education institutions. One is the Amgen Biotech Experience (see AmgenBiotechExperience.com), which partners with higher education institutions across several Amgen communities, and empowers high school science teachers to bring biotechnology labs to their students utilizing research–grade equipment. This program now reaches over 60,000 students a year with hands–on labs.

Moving Forward

Higher education and businesses must continue to partner if we are to advance a jobs–driven economy. One path towards this is to fully participate in effective large–scale partnerships committed to strengthening education and building the future workforce. The Amgen Foundation is proud to be a significant partner in 100Kin10 – a networked approach to providing America's classrooms with 100,000 excellent STEM teachers by 2021 – and Change the Equation, which works at the intersection of business and education to ensure that all students are STEM literate. A second path is to explore how your industry or company can participate in advancing this important issue, including partnering with relevant stakeholders such as universities in your communities, and exploring how to best leverage the competencies your employees and organization can bring. Developing tomorrow's workforce is every sector's responsibility – our future success will depend upon it.

About Amgen

Amgen is committed to unlocking the potential of biology for patients suffering from serious illnesses by discovering, developing, manufacturing and delivering innovative human therapeutics. The Amgen Foundation, operating since 1991, is an integral component of Amgen's commitment to dramatically improve people's lives and the principal channel for Amgen's corporate philanthropy. To date, the Foundation has contributed over $200 million to non–profit organizations globally that reflect Amgen's core values, and complement the company's dedication to impacting lives in inspiring and innovative ways.

The Amgen Foundation seeks to advance excellence in science education to inspire the next generation of innovators, and invest in strengthening communities where Amgen staff members live and work. The Foundation places a strong emphasis on strengthening science education and is committed to investing in meaningful, evidence–based initiatives that make a difference at the local, national, and international levels.

To that end, the Amgen Foundation has contributed over $100 million to advancing science education programming globally. Learn more about the Amgen Foundation's deep commitment to science education at www.amgeninspires.com.

About the Author

Scott M. Heimlich is Vice President of the Amgen Foundation. He is responsible for the strategic management and direction of the science education portfolio for the Amgen Foundation, the principal philanthropic arm of Amgen Inc., including the development and oversight of key initiatives at the K–12 and higher education levels. He was the principal architect of the Amgen Scholars Program, the Foundation's largest initiative, providing undergraduates with access to research opportunities at premier educational institutions across the world. He led the U.S. program's expansion to Europe and Japan, and today continues to oversee the $50 million international program. Under his leadership, the Amgen Biotech Experience has transformed from a local program into a multi–site, international initiative bringing biotechnology to over 60,000 secondary students a year. With these and many other initiatives, the Foundation's commitment to science education recently surpassed the $100 million milestone.

Heimlich serves on The Conference Board Business–Education Council and Southern California Grantmakers STEM + Arts Advisory Committee, and leads the Foundation's commitment to STEM education networks such as 100Kin10 and Change the Equation. Prior to joining Amgen in 2005, he served in positions at the University of California, Los Angeles, Los Angeles Pierce College, University of Southern California, and a junior high school in Japan. He holds a bachelor's degree, master's degree, and doctorate in education from the University of California, Los Angeles.

Collaborate in the Classroom: Compete in the Marketplace
By: Dr. Bryan Albrecht, President and Chief Executive Officer,
Gateway Technical College

STEM partnerships demonstrate the potential to unlock growth in education and workforce development by integrating the knowledge and skills of STEM in ways that provide students with a pathway to technical careers.

Our greatest potential strength in the global competition for jobs remains the American workforce. The best way to enable that workforce in this competition is technical education. I am convinced STEM education has never, ever been more important. It is an imperative to secure our nation's viability in the competitive global economy.
— Nick Pinchuk, Chairman and Chief Operating Officer
Snap–on Incorporated

Driven by innovation, technology and human capital, the STEM partnership between Gateway Technical College and Snap–on is intended to inspire commitment by educators, community leaders and employers of STEM talent from both the public and private sector. Technical partnerships, technical education and pre–engineering will generate expanded capabilities that meet the needs of our nation today and will help ensure a path to greater prosperity going forward.

By working together, Gateway Technical College and Snap–on serve as a model of cooperation in developing new ideas and innovative partnerships that have influenced hundreds of schools and thousands of teachers K–16 throughout the country. As a member of STEMconnector®, Gateway and Snap–on are active in sharing their story with education and industry leaders to engage a community of learners about the importance of a STEM educated citizenry.

Founded in 1920 and headquartered in Kenosha, Wisconsin, Snap–on is a leading global innovator, manufacturer and marketer of tools, equipment, diagnostics, repair information and systems solutions for professional users performing critical tasks. Snap–on has a storied history in partnering with education and education associations. Gateway Technical College, also located in Kenosha, was founded in 1911 and has been an educational partner with Snap–on since the 1960s.

That partnership evolved into a comprehensive and strategic relationship with a shared belief in the importance of career and technical education and the expansion of STEM learning. Snap–on, a company whose growth is driven by innovation that depends on the underlying technical capability, values the importance of education at all levels in creating the intellectual capital that American companies need to compete. This belief pointed the way to a model with national and international reach while at the same time having a local input. As a result, the National Coalition of Certification Centers (NC3) was formed and Gateway began training and certifying high school, community and technical college instructors in Snap–on diagnostics throughout the nation. From that base, currently more than 200 high schools and colleges are delivering one or more of the now 38 Snap–on certifications developed through NC3. To date, more than 900 high school, community and technical instructors have been Snap–on certified, along with over 16,000 student technicians.

Gateway Technical College, in partnership with Snap–on, has invested in a new facility with a name that reminds us of our work still to be completed. The Horizon Center represents the transformation of Gateway's automotive and aviation programs. The horizon is where the land (auto) and sky (aviation) meet and is forever changing, keeping lifelong learning at the center of the Horizon Center mission.

Expanding on the original vision for the both NC3 and the Horizon Center, Gateway Technical College and Snap–on have broadened their partnership to include STEM camps for elementary and middle school students as well as integrated manufacturing and engineering programs for high school and college-level students. STEM camps operated in partnership with the Kenosha Boys & Girls Club have served as a vehicle for enriching its summer camps. Youth interested in science and engineering are encouraged to participate in a week–long STEM experience led by Gateway faculty, enhanced with community field trips. The STEM camps are designed to inspire creativity and hands–on use of tools and materials. STEM students have designed and built solar cars, planned and prepared community agricultural projects, and participated in maker camps utilizing 3D printers to bring engineering designs to life. Students engaged in this experience have expressed a real excitement toward learning how products are designed, built and work. Snap–on serves as the sponsor and provides the funding to support the teacher, materials and out–of–classroom experiences. The first year, 30 students participated and the number doubled to 60 the second year. It is anticipated that by adding additional camps and expanding the age groups eligible, the STEM camps could reach 300 students each summer.

Another example of the partnership between Gateway Technical College and Snap–on is the development of the iMET Center. The name iMET stands for integrated Manufacturing and Engineering Technology and serves as an acronym for Gateway's uniquely positioned advanced technology center located in Sturtevant, Wisconsin. This state–of–the–art facility serves as Gateway's center for engineering and technical training. Snap–on has partnered in the development of Mechatronics, Fab, CNC and Metrology labs. Each of these labs focuses on the integration of STEM skills to improve the educational outcomes of the students in engineering and manufacturing programs. Students now have the opportunity to design, prototype, test, re–engineer, and manufacture products from ideas they have generated. The iMET Center also provides students direct contact with industry professionals through seminars and workshops. Snap–on associates participate regularly in these discussions on patent protection and additive manufacturing.

Gateway Technical College and Snap–on share a common set of values as they relate to STEM education. "STEM efforts at Gateway are helping us to meet the need for more engineers, scientists and technicians, and address the skills gap employers are challenged with," Bryan Albrecht, President of Gateway Technical College. Our call to action is for everyone concerned about our economic prosperity, our educational competitiveness and our ability to sustain career opportunities for future generations to get involved by becoming a learner and champion for STEM in your local school and community. Snap–on's leadership in building a STEM community has fostered many new partnerships for Gateway and educational institutions across the country. "Our community leaders respect Snap–on and the leadership it provides for education and business," Debbie Davidson, Vice President Workforce and Economic Development for Gateway Technical College.

Gateway and Snap–on have made a commitment to leverage their core values and individual strengths to promote STEM education as a pathway for individual and national economic success. From elementary school STEM camps and middle school robotics competitions, to "Project Lead the Way" high school program support, Gateway and Snap–on are champions for STEM teaching and learning. Snap–on donates tools and equipment and supports a student industry certification program, while Snap–on associates are involved in supporting local schools by hosting corporate tours, serving as youth mentors and as classroom speakers. STEM provides a common platform for education and industry to work together to ensure economic prosperity for all. Gateway Technical College and Snap–on have recognized this value and are partnering and providing that opportunity for all learners.

Action Items
It is imperative that education and business work together to advance a common agenda to drive local economies. There are several actions that can amplify this effort. Both colleges and business are in leadership positions to inform policy makers on the importance of investing in training to broaden the talent pipeline for regional competitiveness. Business and industry leaders have a perspective that can drive curriculum and training standards. The delivery of these standards can be influenced by serving on local education advisory committees, serving as training mentors, providing technical experts to work with instructors, securing internship opportunities and developing specific training programs and certifications. Educators must also be willing to invest time and energy in understanding the changing talent needs of local employers. This can be accomplished through focus groups to assess training needs, participating in teacher externships to gain first–hand experience, curriculum cross-walking with job skill assessments and skill development assessments in partnership with employer HR departments.

Job driven economies begin with understanding the current job skill requirements and assessing future skill development opportunities. Up–skilling the workforce is a shared responsibility. Employers investing in current workers can lead to skills advancement, which grows the organization and opens up entry-level opportunities to expand the workforce with new talent. Colleges must be ready at both ends of the spectrum to meet this need. Advanced skills in diagnostics, mechatronics or additive manufacturing is just as importation as entry-level skills in precision measurement, computer applications and safety. The balance between what is taught and what is necessary to acquire a job is largely dependent on a strong line of communication between employers and educators. There is no question that jobs are the common denominator for a strong economy. Understanding and communicating the necessary inputs, along with high levels of performance accountability, will determine the success of training candidates in achieving employment and advancing the economic value of employers.

About Gateway Technical College

Gateway Technical College provides quality technical education to the residents of its district, which is comprised of the southeastern Wisconsin counties of Kenosha, Racine, and Walworth. Gateway is one of sixteen technical college districts, which comprise the Wisconsin Technical College System. Gateway is a taxpayer–supported institution of postsecondary education, offering more than 60 degree and diploma programs, as well as nearly 50 certificate programs. Gateway provides you with almost limitless alternatives for your educational and employment future.

Associate of Applied Science Degrees, and Technical Diplomas are awarded upon successful completion of individual program requirements. In addition, a wide variety of Adult Continuing Education (ACE) noncredit classes, workshops, and seminars are offered to assist Gateway District residents in expanding and augmenting occupational skills, or to assist in the improvement of their chosen lifestyles.

About the Author

Dr. Bryan Albrecht serves as the President and Chief Executive Officer of Gateway Technical College. Gateway is located in Southeast Wisconsin and serves approximately 25,000 students annually. Gateway is known for having strong partnerships with the business community and establishing a culture of innovation. Under his leadership Gateway has expanded programs and services, built a national industry training network, and enhanced the talent pipeline from high school through post-graduate-level studies.

President Albrecht serves on Southeast Wisconsin's local Workforce Board, as well as the National Manufacturing Institute's Advisory Board, the National Occupational Competency Testing Board, the National STEM Academy Advisory Board, and the National Center for Occupational Research and Development Board.

His experience has led him to testify before the U.S. Congress on career and technical education issues, as well as be named a Distinguished Educator by the International Technology and Engineering Association.

Dr. Albrecht earned his Bachelors, Masters, and Education Specialist degrees from the University of Wisconsin–Stout and his Doctorate of Education from the University of Minnesota.

CHAPTER TEN

Lifelong Learning and
Competency Based Education

"I think businesses are the critical factor. The higher education players have to learn to listen and learn from the businesses from the beginning. In the past, they only went to the business with the end product; hire my graduate. But today and tomorrow they will have to go to them not just once but over and over again as they refine and develop their curriculum to meet the accelerated changes that are happening in the workplace."

– Jane Oates, VP for External Affairs
Apollo Education Group

Got Skills? The Workforce Revolution
By: Jamai Blivin, Chief Executive Officer, Innovate+Educate

Education and employment in the United States has never seen such a dilemma. As 2014 draws to a close, employers are struggling more than ever as they claim they cannot find skilled workers for the many open positions in high demand fields. At the same time, billions of dollars are piling into training and education resources, with no real certainty that business understands the training or how it relates to success in employability. The archaic labels that have worked previously (including degree and years of experience) are knocking many qualified jobseekers out of opportunity, and thus we have (drum roll) ......a Workforce Revolution.

What exactly is a revolution? As defined by Wikipedia: A revolution (from the Latin "revolution", meaning "a turnaround") is a fundamental change in power or organizational structures that takes place in a relatively short period of time. Aristotle described two types of political revolution 1) complete change from one constitution to another and 2) modification of an existing constitution.

To that end, we predict that the big change in power (and the full launch of the Revolution) is that of an industry–driven skills to employment system that illuminates the critical skills necessary for our own country's global competitiveness. This new system *must* be demand driven and will require systemic change from the demand side players (businesses small to large) for true success.

What do we mean by success? First, let's look at the statistics that show the tremendous need for this revolution:

- Students are demanding more direct connections with employers: 87.9 percent of college freshman cited getting a better job as a vital reason for pursuing a college degree. (American Freshman Survey, 2012) which is 17 percent higher than in the same survey questionnaire six years prior.

- Students' demographics are shifting. The National Center for Education Statistics projects that by 2020, 42 percent of all college students will be 25 or older.

- The nontraditional student (18–22 year old not enrolled fulltime, do not live on campus, must work in school is somewhere around 71 percent of all college–going students in the U.S. (Hire Education, Clayton Christensen, 2014)

- There are approximately 37 million American adults with some college but no degree. (Hire Education, Clayton Christensen, 2014) Yet, job postings still require a degree – over and over.

- Only 36 percent of full–time students enrolled at four–year universities, 19 percent at other universities, and a shocking 4 percent of students at two–year institutions graduate on time. For those that do graduate with a bachelor's degree, 54 percent of those under the age of 28 are either underemployed or unemployed. (Managing the Talent Pipeline: A New Approach to Closing the Skills Gap, U. S. Chamber of Commerce Foundation, November 2014)

These stats alone show that the demographics of education in our country are changing. So, let's analyze now what success could look like:

- Success is a system in which the demand side is able to articulate entry level to mid skill core foundational skills.

- The demand side then agrees to a framework that is transferable across many job sectors in the U.S., specifically the high demand job sectors. Why not? We can validate that 95 percent of all U.S. jobs require 3 to 5 of the same core foundational skills for employability success. (Innovate+Educate research, 2011–2014).

- These core foundation skills should be front and center for success in education and training, assuring that the education and training partners can assure that students and learners can achieve the competency required to be job ready.

- Job postings begin to be skills and competency based rather than only including education (degree and specificity of degree) and experience. Both of these prove to be key barriers to employment.

- Competency based employment uses real labor data provided by groups such as Burning Glass, Wanted Analytics and EMSI to show where the jobs are, what the skills are required for those jobs, and break down those job postings into a language understandable between supply/demand.

- The job descriptions begin being re–written in a skills to competencies based language to assure more accurate navigation for the job seeker and more predictive hiring for the employer, thus creating a new talent demand/supply system in the U.S. based on skills and competencies.

- Higher education institutions and training partners begin to coordinate their own teaching and training to meet the demand side of the labor equation and assuring a more accurate, qualified candidate for jobs upon graduation.

- A portfolio of validated assessments is identified (or built) that can measure these qualifications and skills to assure that the employer can trust hiring by competencies

- A portfolio of free to low cost training curriculum or training modules is available that assures the jobseeker can train/skill up to assure they have the job competencies required or preferred by the employer.

- Industry re–directs their own training and resources to assure that once the core foundation skills have been hired, they can train specifically to the jobs within the company and provide a pathway to high level jobs that "grows their own" into higher level positions within the company based on skills and competencies.

Call to Action

In closing, this is a call to action to challenge business and industry, higher education and national partners to focus on a new model of education to employment – with a demand driven focus on the key "win" at the end.

That win is defined as a JOB. And a JOB filled by a strong, skilled candidate that has tremendous potential for economic success.

About Innovate+Educate

Innovate+Educate is a national 501c3 non–profit founded in 2009 by Chief Operating Officer Jamai Blivin. With a focus on industry at the helm, the board of top Fortune 500 companies created a vision for having industry lead as a key driver in the solutions around STEM education and workforce. In October 2013, the Innovate+Educate Board of Directors voted and approved to change its strategic vision and mission to focus on employer–led strategies to close the national skills gap. The mission of I+E is to implement research based–demand–led strategies that lead to the national adoption of competency–based hiring and training by employers. A natural outcome is career–building skills for individuals, transferrable across multiple sectors. I+E recognizes that STEM jobs in high demand are key to closing the skills gap, and the organization's focus is on entry to mid skill entry to those jobs, and creating a pathway that will help lead to economic prosperity. The work focuses on serving as the integrator for regional skills–to–jobs pilots that will validate a new employment system in the U.S. based on skills and competencies.

The organization was launched to place industry as a key driver in promoting and implementing systemic change in education and workforce. Since that time, Innovate+Educate has become a leading voice across States for education to employment strategies with a focus on new employment pathways in high demand fields.

About the Author

Jamai Blivin is the Chief Executive Officer of Innovate+Educate, an organization she founded in partnership with lead executives Jami Grindatto (Intel) and Kim Admire (Lockheed Martin) after returning to the Southwest in 2008.

Jamai is a frequent speaker at industry conferences and educational conferences sharing her passion and vision for meaningful industry partnerships, with a focus on community and regional ecosystems. In 2010, Innovate+ Educate was nominated for and received the New Mexico Business Weekly's "Small Business Heavyweights". I+E's recent work for Talent Albuquerque was recognized by the White House at the signing of the nation's Workforce and Innovation Opportunity Act on July 22, 2014.

Jamai holds a BSBA and MBA in Finance from the University of Arkansas. She and her husband share their lives with seven children (five currently in college on their own education to employment journeys) and two still at home (ages 15 and 10). They reside in Santa Fe, NM.

Customized or Standardized: How Should Colleges Offer Industry Training?

By: Dr. Dane Boyington, Co–founder and Chief Technical Officer, Thinking Media &
Sheila Boyington, Co–founder and President, Thinking Media

Businesses increasingly want to hire employees that have the exact skills and experience needed on the job in order to reduce post–hire training time and costs. Community colleges and trade organizations are moving towards standardized credentials in order to supply these workers more quickly. However there is often a view that there must be a tradeoff between providing industrial training that is customized for specific business clients versus offering standardized curriculum resulting in portable credentials. The ideal solution provides the exact training that the business needs while still offering the trainee a portable credential that advances the person's lifelong learning portfolio.

We know that STEM jobs are growing nationally at a pace that far outstrips other job categories. It is also widely acknowledged there is a corresponding shortage of workers needed to fill these jobs. A recent study by the job search firm Indeed[93] shows that the U.S. loses $1.6 billion in productivity yearly due to unfilled positions. A third of job openings remain vacant for three months or longer. In the manufacturing industry, about 600,000 skilled positions were unfilled in 2012.[94]

These positions remain unfilled due to a lack of qualified applicants. While there is much debate about the wisdom of importing talent from other countries, it is universally agreed that it is our collective responsibility to prepare as many of our own citizens for these positions as is possible. This is a responsibility that is shared between higher education and industry itself. Traditionally, higher education endows students with general knowledge and transferrable skills. Then businesses take these individuals and provide the industry– and business–specific knowledge that allows them to be productive in the work world.

The responsibility of developing employees is the source of much of current debate over the level of available STEM workers. Some claim that the perceived lack of workers is due to the increasing demands of industry that applicants must already have exact skills needed to become productive on day one.[95] Others believe it is that students do not have the right skills required for modern industry.[96] An ASTD 2014 report indicates manufacturing organizations, which are typically large organizations, report an average spending of $535 and providing 27 hours of training per employee.[97] However the U.S. Small Business Administration reports that small businesses have generated almost two–thirds of net new jobs over the past 17 years.[98] These smaller employers do not have the resources to provide today's sophisticated technology training. A 2011 Accenture survey of U.S. employees found that only 21 percent had received employer–provided formal training in the previous five years.[99] This results in the often–cited issue that employers want employees with experience, but few are willing to provide that initial experience.

Many increasingly realize that industry–education partnerships are the only way to solve this issue.[100] The component of the American education system that has the primary responsibility for implementing industry–education partnerships are community colleges.

In 2010, President Barack Obama set a national goal of increasing the number of community college degrees and certificates by 5 million over the next decade. "In the coming years," he added, "jobs requiring at least an associate degree are projected to grow twice as fast as jobs requiring no college experience. We will not fill those jobs - or keep those jobs on our shores - without the training offered by community colleges." The colleges have the flexibility to provide both formal academic education and the industry–specific training that businesses want. In 2011–12 community colleges awarded 770,797 Associates degrees and 436,037 certificates.[101] Of 12.8 million community college students, 5 million are enrolled in non–credit trade programs.

Businesses have embraced the community colleges as efficient ways to shift training costs off of their books. Through a combination of federal grants such as the Trade Act (TAACCCT) and industry support, colleges have developed training programs that provide employers just the skills and experience that industry wants. Examples of such programs are now becoming numerous and are demonstrating tremendous success. In New York State, Hudson Valley Community College and General Electric are one such example. According to a new joint project between the two entities, GE is looking to install a 50kW class fuel cell power generation demonstration system at HVCC's TEC–SMART facility in Malta, NY. The college will use that system to provide training for students, developing a curriculum in partnership with GE.[102] Gateway Tech in Wisconsin has a program that trains students to work for the Snap–On Corporation. According to the American Association of Community Colleges, when you visit the students working in Gateway's program, "you'd think you're in a Snap–On plant." The AACC has provided a useful listing of a number of additional examples of these partnerships online.[103]

These programs have the advantage of providing the business the exact skills needed, often taught on exactly the same or similar equipment as what the student will see in the actual workplace.

However does this provide the learning with the ideal combination of skills and experience?

If a worker learns how to work in a Snap–On plant, how does that serve the worker if he or she moves to a different location?

The answer to this is, of course, industry–recognized credentials. In the past credentials were largely expressed as college degrees, but today many new technical and industrial skills these are neither required for jobs nor awarded as part of industrial training. The new credential currency is stackable, portable credentials such as those suggested by the Manufacturing Institute.[104]

As an example, Wayne Community College in Goldsboro, N.C., is partnering with global aerospace and defense leader AAR to provide an eight–week welding certificate program to address a shortage of welders at AAR Mobility Systems. Under the customized curriculum, incumbent workers from AAR who complete the course can test for their welding certificate and immediately increase their salaries by as much as $4.50 per hour. The fast–track welding curriculum also is available to non–AAR employees through Wayne Community College's adult continuing education initiatives.

In Tennessee, Chattanooga State Community College has partnered with Volkswagen to operate the training center for VW's new North American assembly plant. Of 61 VW training facilities worldwide, this is the only one that is not operated by VW itself. With Chattanooga State's help, the new factory went from groundbreaking to producing the Motor Trend Car of the Year in just over two years. Chattanooga State also is assisting Wacker Chemical with training for a new polysilicon chemical facility. To train chemical operators before the plant was built, the college created a complete chemical distillation pilot plant and training facility, designed after Wacker's process, on the college campus. Graduates of this program not only receive U.S.–based certifications, but also receive chemical operator certification from the German Chamber of Commerce.

Even if no single employer is large enough to require or wishes to sponsor a custom training program, colleges can form consortiums of similar businesses to provide training for a single local industry. Air Washington, a consortium of multiple community colleges, aerospace technology centers, employers and the International Association of Machinists and Aerospace Workers union are designing and implementing an education and training program to meet local aerospace industry needs for advanced manufacturing/machining, aircraft assembly, aircraft maintenance, composites, and electronics. Air Washington is developing and aligning curricula to meet industry needs and European Aviation Safety Agency (EASA) standards.

In another example, DuPont is working closely with West Virginia University at Parkersburg to develop curriculum for the skills needed to meet the demands of polymer companies in and around Parkersburg, West Virginia. The program gives selected students the opportunity to earn a 30–hour certificate of applied science in chemical and polymer operator technology.

These programs all provide the student with the specific skills that local employers want, but also provide a portable credential that can create a documentation of the learning along a career pathway for lifelong learners. In order to provide these credentials and skills to workers in the most efficient path, the training programs are often available on an as–needed basis, and are not necessarily confined to the standard academic school year calendar. Furthermore, students can progress along a timeline that fits the needs of both the individual and the hiring company. Ideally progress is based on achieving specific competencies instead of spending a designed amount of time in the classroom. Learning is confirmed through secure assessments or skills demonstrations. However care must be taken to design these custom programs carefully to ensure that the business and certification needs are met and documented. Several models have been developed as a guide through this process.[105]

Integrating portable credentials into customized training programs provide advantages to the business, the student, the college and the entire community.

BUSINESSES
Are assured that the training includes a complete set of competencies and that achievement of these competencies has been reliably measured and documented.
STUDENTS
Receive portable, stackable credentials that can be used as the basis of future training or employment at a variety of locations.
COLLEGES
Have modular curriculum that is used to prepare for credentials, therefore similar training can also be offered to other business partners.
COMMUNITY
Benefits by having a workforce that has demonstrable skills that will attract similar business in related industries to the area.

While the inclusion of standardized credentials in a customized industry training program may involve a small amount of up–front planning, the long–term benefits will pay dividends to all involved.

Action Items

- **Establish training partnerships** between community colleges and local businesses that focus on high–demand jobs. Create programs that specifically address the needs of the business.

- **For larger employers, do not rely solely on pre–existing courses or programs**. Create programs that specifically address their needs and, where possible, using similar equipment or on–site internships.

- **For smaller employers, seek to group related partners together** to create a program for local industry groups. Seek agreement on mutual a curriculum.

- **Follow standard guidelines** to build a successful competency–based program.

- **Provide successful students with industry–recognized portable credentials,** even if the business does not specifically require them. Use the credentials to demonstrate to the client business the accuracy and value of the training. Seek other businesses that utilize similar skills, and market your students and training programs to these.

About Thinking Media

Thinking Media is the creator of Learning Blade®, a STEM career education curriculum for middle/high schools, validated by BattelleEd and suggested by ACT. As the creators of the ACT's KeyTrain® and Career Ready 101® curriculum systems, serving as past Vice Presidents for ACT WorkKeys®, and early participants on the design/implementation teams of the skills certification systems across the country, owners Dr. Dane and Sheila Boyington have unparalleled experience. Thinking Media and the Boyington's have led many states to the National Career Readiness Certificate system allowing job seekers to certify their skills. For over 15 years Thinking Media has focused on the use of technology to provide resources in the education, healthcare and technology fields. Thinking Media created the KeyTrain® Curricula System that was acquired by ACT (the college testing company) where he served as Vice President until 2012.

About the Authors

Sheila Boyington, MS, PE is co–Founder and President of Thinking Media. Thinking Media was the creator of KeyTrain® that was acquired by ACT (where she also served as Vice President until 2012) and has been hailed as the most effective system for improving basic skills, and was used by millions of students/clients in high schools, community colleges, one stops and major corporations in throughout the United States and abroad. Sheila is well–known for her passion, strong management and leadership skills. Those skills were used to gain high adoption of the Thinking Media tools.

Dane Boyington, PhD, is co–Founder and Chief Technical Officer of Thinking Media, a successful company focusing on e–learning development designed to improve workplace literacy for Fortune 500 industrial companies and government. Dane is the visionary thought–leader for Thinking Media and leads the design and development of the tools created. Dane holds a doctorate in Chemical Engineering from the University of California at Berkeley, and a B.S.in Chemical Engineering from the University of Florida with high honors. Dane also held technical manager positions at DuPont prior to founding Thinking Media.

The Boyington's are also well known for their passion in recognizing the value of skills certification and have worked to develop materials that have been used to create some of the most significant, innovative tools in demand–driven education systems and career readiness initiatives. In addition to their work as Thinking Media, the Boyington's hold advanced engineering degrees from the University of Florida and University of California, Berkeley. They serve as National Senior Advisors to STEMconnector® and the Million Women Mentors (MWM) ® Initiative.

Competency–Based Education: A Catalyst for Change

By: Melissa Goldberg, Senior Workforce Strategist, College for America, and
Julian L. Alssid, Chief Workforce Strategist, College for America

For the past 15 years, Workforce Strategy Center - now a part of the non–profit College for America at Southern New Hampshire University - has been striving to build effective workforce development systems to strengthen the economy and advance education and career outcomes for students. After nearly two decades of consulting, researching and documenting promising practices, among hundreds of university–employer partnerships, we have seen what works (and what doesn't).

Many of the models we have documented and disseminated have become broadly accepted or adopted by policy makers - including bridge programs, career pathways, and the use of labor market intelligence in higher education and workforce development.

But, much work remains to be done. Businesses today point to challenges in recruiting and promoting skilled workers. Many, if not most, would argue that the skills gap is increasing. These challenges are exacerbated by a perception gap between the business and educational communities. A Gallup poll conducted for the Lumina Foundation released earlier this year revealed that 14 percent of Americans - and only 11 percent of business leaders - strongly agree that graduates have the necessary skills and competencies to succeed in the workplace. That is in stark contrast to another poll conducted on behalf of Inside Higher Ed, indicating that 96 percent of academic officers believe that they are effectively preparing students for success in the workplace.

Today's employers expect practical skills, not just theory - proof of both the ability to learn and the ability to execute. And they aren't getting it. Every day they see well–screened, seemingly well–qualified graduates filter through their doors - without the basic skills sets expected.

In the Gallup/Lumina poll, 79 percent of business leaders report that a job candidate's applied skills in the field are very important. And College for America commissioned a survey of more than 400 HR and director–level leaders, revealing that 85 percent of respondents identified finding well–qualified applicants as a key challenge.

It is as if employers and educators come from different worlds and speak different languages. In the end, though, they share an overlapping goal: to develop savvy, skilled people who can contribute to the success of an organization and society. But this language barrier has prevented business leaders and educators from entering into valuable partnerships. As consultants and researchers, we saw a need for a common language. The solution? A renewed focus on competency–based education. The catalyst for change emerged for us in March 2013 when we merged our consulting think tank with Southern New Hampshire University (SNHU) to build College for America (CfA).

CfA is a non–profit college created to better connect workforce research, higher education, and labor market needs - and to remove barriers that prevent 47 million adult workers from earning a college degree.[106] Designed as a business–to–business model, the college partners with employers to offer employees a chance at a degree - tapping into their potential, filling the talent pipeline, and boosting the bottom line. The postsecondary school offers accreditor–approved associate of arts and Bachelor of Arts degrees that require mastery of competencies through real–world, business– and industry–oriented projects.

Early returns are promising. Since launching in January 2013, CfA has enrolled more than 1,000 students, graduating more than 30 as of October 2014. Based on a survey of these first graduates, more than half have been promoted or taken on increased responsibilities; 70 percent have new career goals; and 20 have enrolled in a CfA BA program.

One distinguishing factor of CfA is its curriculum development process, which involves primary and secondary labor market analysis, subject matter expert review, and employer input and feedback. The result? Certificates and degrees based on industry–informed competencies and rigorous academic requirements. Businesses value them because they are delivered in a practical, hands–on, self–directed fashion. Consider CfA's partnership with the University of Pennsylvania Health System (Penn Medicine).

Penn Medicine, consistently ranked as one of the nation's best hospitals by U.S. News & World Report, is dedicated to promoting continuous learning and improvement within its health system. It established the Penn Medicine Academy to help the system continually improve care delivery and patient outcomes, make Penn Medicine a better place to work, and train staff to deliver care in a consistent and standardized way.

"For practice management in ambulatory settings, employees tend to learn important competencies through experience, so they don't always acquire the knowledge, skills, and behaviors in a consistent way," said Judy Schueler, Vice President of Organizational Development & Human Resources at Penn Medicine. Across the healthcare industry, patient service representatives, financial business representatives, and practice coordinators are learning as they go - but their work is becoming increasingly important to improving care quality and the patient experience.

Consequently, Penn Medicine Academy seeks out partners and models that help it train and educate its workforce in a consistent, standardized way. So when Schueler learned about CfA - a competency–based, workplace–applicable degree program with degree options specifically for nonclinical healthcare workers - she knew it would be a great addition to the Academy.

"Unlike existing business degrees in healthcare, the College for America degree focuses on helping employees manage a physician or ambulatory practice, coupling that education with an apprenticeship kind of model through real–world projects," Schueler shared. "I know of no other degree program in the country that really focuses on the right blocks of knowledge in practice management like the Bachelor of Arts in Healthcare Management." With the program's competency requirements spanning regulatory requirements in an ambulatory setting, revenue billing and cycles, understanding how to improve the patient experience, responding to patient satisfaction surveys, value–based purchasing, and more, Schueler was sure that Penn Medicine Academy needed to bring in CfA.

Penn Medicine worked with CfA to launch a pilot program in February 2014. Its intent is to open up enrollment to all employees across the system who can benefit from a degree. "While our employees have never said, 'I wish I could have a competency–based education program,' they have said that they want an accessible program for this point in their lives - one that gives value to the work that they've already done," said Frances Graham, Director of Workforce Development at Penn Medicine.

CfA requires that students master every competency, regardless of time, in order to earn a degree, giving Penn Medicine more confidence in employees who have proved mastery of workplace–relevant competencies. "People draw conclusions about what employees know based upon a resume, but you don't want to confuse a resume with reality," Judy Schueler stated. "A College for America degree validates skill, knowledge, and behavior."

If we are going to advance a jobs–driven economy, business leaders and educators will need to work in partnership to align educational programs with business needs. To do so, they need to set joint goals and establish a common language for their work together. We suggest that competencies become the foundation of that common language as they have meaning in both educational and business settings.

Building on that common language, business leaders must provide input and context about skills needs in the workplace. Educators should gather that input and create rigorous, workplace relevant curricula that allow students to demonstrate they have mastered the competencies required in the labor market.

About College for America
At College for America we work to better connect workforce research, higher education, and labor market needs. We partner with employers to offer their employees rigorous college degree programs and an online learning model that is affordable, self–scheduled, and built to develop competencies through project–based, real–world learning.

The liberal arts degree programs help existing STEM workers and other students build promotable skills by emphasizing competencies in problem solving, critical thinking, and communication. Students advance by demonstrating what they know, instead of time logged in a course. That means they can breeze through competencies they've already mastered on the job, but they can take extra time and support working on skills they haven't yet developed. Students demonstrate competencies by submitting projects, which receive quick, rigorous feedback by professional educators. Mastery of every competency is required to earn their degree. To help with the transition of returning to school, every student is assigned a Learning Coach.

Founded with support from a Bill & Melinda Gates Foundation/EDUCAUSE grant in 2012, College for America is helping more than 60 employers nationwide develop talent and build leadership.

About the Authors

Melissa Goldberg, Senior Workforce Strategist at College for America, has more than 20 years of experience advising executives, as well as researching, documenting, and disseminating promising practices in the field of workforce development. At College for America she works to ensure that degrees and certificates have relevance in the labor market. For the past decade, Melissa served as Senior Associate at Workforce Strategy Center, where she facilitated state and regional strategic planning efforts and provided technical assistance to foundations, federal agencies, businesses, workforce boards, and community colleges across the country. She authored many studies highlighting promising practices in employer–driven workforce development programs. Her earlier work included leading community college business outreach and continuing education operations focused on establishing educational solutions to advance career prospects for unemployed and underemployed individuals. Melissa earned her M.P.A. at New York University's Wagner School for Public Service.

Julian L. Alssid is Chief Workforce Strategist at College for America at Southern New Hampshire University (CfA). Julian is responsible for ensuring that CfA's offerings have labor market relevance. He also oversees CfA's Signature Initiatives - partnerships with large intermediaries and employers that expand the scope and scale of CfA as a competency–based solution for higher education. Julian is a nationally recognized expert in workforce development innovation and policy. Julian founded and directed Workforce Strategy Center where he advised over 20 states on workforce policy and established himself as a leader in promoting effective, practical solutions for implementing talent development strategies. Julian has authored major studies on workforce strategy. His views on engaging employers, online education, and addressing the skills gap have received extensive attention in national and local media, and he speaks and writes regularly on the need for policy and educational reform in the field.

CHAPTER ELEVEN

The Diversity Opportunity

"By virtue of providing a robust, career–relevant STEM curriculum to our current student population – a majority of female and minorities –Colorado Technical University is poised to make a difference in the underrepresented populations in the STEM education and workplace."

– Cami Jacobson, Vice President Industry Strategy, Colorado Technical University

Access to Success: Building the Pipeline for Women in STEM
By: Linda Hallman, Executive Director and Chief Executive Officer,
American Association of University Women (AAUW)

When it comes to diversity in the STEM world, the challenges are well established: The sector remains dominated by white and, to a lesser extent, Asian men, while struggling to fill its growing workforce needs.

More than 80 percent of all STEM jobs are in the fields of computing and engineering, yet women make up just 25 percent of the computing workforce and 14 percent of the engineering workforce. The number of African American, Hispanic, and Native American women in these fields is even more discouraging.[107]

The messages women receive every day from parents, teachers, professors, and employers - and even their toys and t–shirts - make it clear that women don't belong in STEM, even though computer science and programming were literally invented by women. Additionally, stereotypes about women's abilities persist, to great negative effect, despite studies showing that women perform as well as men on math and science tests and, in some cases, outperform them.

But improving diversity in STEM fields isn't simply the right thing to do; it's the smart thing to do. In this segment of the economy, where jobs often outnumber qualified applicants, increasing the number of women and minorities would greatly increase the size of the available talent pool. More importantly, companies would be bringing a diverse set of minds and experiences to bear on the most challenging issues of the day. When airbags were first introduced, for example, a predominantly male engineering group made devices that fit male bodies - and failed to prevent the deaths of thousands of women and children.

The encouraging news is that these industries are poised and ready to do what needs to be done to recruit more women, as evidenced by the recent high–profile release of diversity numbers by big–name tech companies and increased corporate investment in pipeline–building projects. The existence of STEMconnector®'s STEM Higher Education Council, which brings together higher education and businesses to prepare students to become successful STEM professionals, certainly demonstrates this commitment.

For schools and businesses ready to take the next step, there's still ample low–hanging fruit out there. Community colleges provide a largely untapped font of potential talent: 40 percent of all undergraduates attend community colleges, including 4 million women. In addition, community colleges educate the most diverse student body, with 32 percent of students identifying as African American, Hispanic, or Native American.

By more deliberately shaping the path from education to career for community college students, two– and four–year colleges can help more students successfully transition into the often satisfying and well–paying careers in the STEM fields. Right now, women in community colleges remain clustered in traditionally "female" and low–paying fields such as cosmetology, nursing, and education; many of them don't even realize that other options exist, while others are discouraged by stereotypes and a lack of support if they do attempt to enter a nontraditional field.

AAUW's research report *Access to Success: Women in Community Colleges* provides research–backed recommendations for increasing the number of women who select and persist in STEM fields and also highlights existing programs that have shown encouraging results in increasing women's entry and resilience in STEM fields. The following recommendations can help two– and four–year schools not only keep women in STEM classrooms but also direct students toward a rewarding STEM career.

- **Actively recruit more women into nontraditional and STEM fields.** Many women may not initially express an interest in nontraditional or STEM fields, but colleges can enhance outreach and marketing to encourage women to enter these fields by developing recruitment materials that feature women and help demystify unfamiliar fields for women students. Recruitment materials should also include information on job opportunities, earnings, and educational requirements for nontraditional and STEM fields.

- **Ensure that institutional practices such as academic and career advising do not reinforce stereotypes or promote discrimination of women.** Academic advisers are a key point of contact for students, and academic advising promotes student success. Academic and career advisers, including faculty, can play a major role in increasing women's participation in fields where they are underrepresented. Academic advisers should be educated about occupational segregation, gender bias, and the importance of promoting nontraditional careers to women and men.

- **Develop educational and career pathways to help students navigate STEM curricula.** Program directors can map course and program requirements so that students have a clear path to earning a degree and entering a career in STEM. Career pathway maps should also include the kinds of jobs and wages students can expect from the degree they plan to earn. Research suggests that this kind of information can help motivate students to persist until they achieve their goal.

- **Use creative instructional approaches, like learning communities, to support students.** Learning communities can foster women's success in STEM. These communities provide much–needed peer support, create a sense of community, and help promote feelings of belonging among students. Women who have support and feel like they belong in STEM fields are more likely to stay in these fields. Introductory courses that require little or no experience in technical fields are a good way to attract students and nurture their interest.

- **Expose women in nontraditional fields to role models and mentors.** Research suggests that women who persevere in nontraditional fields must be resilient, despite the barriers they face. Successful women in nontraditional and STEM fields can serve as role models and mentors for female students, offer suggestions and strategies for success, and reinforce the message that women can be successful in these fields.

- **Partner with local employers to connect students to available opportunities.** Students depend on their schools for information about which programs and credentials prepare them for jobs and careers. Local employers can share information with colleges and universities on the skills they need, job openings, and wage information, which schools can then use to decide which programs and courses will be useful to students.

The Mathematics, Engineering, Science, Achievement Community College Program (MCCP), in place at 36 California community colleges, illustrates the potential success of these recommendations. MCCP focuses on supporting men and women students from their first enrollment until they successfully transfer to a four–year institution. The pillars of the program include peer support through learning communities, active academic support and tutoring, and transfer support. Program managers set up learning communities of students who take their math and science courses together, which facilitates relationships among students and with faculty.

In addition, MCCP welcomes students with limited math skills or experience, a common characteristic of traditionally underrepresented populations, who are less likely to have had access to advanced math and science courses in high school. Most MCCP students begin college math with introductory algebra, and the program provides academic tutoring and advising while closely monitoring student progress, allowing students to catch up and successfully complete the more–advanced requirements of later courses.

This kind of successful intervention isn't just limited to community colleges. Carnegie Mellon University saw similar success when it relaxed admissions standards related to previous computer programming experience and instead offered introductory courses on the subject. From 1995 to 2000, the university saw the number of women in the School of Computer Science grow from 7 percent to 42 percent.

The changes really are that simple. By breaking down artificial barriers to entry, by extending a welcoming hand and being willing to offer some training, and by simply questioning the predominant culture of "brogrammers," colleges, universities, and companies can take huge steps toward solving one of the biggest problems facing the STEM industry in the United States. Some of these programs are already in place at schools all over the country, but for everyone else, what are you waiting for?

About The American Association of University Women

The American Association of University Women (AAUW) is the nation's leading voice promoting equity and education for women and girls. Since their founding in 1881, AAUW members have examined and taken positions on the fundamental issues of the day - educational, social, economic, and political.

Their nonpartisan, non–profit organization has more than 170,000 members and supporters across the United States, as well as 1,000 local branches and over 800 college and university partners. Throughout their history, AAUW members have examined and taken positions on the fundamental issues of the day - educational, social, economic, and political.

About the Author

Linda D. Hallman is the Executive Director and Chief Executive Officer of AAUW. For more than 25 years, Hallman has made her mark as an association innovator. She has led a variety of associations, focusing on creating high–performance individuals, teams, programs, and governance in the fields of health care and horticulture.

Before taking the helm of AAUW, Hallman served as president and Chief Operating Officer of the American Medical Women's Association. From 1997 to 2002 she served as Chief Operating Officer of the American Horticultural Society, and from 1988 to 1997 she held virtually every leadership position with the American College of Health Care Administrators. Hallman began her career as a soprano soloist with the United States Army Band, "Pershing's Own," at Fort Myer, Virginia. A native of Washington, D.C., Hallman received her bachelor's degree in music education from Indiana University in Bloomington, Indiana, and her master's degree in organizational management from George Washington University in Washington, D.C. She is also a certified association executive (CAE).

Hallman is a frequent speaker on women's issues, finance, leadership, and management, and she is an expert on creating extraordinary membership experiences and cultures, organizational strategies, alliance building, and fundraising. In 2013, STEMconnector® recognized her as one of 100 Women Leaders in STEM®.

Advancing Girls and Young Women in STEM
By Julie Kantor, Vice President and Chief Partnership Officer,
STEMconnector® and Million Women Mentors and
MacKenzie Moore, Associate, Business Development,
STEMconnector® and Million Women Mentors

The simple truth is that our nation faces a major gap in the number of women and girls going into the fields that make up STEM – Science, Technology, Engineering, and Math.
- Blair Christie, SVP and Chief Marketing Officer, Cisco Systems

Mentor duty should be the new jury duty.
– Brandon Busteed, Gallup Education

Women in STEM
As girls grow up, they are told they can be anything, work in any job, in any environment and achieve any goals they set for themselves. But, as girls grow up and enter college STEM classes they often feel pushed out by boys and pulled out by girlfriends and sometimes faculty comments. According to the US Department of Commerce, Economics and Statistics Administration, women make up 50% of the workforce, yet women only account for 24% of the STEM workforce and 50% of women drop out of STEM positions in the first 10 years. However, given that 71% of jobs in 2018 will require STEM skills and STEM jobs pay women better (we learned from the White House women in STEM make 92 cents for every dollar a man makes versus the average of 76 cents on a dollar), advancing girls and young women in STEM will be critical.[108]

Working with partner, My College Options, we shared with the nation that in 2013, 15% of high school female seniors reported that they were interested in pursuing a STEM career vs. 44% of the boys. Over 70% of the girls selected sciences and boys were eight times more likely to select technology and engineering as their area of interest. What really surprised us and we see this as a huge opportunity for our nation, was that only 4% of the 368,000 girls in the survey said they were encouraged in STEM by a mentor. We also know from The National Mentoring Partnership that only 1:3 college students graduate with a mentor. We can do something about this![109]

Mentoring: A Solution
Mentoring is a vital tool to recruiting and retaining more women in STEM fields. Mentoring counters negative stereotypes, shows STEM careers are hard yet rewarding, and offers insight into the various pathways (educational, internships, etc.) to achieve a successful STEM career. To reaffirm Linda D. Hallman, CAE, Executive Director and CEO of the American Association of University Women, "We need to do more than just tell young girls that they can be engineers, rocket scientists, or computer programmers. Mentors can inspire girls and give them an insider's view of what it's like to work in STEM." Furthermore, mentoring has been a proven tool in retention of employees. Key findings by a study done by Wharton School of Business on Sun Microsystems (now part of Oracle) include:

- Employees who mentored were promoted 6 times more than their peers who did not mentor

- Employees who were mentored were promoted 5 times more often than their peers who did not have a mentor

- 25% of employees who mentored received a salary grade change (opposed to 5% of employees who did not mentor)

- Employees who participated in the mentoring program had a retention rate that was 20% higher than those who did not mentor

This groundbreaking study shows the win-win to the mentor, the mentee, and the corporation. It's more than good business, it's good for business.

The Million Women Mentors Story & Vision Ahead

Million Women Mentors, an initiative of STEMconnector®, is a collaboration of over 30 corporate sponsors and 56 partners including Arizona State University, Howard University, United Negro College Foundation, First Robotics, Black Girls Code, Mentornet, National Girls Collaborative Project and more who reach over 30 million girls and young women. This initiative will support the engagement of one million women and men in STEM to serve as mentors by 2018. Our shared vision is to serve at least one million girls and young women throughout the middle school to work age continuum in mentorship with five suggested pathways and a minimum of 20 hours. Companies like Tata Consultancy Services are taking the pledge to mentor over 15,000 girls and young women in STEM. Apollo Education Group stepped up with 4,000 pledges and National Girls Collaborative at 90,000 with 20 States mobilized and the State of Tennessee with 10,000. Lieutenant Governor Kim Reynolds of Iowa stepped up with a pledge of 5,000 and the mobilization of a blueprint action plan and leadership council leveraging corporate engagement. Her leadership has inspired several other Lt. Governors. TCS, PepsiCo, Sodexo, Apollo Group, Cisco and others are leading the way as Vice Chairs of the newly formed MWM Leadership Council.

Tata Consultancy Service's President of North America, United Kingdom and Europe, Surya Kant, says, "Our partnership with Million Women Mentors is a part of our company's commitment to diversity and inclusion. Through MWM, we are encouraging our associates to mentor women and girls by sharing their passion and experiences in IT, inspiring mentees to pursue STEM education and careers. We are committed to having our employees in the United States and across the globe participate in mentorship programs to improve the employability of women and girls, and understand that this effort will require action from everyone, men and women alike."

Advancing a Jobs-Driven Economy

Launched January 8ᵗʰ, 2014, Million Women Mentors and the Leadership Council have significant goals between now and 2018. Through this initiative, Million Women Mentors will:

- Lead a national call to action for corporations, organizations, government entities and state working teams to join MWM and capture metrics around mentoring girls and young women in STEM

- Provide an automated, scalable and easy-to-use platform to eliminate barriers and provide large numbers of STEM professionals (male and female) with tools to becoming effective mentors in partnership with 56 organizations reaching over 30 million girls/young women

- In January 2015, launch technology to match participating corporations and organizations to scaled non-profit partners and educational institutions in need of STEM mentors and role models

- Recognize best practices and 'who is doing what' in mentoring girls (middle school through careers in STEM learning)

Mentor + Sponsor = Mentoring 2.0 in a Jobs-Driven Economy

At Million Women Mentors, we have learned some valuable lessons our first year as we work closely with hundreds of corporations, thought leaders, and valued partners.

We have learned we all need to advocate for internships, European apprenticeship models and job shadowing for experiential learning and for starting younger (Gallup Education shared with us that only 4% of high school students were in internships last year and US Department of Labor just announced 100m for apprenticeship programs).

We learned from Economist Sylvia Ann Hewlett that "men are 46 percent more likely to have an active sponsor who throws opportunities their way and speaks highly of them behind closed doors." Essentially a mentor speaks *with* you and a sponsor speaks *about* you as an advocate and champion. An important distinction!

One of biggest lessons learned is that many companies and government entities do not currently have formal ways of capturing their mentoring activities. We need to move mentoring as a strategy to advance a diverse pipeline in STEM. 'You get what you measure.' so moving mentoring from the informal space to measurable programming is paramount.

We will also advocate for reverse mentoring as we have seen how much we all learn every day from a millennial workforce with superior technology skills and diverse thinking. Peer mentoring groups have also shown a clear win-win.

As we shared earlier from the Wharton study, mentors are six times more likely to be promoted and retention rates of employees both the mentees and mentors are 20% higher. So to advance a jobs-driven economy we share that mentoring is not just good to do for others, it is good for business.

We learned that we need to elevate further partnerships between Universities and Corporate America that offer training and a clear pathway to jobs.

We hope you will join us in this collective and carve out your role in this journey.

Call to Action
Go to www.MillionWomenMentors.org and take the pledge to be a mentor!

About Million Women Mentors
Million Women Mentors, launched as an initiative of STEMconnector®, supports the engagement of one million women (and men) in STEM to serve as mentors by 2018. Million Women Mentors is a collaborative of 56 partners (reaching over 30 million girls and young women), 30 sponsors, and 30 state leadership teams. The Million Women Mentors Leadership Council is chaired by Cisco, PepsiCo, Sodexo, Apollo Education and Tata Consultancy Services. Over 200,000 pledges to mentor girls and young women in STEM have been entered to date. Thirteen US Senators and Congresswomen supported us during our launch on January 8th, 2014.

About the Author
Julie Kantor is a veteran leader and tireless ambassador of STEM education, entrepreneurship and building of America's skilled workforce, serving in CXO roles since 1992. As Vice President and Chief Partnership Officer at STEMconnector® & Million Women Mentors (division of Diversified Search LLC), Julie and team bring together corporate America, government, higher education and national nonprofits as members to better convene key players in the STEM universe and consult around smart STEM investments.

Julie is known in the community as a people person, a brand-builder, tech savvy, national thought leader, writer for Huffington Post and networked entrepreneur with a proven track record.

Kantor was recognized by President Obama for her 20 year career in education in April of 2012 and honored by the Center for Innovative Technology (CIT) as 2012 CIT GAP 50 Winner. Before joining STEMconnector®, Julie launched Network for Teaching Entrepreneurship (NFTE) in Boston, took over the Washington, DC, region of NFTE in 1995 and spent 20 years scaling youth entrepreneurship education to many U.S. cities and raising $20 million. Julie was a catalyst in expanding NFTE programs in India, Baltimore, Philadelphia and Boston.

MacKenzie Moore is an Associate of Business Development at STEMconnector® and Million Women Mentors. She is a passionate and dedicated individual and focused on advancing girls and young women in STEM fields. Born and raised in Jackson, Wyoming she ran a math-tutoring program called Jackson Mathematics targeting tier two students in Teton County School District. She's also been a leader and advocate for environmental movements and engaging high school students in community service and outreach efforts.

The Million Women Mentors team leaders also include: Edie Fraser - CEO, Lorena Fimbres - Vice President and Chief Business Development Officer, Dr. Talmesha Richards - Chief Academic and Diversity Officer and Sheila and Dr. Dane Boyington - Senior Advisors.

The Innovation Crisis and the Importance of
Empowering Women in STEM Fields
By: Dr. Wayne Frederick, President, Howard University

The fields of STEM are keys to the future success of the world. Every day, an economist or policy maker is explaining the importance of fielding a reliable stream of talent in the STEM professions and encouraging young people to get involved in these areas. Although the United States currently has a global competitive advantage, which is a direct result of the knowledge, power and innovation of its workforce, as other countries become more technologically advanced, it is clear that the United States must do more. Not only must we do more, we must also improve our means of generating interest in these areas. More specifically, we must do a better job of infusing STEM into academic coursework and teaching youth about the importance of STEM early in the education process.

Currently, American schools are not keeping pace with technological improvements in innovation and competency. While primary and secondary schools, as well as colleges and universities throughout the country are investing more money in research and man–power to generate interest in and promote these disciplines among the next generation of leaders, more work is required. Specifically, more must be done to encourage minorities and women to pursue STEM careers. When you look at the current composition of those working in STEM areas, the vast majority of STEM professionals are men. When you visit laboratories, spend time in Silicon Valley and review the enrollment data regarding students in STEM advanced degree programs, you see very few women. Further, a number of publications, including the New York Times[110] and the Boston Globe,[111] have discussed the dearth of women in the STEM fields and the need for more female leaders in these areas. While this problem has been identified, the key questions are why does this problem exist and how do we rectify it?

The answer to the first question regarding why the gender disparity exists varies. It may be attributed to bias in hiring and promoting women in STEM–related fields. The answer may also be that some colleges and universities fail to provide learning experiences that adequately prepare students to get jobs and succeed in STEM professions. Yet, another reason may be the subconscious belief that STEM fields are men's fields, which can ultimately deter women from studying these subjects. While there is no one definitive answer, each of these reasons contributes to the low number of women in STEM fields. Therefore, each contributing factor must be addressed to ensure that women become more visible, active and present in the growth and future success of STEM.

Howard University is committed to addressing these contributing factors. We believe that women are an integral part of the future success of the STEM fields and believe that it is imperative for us to encourage minority and female students to pursue professions in STEM. We believe that the STEM fields need more women leaders and intend to use our talent and resources to inform, advise, and assist students interested in being future leaders in these fields.

To that end, Howard offers a number of advanced degree programs in the sciences, various engineering disciplines and computer science. We also graduate more African–American students with bachelor's degrees, who have gone on to earn doctorates in STEM fields than any other school in the country. We do this by providing a supportive environment that offers extensive academic advisement, internship and occupational opportunities, mentoring and a safe space for students to learn, grow and progress. For example, we believe that the female students enrolled in the College of Engineering, Architecture and Computer Science (CEACS) are successful, in part, because they have such phenomenal female role models in the dean and the female department chairs and faculty who have exemplary records of scholarship, achievement and excellence in these fields.

Additionally, we strive to provide our students with educational opportunities designed to prepare them for a successful professional career. This is particularly important to us because many of our students are the first members of their families to attend college; therefore, their time at Howard University is not only a time of academic enhancement but also a time of growth and transformation. For this reason, our course work is not only about lectures and books but also about hands–on experiences that are made possible through our relationships with leading companies in the STEM fields. For example, Yahoo donated 125 servers to power a new Yahoo Data Center at Howard University; these servers will be utilized by our computer science and engineering students as they strive to uncover and understand the latest advances in technology. Similarly, Google sponsors an engineer–in–residence program, which gives our students opportunities to gain insights from industry professionals. These are just a few examples of the University–private industry partnerships we have created to connect our students with companies that actively engage in STEM work and help them succeed in being STEM leaders. Their success is our top priority and that is why we are always looking for new and innovative ways to continue providing the resources, tools and opportunities required for them to excel academically.

While partnerships are an integral part of our course curricula in STEM fields, we are also constantly developing new programs designed to generate greater interest in these areas and lead students on a path to successful careers. We recently launched two new STEM–based academic programs. The first program is the Howard University Science, Engineering and Mathematics program (HUSEM). This is an interdisciplinary initiative involving our College of Arts and Sciences and the College of Engineering, Architecture, and Computer Science; its purpose is to encourage students to consider pursuing graduate studies in the STEM fields. The second program is the Global Education Awareness and Research Undergraduate Program (GEAR UP). GEAR UP was created to leverage Howard University's international profile by providing global, cutting–edge research opportunities to our students. To that end, students in this program travel across the world to conduct research on subjects ranging from hair loss to cyber security.

Advancing a Jobs-Driven Economy

We developed these programs after receiving funding from the National Science Foundation (NSF) and are extremely excited about their future. We believe that these programs will enable us to show other colleges and universities that, through a concerted effort, we can meet our nation's innovation crisis, contribute to the gainful employment of our youth and close the skills deficit facing the private industry involved in STEM work.

While closing the gap between men and women in the STEM fields requires that we provide students with education and hands–on experiences, we must also provide faculty with greater support and more research opportunities. In furtherance of that objective, NSF awarded the university an ADVANCE–IT grant, which allows us to provide workshops and professional development opportunities for our faculty. The ADVANCE–IT program also enables us to offer a mentor program, which makes it possible for researchers and junior faculty to receive support from our senior faculty members. Nurturing the promising careers of up and coming STEM professionals contributes to the creation of a culture that ensures the identification of and support for talent. In addition, it allows us to create robust succession plans that include more women in our STEM departments and increase the number of female leaders in STEM professions.

We recognize that STEM is the future and it is our responsibility to educate, encourage and empower students interested in these fields. Howard is committed to achieving these goals and will continue to build strategic alliances, implement innovative programs and provide the requisite support to our students and faculty to ensure that we are at the forefront of producing the STEM leaders of tomorrow.

Action Items

Two things private industry can do with universities to advance a jobs–driven economy:

- Create partnerships that better align academic programming with the skills required to make students successful professionals in STEM careers.

- Partner on infrastructure investments that create opportunities for advanced graduate study and research in STEM.

About Howard University

Founded in 1867, Howard University is a private, research university that is comprised of 13 schools and colleges. Students pursue studies in more than 120 areas leading to undergraduate, graduate and professional degrees. Since 1998, the University has produced two Rhodes Scholars, two Truman Scholars, a Marshall Scholar, 30 Fulbright Scholars and 11 Pickering Fellows. Howard also produces more on campus African–American Ph.D. recipients than any other university in the United States.

About the Author

As the 17th President of Howard University, Dr. Wayne A.I. Frederick is dedicated to strengthening the University's position as a world–renowned academic and research institution.

Under his leadership, there is a renewed commitment to academic excellence and access to an affordable education. He launched Howard's Center for Academic Excellence, created to provide student retention support services and increase undergraduate success. He also introduced the Graduation & Retention Access for Continued Excellence (GRACE) grant program, which provides need–based funding to increase on–time graduation.

Dr. Frederick was born in Port of Spain, Trinidad, and was admitted to Howard at age 16 with a dream of becoming a physician. His passion to heal was driven by sickle cell anemia, a hereditary disease he has lived with since birth. He earned a Bachelor of Science degree, a Doctor of Medicine and completed his surgical residency training at Howard University Hospital. After fulfilling his post–doctoral research and surgical oncology fellowships at the University of Texas MD Anderson Cancer Center, Dr. Frederick became Associate Director of the Cancer Center at University of Connecticut, where he also served on the Department of Surgery faculty.

Effective Outreach for Middle and High School Latinas
By: Dr. Maria Harper–Marinick, Executive Vice Chancellor and Provost,
Maricopa County Community College District

Research continues to show that Latinas, as compared to other underrepresented females, are less likely to enroll in STEM, despite being a part of the largest minority group in the U.S. Industry and Education alike are also finding that there are, and continue to be, many social and cultural barriers that make it especially difficult for young Latinas to break into male–dominated STEM career paths.

In Arizona, this issue is particularly prominent and caught the attention of a major local employer, Intel Corporation. After participating at a national Hispanic Women's Conference in 2001, key Intel employees noticed that Hispanic pre–college girls were not fully aware of the opportunities available beyond traditional roles and the stereotype mirrors often upheld by the mass media and society in general. These employees sought to make a difference and created the Latina Outreach Working Group (LOWG) within the Intel Latino Network employee group structure.

At the Maricopa Community Colleges, leaders recognized the trend as well. Higher dropout rates among Hispanic students led to the development of more support services and preparation for this at–risk group. More needs to be done, however, to support women.

> *All too often, there is the perception that these professions are not considered traditional careers for Latinas.*
> - Maria Reyes, Founding Member of the *Hermanas* Conference and Dean of Career & Technical Education, Chandler–Gilbert Community College

Passion and dedication to make a difference led these two leaders to develop the *Hermanas: Diseña Tu Futuro* (Design Your Future) Conference. The mission: to increase the number of underrepresented females in STEM fields, inspiring these women to pursue an engineering and science education and envision future careers in a technical field.

Now running for 11 years, *Hermanas* specifically targets Latinas in middle and high school, and creates a unique experience designed by Latinas for Latinas.

The one day conference invites girls to a community college campus to learn more about possible education and career paths in STEM and listen to other Latinas who have succeeded at these careers. Components of the *Hermanas* Conference includes:

- **Latina Town Hall** – one–on–one conversations with professional Latinas in STEM industries. This is an essential component of the *Hermanas* Conference; it allows participants to express fears and concerns in a safe setting with a role model they can relate to.

- **Education Resource Fair** – pathways available through the community colleges and articulation paths into 4–year universities.

- **Hands–on Activities** – 45 to 60 minute workshops led by college faculty that expose participants to STEM concepts.

- **Student Success or Parent Preparation Seminars** – Presentations on how to succeed in high school and explanations of college and financial aid, scholarships support, and resources.

Maricopa Community Colleges have a long–standing commitment to develop and implement best practices in STEM programs and outreach. The *Hermanas* model implements these strategies through four key building blocks to create possible stepping stones for a Latina's pathway to a 4–year STEM degree. A pre–college event, on a college campus (created with underrepresented students in mind), that provides information on STEM education and careers, creates a holistic experience for students, families, and the community. The *Hermanas* approach, with interaction between participants, parents, education and industry leaders, also allows for a more seamless transition from middle through high school to college.

> *For girls who may often be intimidated by non–traditional professions, male–dominated fields, or who lack the financial resources or preparation to enroll in college, the Hermanas Conference provides effective tools and practical pathways that enable them to successfully navigate these challenges,*
> – Gabriela Gonzalez, Founding Member of the *Hermanas* Conference and Current Program Manager at Intel

Impact of the *Hermanas* Conference
Participants of the *Hermanas* Conference from 2007 to 2014 self–report their knowledge and confirm their confidence in STEM, specifically engineering:

	Before *Hermanas*	After *Hermanas*
"I know what an engineer or scientist does"	35 percent	93 percent
"I CAN be an engineer or scientist"	51 percent	91 percent

Impact of the *Hermanas* Conference is measured by:

- Registration in one of ten Maricopa Community Colleges – 65 percent of Hermanas participants.

- Participation from area high schools at a rate that meets or exceeds the overall participation rate from that high school.

- Pursuit of a STEM–based area of study as a stated major.

Evidence that Supports the Success of the *Hermanas* Initiative

What started as a singular event with one sponsor in 2005, has now been expanded to four colleges. Chandler Gilbert and Estrella Mountain now offer middle and high school conferences. South Mountain joined with a high school program followed by the newest college, Phoenix College in 2014. Financial support has also grown to include sponsorship from the Qwest Foundation, Cardinals Charity, IBM, Avnet, and the APS foundation.

Interest in the *Hermanas* Conference continues to grow, as shown by the increasing number of participants in Arizona's programs:

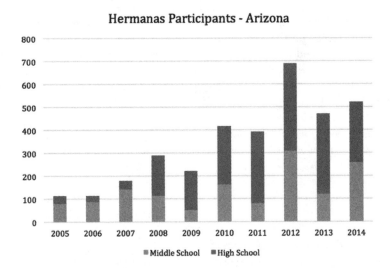

Hermanas Participants - Arizona

Creating a Replicable Model

Educators and industry see value in the *Hermanas* initiative because it is an effective way to reach underrepresented female students. Every year, hundreds of volunteers from the Maricopa Community Colleges, neighboring communities, and Intel employees (a main sponsor of the Arizona program) support the conference because they see the importance of working directly with underrepresented students. Intel employees alone have logged over 13,000 hours to volunteer for the conference.

In addition, *Hermanas* provides visibility to Latina role models within an organization and provides a mechanism for leaders in education and industry to connect with their communities. Dr. Maria Harper–Marinick, Executive Vice–Chancellor and Provost of the Maricopa Community Colleges says, "As Hispanic professionals, we can communicate, we can educate, and we can support our communities to ensure there is access for all."

Based on the successes of the Arizona efforts, this effective and balanced partnership has recently been produced for high school students in Oregon and California.

The model has a low cost (approximately $45 per student) and a high return on investment. The conference can be replicated with the following resources: 2–3 key industry partners (who provide funding, volunteer hours, and role models), community college participation (to provide conference support, faculty participation to teach conference workshops), K–12 buy–in, and of course, participants from local high schools.

Action Items

- Further develop the *Noche de Colegio* (College Night) event. *Noche de Colegio* is a special invitation to *Hermanas* participants and their parents to learn more about college paths and resources. Increased communication with past *Hermanas* participants ensure the proper resources are in place to help *Hermanas* students succeed. These efforts would allow for a more direct pipeline from high schools into college.

- Develop a middle school continuation for 3–4 days during the summer using the *Hermanas* model (hands–on activities, Latina Town Hall, and the community college experience). The *Hermanas* Conference is a successful first step in generating more interest in STEM, but we need to develop more opportunities that will continue to engage middle school participants, especially those that express a willingness to pursue other extra–curricular activities. The summer experience should have windows into a diversity of STEM careers.

About Maricopa Community Colleges

Consisting of ten colleges and two skill centers, the Maricopa Community Colleges (MCCCD) is the largest provider of workforce training in the State of Arizona. MCCCD currently offers over 900 Associate degree and certificate programs in occupational areas, including nearly 400 in STEM–related fields. Main STEM areas include: architecture and construction, engineering and technology, biological and health sciences, information technology, and manufacturing. MCCCD anticipates an approximate growth rate of 5 percent in all STEM areas per year over the next ten years.

A sample of main programs and services offered by MCCCD which build a STEM–related pipeline of students from secondary school and on to four–year universities and the workplace includes: National Science Foundation Grants, Department of Labor Trade Adjustment Assistance Community College and Career Training Grants, and a National Information, Security, and Geospatial Technology Consortium (NISGTC) Grant.

MCCCD has several successful partnerships with many colleges, universities, and businesses in providing comprehensive educational opportunities. A sample of these partnerships includes: the Arizona Precision Manufacturing Apprenticeship Program (a partnership between MCCCD and local employers), Translational Genomics Research Institute (TGEN) Partnership which focuses on pipeline development including student internships, and Automotive Program Partnerships which provide apprenticeships and on–the–job training.

About the Author

Maria Harper–Marinick, Ph.D., is Executive Vice Chancellor and Provost for the Maricopa County Community College District. She works closely with the Chancellor to develop and implement the District's strategic plan; lead initiatives to enhance access and increase student success; and build the stature and recognition of the District and its ten colleges locally, nationally, and internationally. Dr. Harper–Marinick also provides oversight for all areas within academic and student affairs; institutional effectiveness and research; university relations and transfer; grants development; international education; high school to college pathways programs; workforce development; and small business development.

Dr. Harper–Marinick serves on several boards and councils including the federal Advisory Committee on Student Financial Assistance (Chair) by appointment of U.S. Secretary of Education Arne Duncan; National Community College Hispanic Council (President–Elect); American Association for Community Colleges' Commission on Diversity, Inclusion, and Equity; Arizona Minority Education Policy Analysis Center; among others.

Dr. Harper–Marinick came to Arizona State University (ASU) as a Fulbright Scholar in 1982. She has authored scholarly articles and chapters and presented at national conferences. Dr. Harper–Marinick has been the recipient of awards and recognition, most recently she was recognized by ASU's Morrison Institute for Public Policy as a Distinguished Associate (2014). In 2014, she was selected as one of the 50 Most Influential Women in Arizona Business by the AZ Business Magazine, highlighted by the Phoenix Business Journal in their Executive Profiles, and featured in an article by Dana Wilkie in the International Educator titled "Women Making Their Marks."

Driving Quality Hispanic Talent to Jobs

By: Richard Morley, Chief Executive Officer,
Society of Hispanic Professional Engineers (SHPE)

SHPE has connected Hispanic STEM talent to corporate America for over 40 years. Our partnerships with businesses, higher education, government entities and other organizations that share our mission is a proven model for advancing a jobs-driven economy.

While other organizations work to improve STEM programs in K–12 or higher education, increase student access, retention and persistence, improve Hispanic corporate visibility and raise the overall quality of life for Hispanics in America - all critical work - SHPE works at the very nexus of specific STEM related jobs and the need for talent, diversity and inclusion in corporate America. Our entire value model is built around advancing a jobs-driven economy and providing the highest quality Hispanic talent for those STEM jobs.

Studies by Forbes,[112] McKinsey[113] and the Harvard Business School[114] among others show that a diverse workforce is critical for an organization's ability to innovate and adapt in today's fast–changing environment. Diversity fosters innovation and innovation drives business success. For SHPE's most successful business partners, diversity and inclusion is a mentality, a corporate strategy that breeds innovation and competitive advantage, and not just a set of numbers to meet for talent acquisition.

SHPE's 336 (and growing) graduate and undergraduate chapters at universities and colleges across the country engage students in academic excellence in STEM. However, SHPE's programs go far beyond just academic success. Our work addresses the gap ranked highest among corporate executives: the need for soft skills such as leadership, writing and presentations, critical thinking and teamwork:

> *Data from the American Society for Training and Development's member survey shows that leadership and executive skills, managerial and supervisory skills, and profession– or industry–specific skills are ranked as the highest areas for skills gaps. It is important to note that managerial and supervisory skills are of most concern to the majority of respondents: they ranked skills in this area as the first or second biggest gaps.[115]*

While our laser focus is on providing the highest quality Hispanic STEM talent at entry–level and graduate degree positions for a jobs-driven economy, our programs encompass K–12, college/university programs, corporate professional development and consulting for strategic advantage through corporate diversity and inclusion.

Higher education can help drive high quality Hispanic STEM talent by understanding SHPE's model of matching talent to corporate diversity and inclusion strategies, and by supporting SHPE and other diversity and inclusion professional societies (SWE and NSBE) on campus.

Seeding the Pipeline

Our college and university student led chapters across the nation are the backbone of SHPE. These college and university chapters are supported and guided by a network of professional development chapters comprised of former SHPE student members and by corporate talent acquisition and diversity and inclusion professionals.

With funding for development, college and professional chapters are providing support and leadership for high school level "SHPE Jr. Chapters" to establish high school (and eventually K–8) chapters and programs. In addition to our flagship SHPE Jr. Chapter Program, Noches de Ciencias (Science Nights) reach thousands of students nationwide. Our plans include growing K–12 STEM pipeline work through collaboration with other mission–aligned organizations, and we invite STEMconnector® partners to join us.

Growing Quality STEM Talent

In the broadest sense SHPE's work provides students an opportunity to belong to and engage in real life business and engineering beyond the classroom. The national studies on student engagement (NSSE)[116] clearly show that engagement influences academic success.

In its fall 2012 issue of *Diversity & Democracy,*[117] the Association of American Colleges and Universities (AACU) focused on civic learning and student engagement, documenting the positive effect of civic engagement and service learning on student success. In many ways the work taking place at SHPE's college and university chapters' mirrors community and service learning initiatives, as students focus on increasing STEM career attainment across the entire Hispanic community.

An online research publication in 2013 in the *Journal of Engineering Education, Strategic Pathways for Success: The Influence of Outside Community on Academic Engagement,* cites that, "Across all institutions, family is the community to which students feel most connected, with friends being a distant second. Students spoke of communities strategically, identifying needs that they meet through participation in communities and linking their participation with increased ability to engage in their academic endeavors." [118]

SHPE is *familia,* a critical element in Hispanic culture. In the truest sense, the SHPE nationwide *familia* and the relationships fostered by SHPE among student peers, academic leaders, corporate role models and other similar mission–driven organizations all combine to create excellence in a model for student success.

To drive Hispanic talent not only in academic success but also in the critical soft skills employers seek, SHPE has created a series of integrated programs that support and bind the SHPE *familia.*

National Institute for Leadership Advancement (NILA)

The National Institute for Leadership Advancement (NILA) is exclusively designed to provide newly–elected student and professional chapter executive board members with the resources for leadership and chapter development. Communication and strategic planning skills are essential to success in both SHPE chapter leadership and along the professional career path.

Regional Leadership Development Conferences (RLDC)

SHPE stages regional leadership development conferences each year for SHPE student and professional chapters to improve their organizational, managerial, and technical skills. They take place in all of the seven SHPE regions throughout the U.S. and Puerto Rico. This program helps attendees develop and improve their pre–college outreach programming efforts and the infrastructure of their SHPE chapters. Additionally, student leaders learn how to interact and network with SHPE's corporate supporters.

Management Growth Training (MGT)

This program offers five days of comprehensive training on everything from project and financial management to dealing with difficult people and interpersonal communications. MGT provides our mid–level professional engineers with the critical skills that produce career advancement and elevate them to higher management levels within their companies. Designed as the 2nd tier in SHPE's Professional Development Strategies Series, the MGT program is currently being revised to offer an even more challenging and beneficial agenda.

Executive Leadership Institute (ELI)

The Executive Leadership Institute's mission is to cultivate an interactive learning environment where current and potential executives are enabled to examine and enhance their leadership and management skills. ELI provides a platform for STEM career professionals to elevate their career to the executive level. This set of courses focuses on developing leadership talent for those who will be competing for executive positions.

National Conference

The annual SHPE National Conference attracts over 5,000 engineering professionals, students and corporate representatives. The conference is an opportunity for engineering companies and corporations to recruit top talent from SHPE membership. It also provides educational, technical and career opportunities for professional and student engineers.

Consulting: Diversity and Inclusion as Corporate Competitive Strategy

Through our many years of work with our corporate partners and sponsors, SHPE utilizes its expertise to help organizations understand strategy and tactics to improve corporate business competitive through diversity and inclusion. In Human Resources departments nationwide, talent acquisition for diversity and inclusion must be viewed by corporations beyond the narrow transactional return on investment (ROI) based on the number of resumes reviewed, interviews conducted and minority hires made. SHPE is in the process of documenting and creating a portfolio of consulting services that focuses on corporate mindset, a growth mindset in diversity and inclusion that is transformational beyond one–dimensional talent acquisition. Ernst & Young has well–documented the need for 21st century strategic innovation and competitiveness in its whitepaper, *The New Global Mindset, Driving Innovation through Diverse Perspectives.*[119]

Advancing a Jobs-Driven Economy

We welcome the STEMconnector® partnership in our national imperative to increase Hispanic degree attainment, and to further STEM careers at the highest levels of excellence in corporate America for Hispanics and other under–represented groups.

About Society of Hispanic Professional Engineers (SHPE)

Celebrating forty years of service, the Society of Hispanic Professional Engineers (SHPE) advocates for and advances Hispanic education, careers and professional development in STEM. As a non–profit sector organization SHPE connects the academic and government public sector with private industry, thus forming a solid networking base across all three sectors strongly positioned for advancing STEM jobs. Coordinating with other under–represented groups in STEM, SHPE partners with the Society for Women Engineers (SWE) and the National Society of Black Engineers (NSBE) among others. Our collaboration with organizations with aligned missions, coupled with SHPE's extraordinarily strong network of academic institutions and government entities, directly tied to our corporate partners who seek underrepresented STEM talent, serves as a strong force in advancing a jobs-driven economy.

SHPE was founded in Los Angeles, California, in 1974 by a group of engineers employed by the City of Los Angeles. Their objective was to form a national organization of professional engineers to serve as STEM talent to business. Today SHPE has a national network of over 400 corporate partners and sponsors and over 336 college and university chapters across the country. With 11,000 members, we connect the highest quality Hispanic STEM talent (undergrad, graduate and early career) with our corporate partners. Over 5,500 people attended SHPE's national conference in Detroit, Michigan, in November 2014, of which many were students looking for jobs and internships, and companies looking to fill positions with high–quality Hispanic STEM candidates.

About the Author

After serving as Executive Director for Irvine Valley College Foundation and Mt. San Antonio College Foundation for the past nine years, Richard Morley was appointed CEO of SHPE on December 1, 2014. At Irvine Valley College Foundation, he increased net assets a total of 39 percent in three years, and at Mt. San Antonio College, net assets quadrupled under Morley's leadership. At both colleges scholarships were substantially increased under his leadership. Mt. San Antonio College (Mt. SAC) is the largest single campus community college district…at 65,000 students, and is the largest Hispanic Serving Institution in the West. Before coming to Mt. SAC Morley served as a consultant in strategic planning, finance and turn around–situations in non–profit management. He co–founded and was President and CEO of CraneMorley, Inc., the largest boutique training and development firm on the West Coast. After selling the company in 1999, Mr. Morley joined the Council for Adult and Experiential Learning as their first Director of Corporate and Foundation Relations. In his early career days he was a high school teacher, and was a staff member of a brand new competency–based high school in the mid–1970s…ground breaking work at the time. Mr. Morley holds two of the highest earned certifications in the non–profit sector, Certified Fund Raising Executive (CFRE) and Certified Specialist in Planned Giving (CSPG). He holds a BS in English Education from Indiana University.

The HBCU STEM Innovation, Commercialization and Entrepreneurship (ICE) Platform and Initiative

By: Dr. Chad Womack, National Director STEM Initiatives
and UNCF–Merck Science Initiative, United Negro College Fund;
Dr. John M. Lee, Vice President, Office for Access
and Success, Association for Public and Land–grant Universities;
Ken Tolson, Member, President Board of Advisors, White House Initiative on
Historically Black Colleges and Universities; and
Dr. George Cooper, Executive Director, White House Initiative on
Historically Black Colleges and Universities

The innovation and tech–economy is projected to produce more jobs and account for most of the economic growth in the U.S. and globally than any other industry sector. In particular, the information and computer technology sector (IT) leads among the tech–sectors driving economic growth, and will likely experience the greatest increase in job growth over the next two decades. Unfortunately, not all communities are benefiting from the rapid growth of jobs and opportunities in the tech–industry. In Silicon Valley, for instance, African–Americans make up less than 2 percent of the tech–workforce in leading companies like Google, Facebook, Yahoo and Twitter. Further, it is clear that for African–Americans and underrepresented minorities the STEM educational feeder systems and pipelines that are the source of tech–workforce talent – K12 and higher education – are not productive at the level of industry demands, and in some cases, are broken all together.

To address these challenges, we have established the HBCU STEM Innovation, Commercialization and Entrepreneurship (or ICE) initiative as a collaborative, enterprise–based and open source platform that will have impact at the student, faculty and institutional/community levels. The mission of the ICE platform is to transform our campuses into high–performance STEM hubs and nodes of innovation and entrepreneurship that will have increased economic impact for the African–American community. The specific goals of the platform are to significantly increase the post–secondary yield of African–Americans pursuing STEM careers; to foster innovation and entrepreneurship across HBCU campuses in a manner that improves the R&D profile, commercialization activities and tech–entrepreneurship performance of HBCUs; and to connect our campuses to economically productive innovation and tech–ecosystems (e.g. Silicon Valley) around the country. Working with our HBCU partners including the White House Initiative on Historically Black Colleges and Universities, and the Association for Public and Land–grant Universities (APLU), the UNCF–led ICE platform has organized leadership across HBCU campuses to address the STEM challenge and raise the performance of our campuses.

The major outcomes and impacts of the ICE platform initiative include:

- Increasing the tech–workforce readiness of HBCU and URM students
- Empowering HBCU students and faculty launch commercial and social ventures that transform their community, environment and society.

Advancing a Jobs-Driven Economy

- Transforming and aligning HBCU STEM curriculum with the innovation and tech–economy; and, on–campus culture to have more of a risk–taking, innovation and entrepreneurship and creates opportunities to connect with the innovation and tech–economy.

- HBCU institutions becoming hubs and nodes of innovation and entrepreneurship, and places where opportunity flow spurs economic growth and social impact in local/regional ecosystems.

History of the ICE Platform Initiative

The HBCU Innovation, Commercialization and Entrepreneurship platform and initiative (or ICE platform) was established in 2013 as a partnership led by the UNCF, Association for Public and Land–grant Universities (APLU) and the White House Initiative on Historically Black Colleges and Universities.

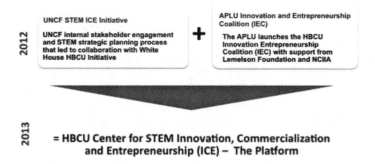

Vision

The vision of the ICE platform is to encourage the emergence of our HBCU campuses into vibrant educational ecosystems driven by innovation and tech–entrepreneurship, aligned with tech–industry demands and expectations, and are connected to Silicon Valley and other innovation ecosystems worldwide. While the ultimate vision is to build capacities for several STEM–industry verticals – including bio/life sciences, artificial intelligence, cybersecurity, automated systems, big data analytics, etc. the immediate focus of the ICE platform is on building and developing the computer science/engineering and IT industry sector vertical.

The ICE Platform Initiative is Framed by 3 Pillars:

1. **STEM Advocacy & Digital Media Platform** – The ICE initiative has established hbcuinnovation.org as the URL and online destination to showcase and highlight STEM, innovation and entrepreneurship activities (students and faculty) across the HBCU landscape and serve as a media bridge that connects the HBCU community to Silicon Valley and other ecosystems. In addition, the ICE platform will leverage opportunities to shape policy at the local and national level to promote African–American excellence in STEM and tech–entrepreneurship.

2. **Pathways to Innovations in STEM and Tech–Entrepreneurship** – This pillar frames our approach to significantly enhance a tech–workforce pipeline that connects highly engaged HBCU students and faculty in the STEM disciplines with Silicon Valley academic and tech–industry stakeholders. The immediate focus will be on computer science/engineering pipelines and pathways that lead towards the IT industry sector(s).

3. **Innovation Hubs and Ecosystems** – The ICE platform will channel capital investments and resources to help seed, grow and develop innovation ecosystems on our campuses in a manner that enhances the value proposition for HBCUs.

Outcomes, Impacts & Scale

The ICE platform is designed to be a market–responsive and scalable initiative whose impact will reach across the entire HBCU community at the student, faculty and institutional levels. The main goal is to empower the next generation of African–American students and faculty as innovators and tech–entrepreneurs that will drive value in the innovation and tech–economy. At the student and faculty level, the ICE platform seeks to align STEM educational outcomes with student preparation for the tech–workforce and faculty as STEM innovators and entrepreneurs. At the institutional level, the ICE platform will enhance R&D, tech–transfer and commercialization capacities among HBCUs that will enhance their value proposition in the post–secondary educational markets and tech–industry sectors.

Level of Impact	STEM Outcomes	ICE Outcomes
Student	• > Numbers of STEM graduates prepared for career success in the tech–workforce • > Mumbers of African–American high school students motivated and prepared to pursue STEM/ comp, science and engineering majors with coding skills	• > Numbers of students engaged and prepared for tech– entrepreneurship, and pursuing new ventures as startup founders

Level of Impact	STEM Outcomes	ICE Outcomes
Faculty	• Increased number and networks of STEM communities of practice/learning communities • Faculty as STEM academic innovators developing new curriculum and methods of delivery	• > Numbers of faculty engaged and prepared to pursue STEM innovations to the market through tech–entrepreneurship
Institution/Community	• Increased R&D investments and expanding R&D portfolios • Robust tech–transfer/ • Commercialization efforts • Networked HBCUs via online STEM educational platform	• Develop culture of managed risk–taking, innovation and ntrepreneurship • Establish a vibrant innovation ecosystem that is networked among other HBCUs and connected to other ecosystems including Silicon Valley

More immediately, the ICE platform seeks to have the following outcomes and impacts in the computer science/engineering and IT industry sector vertical:
- Significantly increase the numbers of HBCU students prepared to pursue careers and tech–entrepreneurship in the IT tech–sector; a particular emphasis will be on supporting students acquiring rigorous coding, programming and software engineering skills.

- Transform and align computer science/engineering curriculum across HBCU campuses with the tech–workforce demands and expectations of Silicon Valley;

- Significantly increase the number of African–American high school students prepared to pursue computer science/engineering as college majors particularly at HBCUs with coding/programming skills.

At every level, the initiative seeks to encourage and empower African–American girls and young women to pursue STEM ICE opportunities, and we will emphasize outreach accordingly.

Programs and Activities:
HBCU ICE Summits (launched Fall, 2013)
We have convened three major events in Silicon Valley including:
- HBCU Innovation Summit – Fall, 2013

- HBCU Innovation and Entrepreneurship Symposium – Spring, 2014
- HBCU Innovation Summit – Fall, 2014

HBCU Innovation Digital Media Platform www.hbcuinnovation.org (launched Fall, 2013) The purpose of the digital media platform is to highlight existing STEM and I.C.E. related activities across the HBCU landscape and to establish a dynamic media portal through which various members of the HBCU innovation community and ecosystem can network and share best practices, events and activities.

HBCU ICE Consortium (launched Spring, 2014)

Led by Dr. John M. Lee/APLU, the IEC was established as a consortium of HBCUs who are committed to pursue strategic development in innovation and tech–entrepreneurship. Initially supported by the Lemelson Foundation, the National Collegiate Inventors and Innovators Alliance (NCIIA) and the National Center for Engineering Pathways to Innovation (Epicenter) located at Stanford University, the IEC represents a growing coalition of HBCUs that are engaged in strategic planning to build innovation ecosystems on their campuses. The ultimate vision is to establish an HBCU–wide venture ecosystem that is directly connected to Silicon Valley and other innovation ecosystems worldwide.

HBCU Computer Science & Engineering Faculty Workshop (launched Fall, 2014)

The HBCU Computer Science/Engineering Faculty Institute will launch at the HBCU I.C.E. Summit in November, 2014. The Institute will establish a community of practice among HBCU computer science/engineering faculty members where best practices, professional development and learning opportunities can be shared. In addition, HBCU faculty members will have access to industry professionals in Silicon Valley and computer science/engineering faculty from tier I level academic institutions.

Action Items

We are excited about the future of the ICE platform initiative. Starting in early 2015, we will be launching the HBCU STEM Scholars Program, Code Academy and Hackathon League as major program efforts to address the needs of students. We will continue the work initiated at the most recent summit and look forward to the next HBCU Innovation Summit in the Fall of 2015 where we will highlight the achievements of our students and faculty across the ICE consortium.

HBCU Code Academy & Hackathon League

The HBCU Coding Academy and Hackathon League represent innovative approaches to directly engage students across the entire HBCU landscape on a semi–virtual platform where they can learn to code/program. Students would have access to a variety of on–line branded 'learn–to–code' platforms (e.g. Treehouse, CODE School, Starter League, Code Academy, etc…) and support from IT professionals from leading Silicon Valley tech–companies serving as mentors and advisors. The emphasis will be on project–based learning and performance–based assessment where students will be encouraged to build their own digital portfolios of work as well as collaborations using developer spaces like GitHub. The HBCU Hackathon League will establish a competitive league among HBCUs where student teams will respond to grand challenges and develop tech–based solutions and compete for prizes and awards.

Advancing a Jobs-Driven Economy

HBCU STEM/Computer Science Scholars Program (to be launched fall, 2014)
The HBCU STEM Scholars Program was launched by a generous gift from the Merck Foundation and represents a STEM pipeline program that identifies students of promise who are motivated to pursue STEM majors at the undergraduate level. Future versions of this program will focus on building a robust pipeline of computer science/engineering majors and students with software programming/coding skills on our campuses that are prepared for internships at Silicon Valley tech–companies. In addition, the program will reach deeper into the STEM pipeline to identify middle and high school students attending schools in communities surrounding our HBCU campuses that are motivated to engage in STEM related programs and activities with an emphasis on computing and design.

About United Negro College Fund (UNCF)

The United Negro College Fund, or UNCF, is an American philanthropic organization that funds scholarships for black students and general scholarship funds for 39 private historically black colleges and universities. The UNCF was incorporated on April 25, 1944 by Frederick D. Patterson (then president of what is now Tuskegee University), Mary McLeod Bethune, and others. The UNCF is headquartered at 1805 7th Street, NW in Washington, DC. In 2005, the UNCF supported approximately 65,000 students at over 900 colleges and universities with approximately $113 million in grants and scholarships. About 60 percent of these students are the first in their families to attend college, and 62 percent have annual family incomes of less than $25,000. UNCF also administers over 450 named scholarships. This is in contrast with the Thurgood Marshall College Fund that raises money for the public historically black colleges and universities.

About the Author

Dr. Chad Womack is a science educator and technology entrepreneur, researcher, and scholar. In his current capacity at the UNCF, Dr. Womack leads the organization's strategic direction to address unmet educational needs in STEM college and career pipeline for African American students.

In addition, Dr. Womack is the Project Lead for the HBCU Startup and Innovation Initiative at the UNCF, a White House and Mitchell Kapor Foundation supported effort to galvanize tech entrepreneurship and commercialization across Historically Black Colleges and Universities.

Prior to joining the UNCF, Dr. Womack Co–Founded the America21 Project, an innovation–based community and economic development non–profit organization dedicated to empowering urban centers and underserved communities through science, technology and innovation. As a national non–profit organization, The America21 Project has launched multiple initiatives in cities through the country. Dr. Womack also serves as a consultant and advisor to the White House, several federal agencies, and local and state governments. Initiatives have included several science educational and training programs designed to address the educational (post-secondary preparation) and human capital needs for the region's biotechnology and life science industry.

CHAPTER TWELVE

Developing STEM Human Capital through State and Federal Action

"We are woefully behind. The only way to change the situation is through public-private partnerships: Industry identifies the needed skills, schools provide the training and public sector creates a supportive policy and funding."

-Klaus Kleinfeld, Chairman and Chief Executive Officer
Alcoa

Excerpt from *100 CEO Leaders in STEM,* a publication by STEMconnector®

Tailoring Employment and Skills Strategies to Produce Quality Jobs
By: Anna Rubin, Policy Analyst,
Organization for Economic Co–operation and Development (OECD)

All Governance Levels have a Role in Building a Stronger More Inclusive Economy
Creating more and better quality jobs is at the top of U.S. policymakers' agendas, as it is for other OECD countries. The decline in the U.S. unemployment rate since its peak during the crisis is promising. However, this hides the fact that a significant number of people appear to have dropped out of the labour market altogether, as evidenced by an overall employment rate that continues to be lower than pre–crisis levels. At the same time, youth unemployment and long–term unemployment also remain considerable challenges.[120]

Additionally, a larger percentage of Americans have a low level of "basic" skills than the OECD Adult Skills Survey (PIACC) cross–country average, which has implications not only for employment and productivity, but also overall health and well–being.[121]

Across the OECD, national governments are seeking to address similar challenges through establishing a stable macroeconomic framework and structural policies that encourage innovation, skills and business development. But the diversity of local conditions must also be taken into account, calling for a response in the U.S. that goes beyond one–size–fits–all federal or state policies. Local policy makers need flexibility, agility and capacity to be able to respond to opportunities and challenges as they arise. They also increasingly need to be able to work across policy "silos", designing strategies that cross–cut employment, training, education and economic development.[122]

The Supply and Demand for Skills Matters – Particularly at the Local Level
A key factor that local policymakers must take into account when designing strategies to boost job creation is how skills are supplied and used in the local labor market. In the context of the knowledge economy, a skilled and entrepreneurial workforce is becoming particularly important to firms' decisions to locate or remain in an area, making hosting a highly skilled workforce key to a community's successful future. But the other side of the coin is also important. A resilient and inclusive economy depends on workers having access to quality employment opportunities that allow them to fully utilize the skills they already have, while also offering opportunities for them to progress and further develop these skills. Where both the supply of and demand for skills is high, employers, workers and the broader community benefit.

To help policy makers better understand these local conditions, the OECD has developed a tool to look at both the supply of and demand for skills at the local level.[123] Looking at both the supply of and demand for skills together can help to paint a more nuanced picture of where conditions are ripe for quality job creation and where specific challenges need to be addressed.

The OECD's Skills Analysis

The OECD LEED programme has developed a statistical tool to help understand the balance between skills supply and demand within local labour markets.[124, 125] According to this methodology, local economies can fall into four different categories: low skills equilibrium, skills deficit, skills surplus and high skills equilibrium.

		Skills Supply	
		Low	High
Skills Demand	High	Skills Deficit	High Skills Equilibrium
	Low	Low Skills Equilibrium	Skills Surplus

In order to approximate the *supply* for skills at the sub–regional (i.e. county) level, the study has used the percentage of the working age population having post–secondary education as an indicator. This was the only indicator available at sub–regional level that was comparable across countries.

In order to approximate the *demand* for skills the following two variables have been combined into a composite index using a weighted average:

- Percentage of population having medium and high skilled occupations

- Income from employment (or where available, GVA per worker)

Both variables were standardised using the inter–decile range method to minimise the influence of outliers.

Data for the skills analysis for the U.S. is taken from the 2012 American Community Survey (ACS) 5–year estimate and from the income and wage estimates published by the Bureau of Economic Analysis.

More information about the methodology is available in the OECD's *Job Creation and Local Economic Development*.[126]

As shown on the map on the next page, using this tool shows that there is considerable variation in skills ecosystems across the United States.

Skills Supply and Demand Analysis, U.S. Counties, 2012

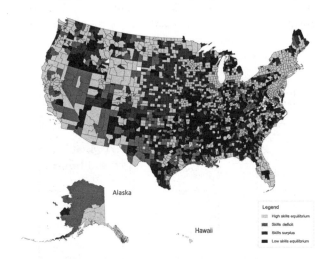

Source: OECD analysis based on 2012 American Community Survey (ACS) 5–year estimate and income and wage estimates published by the Bureau of Economic Analysis –2008–2012 average table CA34 Wage and salary summary.

Approximately one–third of U.S. counties are in a "high skills equilibrium", where a high supply of skills in the labour force is matched by a high level of skilled employment opportunities. These are considered conditions ripe for quality job creation.

Another third show a mismatch between supply and demand. In some of these counties, the workforce has a relatively high level of skills while the demand for skills is relatively low, a situation knows as a skills surplus. This situation can result in a drain of highly skilled workers leaving to pursue opportunities elsewhere. The remainder of these counties are in skills deficit, where employers may not be able to find workers with the level of skills they need.

The final third of counties are in "low skills equilibrium". Often, these areas have a concentration of employers pursuing price–based competition strategies, relying on low–skilled and standardised production. In these places, it may not pay for people to invest in skills when skills are not valued by employers. At the same time, those who do attain skills move away to better quality jobs elsewhere. This can create a vicious cycle, compromising productivity, growth and innovation.

Tailoring and Joining Up Local Strategies is Key
In designing effective local strategies, approaches that work in one skills situation may actually be counterproductive in others. Focusing only on boosting the supply of skills in low skills equilibrium regions, for example, will be of little use unless employers also increase skills utilization through strategies such as moving to higher value–added production and

improving human resource management. While being in high skills equilibrium offers some advantages, this does not necessarily translate into low unemployment. In fact, unemployment may be high, suggesting a need to focus on inclusion and addressing barriers that specific populations face in accessing high skilled employment.

Regardless of the approach taken, actors in only one policy area cannot implement such strategies. Many of the skills challenges that communities face call for coordination across employment, skills and economic development, with a longer–term vision in mind. However, path dependency, a lack of flexibility and capacity, and rigid vertical horizontal accountability can hinder joined–up work.

In its new publication, *Job Creation and Local Economic Development*, the OECD has synthesized research across policy areas such as employment; entrepreneurship and economic development to show how policymakers across governance levels can better align their efforts to boost job creation from the bottom up. It shows not only "what needs to be done", for example to improve skills utilization in firms or promote lifelong learning, but also the governance mechanisms of "how it can be done", from injecting local flexibility into national policy frameworks to improving horizontal accountability at the local level. For policy makers looking to identify new and innovative approaches, this publication provides concrete examples and lessons drawn from communities across the OECD.

About OECD
The OECD provides a forum in which governments can work together to share experiences and seek solutions to common problems. We work with governments to understand what drives economic, social and environmental change. We measure productivity and global flows of trade and investment. We analyse and compare data to predict future trends. We set international standards on a wide range of things, from agriculture and tax to the safety of chemicals.

The OECD Programme on Local Economic and Employment Development (LEED) has advised governments and communities since 1982 on how to respond to economic change and tackle complex problems in a fast–changing world. Its mission is to contribute to the creation of more and better jobs through effective policy implementation, innovative practices, stronger capacities and integrated strategies at a local level. LEED draws on comparative analysis of experiences from five continents in fostering economic growth, employment, and inclusion.

About the Author
Anna Rubin is a policy analyst at the OECD's Local Economic and Employment Development Programme in the Centre for Entrepreneurship, SMEs, and Local Development. Her work focuses on employment, skills and local governance, particularly as it relates to youth. Prior to joining the OECD, she worked with at a variety of policy levels, from working locally with San Francisco's Department of Children, Youth, and their Families to internationally with UNESCO. She has a BA in Psychology and a Master in Public Policy from the University of California Berkeley.

Iowa's STEM Strategy Serves as a Magnet for
Business and Education Partnerships

By: Kimberly K. Reynolds, Lieutenant Governor of Iowa, Co–Chair of Governor's
STEM Advisory Council, Founding Chair of the STEM Food & Ag Council, Chair of
State Efforts for Million Women Mentors, and NLGA Chair–Elect

More than three years ago, Iowa embarked upon a critical journey to create a statewide
STEM strategy. At the heart of this initiative is the Governor's STEM Advisory Council,
which I am honored to co–chair with Mary Andringa, Chairman of Vermeer Corporation.
We serve with 45 visionary, hard–working STEM Council members who understand
that improving Iowa's STEM foundation means a brighter future for students and our
economy.

The Council encourages students to study STEM subjects and consider STEM–related
careers. It also provides a platform for bringing education and business and industry
together to fully prepare our young people for a knowledge–based, global economy.
Nearly 50 companies partner with the Governor's STEM Advisory Council to bring top
quality STEM education to Iowa.

We are extremely fortunate to have very active business leaders immersed in Iowa's
STEM efforts. Their engagement ranges from the devotion of talents, time, and financial
contributions. Many companies host teacher externs in the summer, mentor robotics
teams or computer science clubs, and volunteer in schools.

Our STEM programs depend upon business volunteers and mentors. Those programs
include: IT Academy; Externships; FIRST Tech Challenge; Engineering is Elementary
(EIE); HyperStream; CASE; Project Lead The Way; Hour of Code; the new STEM
Center for Advanced Professional Studies (CAPS) effort; as well as STEM Festivals
across Iowa.

In addition, there is an Active Learning Community of informal and non–formal venues
such as a science center, children's museum, and 4–H that are all focusing on STEM and
the professional development of their staff.

And, the fact that each of Iowa's six STEM regions is overseen by an advisory board
made up of business, industry, and education really unifies our state STEM efforts.
We understand that STEM collaboration is key. Our stakeholders are diverse and
passionate about being involved. They include:

- Business and industry executives;
- Economic development/chamber of commerce organizations;
- Regional workforce development leaders;
- Local government officials;

- Private colleges and universities;

- Community colleges;

- Public University Area Education Agencies;

- Nonprofit and informal learning centers;

- County extension and outreach organizations;

- K–12 students and their parents;

- STEM teachers;

- School board members;

- Libraries; and

- STEM Hub institution representatives, to name just a few.

These individuals and organizations serve as the lifeblood of Iowa's statewide STEM initiative. Our national leadership position in STEM can be attributed to the ongoing synergy created by this extensive network.

Yet, despite the success of harnessing the power behind business, industry, and educational partnerships, we must continue to aggressively use STEM as a tool for economic and human capital development. When I travel across the state, employers tell me about the shortage of well–qualified applicants for middle and high–skill openings. Part of the problem is that it can be very hard for adults and students to identify, on their own, what professional STEM opportunities exist and how to prepare for them.

I believe all Iowans deserve to be empowered with the knowledge and skills in STEM and other subjects that are essential to thrive in the careers of today and tomorrow. STEM is all about expanding opportunity. We must continually communicate that an engaging STEM education opens up rewarding professional possibilities for individuals of all ages.

That approach strengthens the talent pool for STEM business and industry – from start–ups to established companies.

STEM job growth and salaries are promising. In Iowa, STEM jobs will grow from 50,560 in 2010 to a projected 61,500 in 2020, according to the Georgetown University Center on Education and the Workforce. Plus, another 29,000 jobs will be added for health–care professionals.

When it comes to pay, two–thirds of employees with STEM–related associate degrees make more than the average for workers with Non–STEM associate degrees. That's also true for more than 56 percent of workers who have STEM–related bachelor degrees.

One of the ways that we found to actively engage high school students was through STEM business and education partnerships by providing them a chance to consider, observe, and participate in real–life experiences.

Advancing a Jobs-Driven Economy

Just consider Alex Pringnitz, a Spirit Lake High School student in Iowa, who spent two weeks at Polaris Industries to learn about lean manufacturing techniques, including how to make work stations more efficient.

Alex wanted to learn exactly what engineers do as well as find a way to apply physics and give him a purpose for math.

After his experience at Polaris, Alex said: "I liked the experience it gave me; learning about manufacturing. It gave me a new view of Polaris. I've always driven by, but I never knew what was inside. I think everybody should have the option - of a professional experience like this in high school - so they are able to know what they might be getting into before they choose a major in college."

Brian Hines, Director of Operations for the Spirit Lake and Milford Polaris facilities, explained why Polaris opened up its production floor to high school students from Spirit Lake and Okoboji, "It's getting them into the factory and seeing what it's all about. Manufacturing has some great jobs that are challenging, interesting, and fun. You can make a career out of it."

You can see why the Governor's STEM Advisory Council is inspired to promote more of these meaningful partnerships between schools and businesses. Everyone stands to benefit enormously.

Getting this right will help us meet the Council's goal of increasing student interest and achievement in STEM and enhancing STEM economic development. We're doing this by redefining STEM education so it stretches beyond the classroom.

Waukee is the first school district to bring the Center for Advanced Professional Studies (CAPS) programming to Iowa. A CAPS program is designed to broaden students' understanding of career opportunities and support economic development through market–driven curriculum.

It focused on profession–based learning and full immersion into specific industry projects.

The Waukee Community School District had the vision to understand how a CAPS program can drive innovation and entrepreneurialism in Iowa. Their students are able to use their problem–solving and teamwork skills – to master complex content.

They are exploring careers and building a network of professional contacts with business partners in the community. Waukee students can job shadow and participate in internships to bring relevance to what they're studying.

The students also can take courses at area businesses 2.5 hours a day in foundations of insurance and actuarial science; interactive design (combining technology, advertising and marketing); foundations of medicine; or foundations of multidisciplinary design: architecture and engineering. Students do hands–on work on site.

"It's just a great example of how businesses and our education system can work together to produce personalized learning experiences that prepare the next generation for 21st century opportunities," said David Wilkerson, Waukee superintendent.

Waukee's private partners include: Shive–Hattery, DLR Group, DMACC, Des Moines University, FBL Financial Group, CannonDesign, INVISION, and several others.

Opportunities to partner with corporate executives, business professionals and talented teachers help each student prepare for the future. CAPS is making possible for students to better connect what they learn in the classroom with the jobs they may want to pursue someday.

As we head into future, strengthening STEM partnerships between schools and businesses remains one of our top priorities in Iowa.

About the Author

Kim Reynolds, a former state senator and county treasurer, serves as Iowa's 45th Lieutenant Governor. She was elected Iowa's Lieutenant Governor on November 2, 2010. Kim truly understands the importance of fiscal responsibility, job creation, education, and technology.

As Lieutenant Governor, Kim uses her in–depth understanding of Iowa's small towns and urban communities to continually move Iowa forward with bold economic development initiatives. Since 2011, she has helped attract more than $9 billion in private investment to the state. Companies like Facebook, Google, Microsoft, CJ Bio America, Cargill, Mid–American, CF Industries, and Valent Biosciences, have chosen to locate or expand in our state.

Each year, Kim travels to all 99 counties and enthusiastically listens to Iowans of all ages. She actively seeks to learn how Iowa can become an even stronger state. Whether it's meeting with women business owners or rural farmers, Kim embraces the opportunity to gain insights into their concerns or encourage collaboration.

On the global front, Kim knows that one in five Iowa jobs is attributed to international trade. Her travels have taken Kim from China to Germany to South Korea to Vietnam to the Philippines and Thailand. In leading these trade missions, she has established long–term relationships that already are resulting in increased exports, more foreign direct investment and new jobs for Iowans.

Kim tirelessly works to provide access to STEM (Science, Technology, Engineering, and Math) programs for students, especially the underrepresented and underserved. She co–chairs the Governor's STEM Advisory Council in Iowa. Kim also is known throughout the country, as one of the strongest advocates for STEM. Her passion for STEM education was recognized by STEMconnecto® when she was named to their "100 Women Leaders in STEM." In 2013–14, Kim chaired the STEM Food & Ag Council.

Advancing a Jobs-Driven Economy

On the national front, Kim is Chair–Elect for the National Lieutenant Governors Association (NLGA). She also serves on the Education Committee of the Aerospace States Association. The Lieutenant Governor served as president of the Iowa State Treasurers Association in 2000 and later received the "Outstanding County Treasurer in the United States" award.

Kim serves as Honorary Chair of Million Women Mentors – Iowa as well as Honorary Chair of the Employer Volunteer Initiative in Iowa.

A native of St. Charles, Iowa, Kim enjoys her small town roots. Kim and Kevin reside in Osceola. They are proud parents to three daughters and six grandchildren.

Accelerating a Pool of Diverse, Excellent STEM Professionals

By: Lezli Baskerville, President and Chief Executive Officer, National Association for Equal Opportunity in Higher Education (NAFEO)

The growth, development, and diversity of the domestic scientific and engineering (S&E) enterprises are central to the nation's ability to meet the challenges of today while seizing the opportunities of tomorrow. They are fundamental for an excellent, efficient job–driven economy. While the scientific and engineering capability of the United States remains strong, "The dominance of the United States in these fields has lessened as the rest of the world has invested in and grown its research and education capacities."[127] Heretofore, the U.S. has relied on an S & E workforce that was predominantly male, disproportionately White, and Asian. As the proportion of the White males in the S & E workforce has shifted, the U.S. has experienced a growth in the numbers of women in some S & E fields and a greater reliance on international students.[128] Other than in Historically Black Colleges and Universities (HBCUs), there has been no concomitant growth in S&E or STEM degree production among the fastest growing populations in this nation. The National Academy of Sciences et al report, *Expanding Underrepresented Minority Participation,[129]* makes this case poignantly clear:

"Non–U.S. citizens, particularly those from China and India, have accounted for almost all growth in STEM doctorate awards and, in some engineering fields, have for some time comprised the majority of new doctorate awards. Indeed, temporary residents accounted for more than half of the U.S. doctorates in engineering, computer science, and mathematics in 2006."[130]

Historically Black Colleges and Universities (HBCUs) are leading the way in educating African American (AfAm) graduates in scientific, technological, and other fields required for national success. Despite being just three percent of American colleges and universities, HBCUs are the leading baccalaureate institutions of AfAms who earn doctorates in Science and Engineering. They produce 19 percent of AfAm undergraduate science graduates and 20.1 percent of AfAm undergraduate engineering graduates.[131] Forty percent of AfAms receiving four–year degrees in STEM receive them at HBCUs. Of the top ten baccalaureate institutions for blacks who go on to receive a PhD in Science or Engineering, nine of the ten are HBCUs.[132] Twenty–four percent (24 percent) of all PhDs earned each year by AfAms are conferred by twenty–four (24) HBCUs. Most significantly, eighteen of the top twenty-three producers of AfAms who go on to receive science related PhDs are HBCUs. They are also four of the top ten producers of successful AfAm medical school applicants.

HBCUs are as richly diverse as the overall cohort of American higher education institutions. There are 2 and 4–year colleges and universities, public, private, land grant and denominational institutions; undergraduate, graduate and professional schools. HBCUs are among the nation's most racially and ethnically diverse colleges and universities with an average of nearly 25 percent student diversity and in excess of 40 percent faculty diversity. As a group, they educate a disproportionate percentage of low–income and first–generation students – the growing populations of the nation.

Despite their disproportionate graduation rates of blacks in STEM, HBCUs have one eighth (1/8) of the average size of endowments of colleges and universities historically educating primarily white students (HWCUs), and since their founding mostly in the period just after the Civil War, they have not received public or private investments commensurate with their outcomes and impact.

HBCUs do not and have never received a share of federal, state or philanthropic funding proportionate to their mission, output, and impact. Although public funding to HBCUs has increased in absolute terms over the past decade, an entrenched and intractable gap persists between public dollars invested in HBCUs and their HWCU counterparts. See, Gasman, Marybeth, *Comprehensive Funding Approaches for Historically Black Colleges and Universities: A Policy Brief* (University of Pennsylvania Graduate School of Education, 2013). The NSF reports, that six of the top twenty historically and predominantly white institutions receive more federal funds for research than seventy-nine HBCUs combined. The United States Commission on Civil Rights, The National Academy of Sciences and others report persistent inequitable disparities in public funding for HBCUs and their HWCU counterparts.[133]

In order for the United States to realize its education, workforce and economic goals amid the shifting national demographics to becoming "majority minority," and increasingly low–income, first generation families, HBCUs and Predominantly Black Institutions (PBI's) are essential for producing a diverse pipeline of the quality of employees and entrepreneurs America needs to successfully compete in the global economy – people with the content and character needed to move this nation and the world to a peaceful co–existence, toward ecumenism, becoming a sustainable community of One, and "First in the World."

Because HBCUs are doing the lion's share of preparing and graduating African Americans in STEM, they must be supported and strengthened in order to realize their promise of graduating an even larger percentage of U.S. students in S&E and, thereby, leading the nation in meeting its need for excellent, diverse S & E professionals.[134]

Federal and state legislators, public and private, two– and four–year colleges and universities and diverse people worldwide, can and should take the following and other actions to make certain that the nation and world benefit fully from the central role HBCUs and PBIs. They are playing a major role in advancing the jobs–driven economy, accelerating the pool of diverse, excellent STEM professionals,[135] driving healthy, green, sustainable communities, promoting a just society, tolerance and a sense of interconnectivity and interdependence in our neighborhoods and world.

Federal and State Action

The entire STEMconnector® Community should collectively educate federal legislators and industry about the urgency and ROI of establishing and funding Topical Centers of STEM Excellence on the campuses of the 14 HBCUs graduating more than 30 percent of African Americans in STEM. These Centers will collaborate, innovate, and cross–pollinate. This recommendation is supported by the 2010 findings of the National Academy of Sciences Hrabowski Commission and the 2010 Commission on Civil Rights Report on HBCUs and STEM.

GOAL: Federal Legislation passed during first half of 114th Congress establishing fourteen (14) Centers of STEM Excellence on the targeted HBCU campuses.

GOAL: Leading STEM enterprises will fund 6 Multidisciplinary STEM Centers at HBCUs that are not currently among the leading producers of AfAm graduates in STEM, but which are poised to build their capacity in this arena working with and through the Topical Centers of STEAM Excellence (above), through industry and federal laboratories, and to serve as feeders for students going into graduate and professional STEM programs at HBCUs and HWCUs.

- The entire STEMconnector® Community should collectively educate members of the 114th Congress about the value to the establishment of an excellent, diverse jobs–driven economy, of creating, funding and sustaining until they become self–sustaining, Centers of Entrepreneurship and Technology Transfer on ten 10 HBCUs campuses.

GOAL: The 114th Congress will authorize and fund 10 HBCU Centers of Entrepreneurship and Technology Transfer

- The entire STEMconnector® Community should collectively educate federal and state policy makers, policy shapers and opinion makers about the need for investing more public dollars in HBCUs, which yield the highest ROI in educating the growing populations, especially blacks in STEM. The nation and industry must invest proportionately more dollars for STEM research, teaching, training, education, and workforce preparation in HBCUs (and MSIs that are also doing the lion's share of graduating the growing populations of the nation in STEM.

GOAL: As Congress reauthorizes the Elementary and Secondary Education Act and the Higher Education Act, it should adopt an innovative/transformational approach to education funding (elementary/secondary and higher education) that incentivizes disproportionate investments of public and private resources in those institutions that are graduating disproportionate percentages of the growing populations of the nation, including Hispanics, African Americans, Native Americans, Asian Pacific Islanders, low–income students, and first generation students.

- The entire STEMconnector® Community should collectively educate the public and private sectors about the imperative for investing in early STEM education and literacy initiatives, STEM mentoring initiatives that pare college students with middle– and high school students; and increase the numbers of STEM early college pipeline programs.

Advancing a Jobs-Driven Economy

GOAL: The 114th Congress will authorize where appropriate or increase appropriations for investing in early STEM education and literacy initiatives, STEM mentoring initiatives that pare college students with middle– and high school students; and increase the numbers of STEM early college pipeline programs in the schools, colleges and universities educating disproportionate percentages of the growing populations.

Private and/or Public/Private Actions

- Design and execute a social marketing campaign (media, policy, advocacy to change attitudes) highlighting the centrality of HBCUs to realizing the nation's goal of accelerating the graduation of excellent, diverse STEM professionals and making the STEM and sustainability disciplines and professions appealing as attainable, marketable, globally necessary, and "cool." This should be accomplished working through the National Association for Equal Opportunity in Higher Education (NAFEO),[136] the nation's only national membership and advocacy association for all of the HBCUs and PBIs, and in partnership with the nation's leading STEM enterprises, The Ad Council, STEMconnector®, leading minority owned and communications firms and outlets. Entertainers, athletes, other celebrities and icons should be engaged in garnering interest in and securing funding for the initiative. STEM graphic paraphernalia and toy manufacturing and retail industries should be engaged in the campaign.

- Enlist the nation's leading STEM enterprises in funding six Multidisciplinary Centers of STEM Excellence at HBCUs that are not the fourteen leaders in graduating African Americans in STEM, but those that are doing well in this space and are poised to build capacity in this arena and position them to do so working through the fourteen HBCU Topical Centers of STEM Excellence, the federal government, and industry laboratories as well as with the broader universe of leading higher education institutions in STEM. These centers should be incubators and laboratories for testing and adapting the best and promising practices for graduating the growing populations in STEM, and for incubating additional models for accelerating the graduation of blacks and other growing populations in STEM. This should be done working through NAFEO and a partnership of other stakeholder entities it assembles.

- To diversify the STEM professoriate, working through NAFEO, the White House Office of Science & Technology Policy, HBCUs, MSIs and the nation's leading colleges and universities in STEM, foster and support pipeline programs from 2-year HBCUs and other 2-year institutions into and though an HBCU leader in STEM, and into and through one of the STEM graduate programs at an HBCU or HWCU leader in STEM. This is in alignment with the PCAST reports and recommendations, the 2010 findings of the National Academy of Sciences Hrabowski Commission, the 2010 Commission on Civil Rights Report on HBCUs and STEM, and many findings by the United States Congress.

The STEMconnector® Community and its allies must move on all fronts to position HBCUs and MSIs as central components of a national and/or philanthropic strategy to enroll, retain, and graduate minority, low–income, first generation, and other "at–risk students," as well as veterans and students who are differently abled. HBCUs have developed and honed models of successfully educating minority students for more than 150 years, yet, they are undervalued assets in serving students for whom postsecondary education has remained elusive as well as those who can thrive anywhere. The nation will get the most out of its higher education dollars and create greater value for America by investing more in HBCUs that have track records of producing in the most cost–effective and efficient manner, a diverse pipeline of the graduates that our economy needs. This is America's best approach to advancing the jobs–driven economy, STEMming the predominantly male, disproportionately White and Asian U.S. scientific and engineering workforce, and accelerating a pool of diverse, excellent STEM professionals.

About The National Association for Equal Opportunity in Higher Education (NAFEO)

The National Association for Equal Opportunity in Higher Education (NAFEO) is the 501 (c) (3), tax–exempt, not–for–profit umbrella organization of the nation's Historically Black Colleges and Universities (HBCUs) and Predominantly Black Institutions (PBIs). Founded in 1969, NAFEO is the only membership association of its kind, representing the presidents and chancellors of the diverse black colleges and universities: public, private and land–grant, two–year, four–year, graduate and professional, historically and predominantly black colleges and universities.

Whether an institution is one of the 39 private black colleges and universities that belong to UNCF, one of the 47 public colleges and universities that belong to the Thurgood Marshall College Fund; one of the 18 land–grant universities or 19 other public universities that belong to the National Association of State Universities and Land–grant Colleges' Office for the Advancement of Public Black Colleges; a black 2–year institution that belongs to the American Association of Community Colleges; or one of the new Predominantly Black Institutions (PBIs), the institution has a voice and a vote in NAFEO.

NAFEO was founded to provide an international voice for the nation's HBCUs and other equal educational opportunity institutions to place and maintain the issue of equal opportunity in higher education on the national agenda; to advocate policies, programs and practices designed to preserve and enhance HBCUs & PBIs; and to increase the active participation of blacks at every level in the formulation and implementation of policies and programs in American higher education.

About the Author

Lezli Baskerville is a 2014 Harvard University Advanced Leadership Fellow, where she designed a $1B sustainable endowment to fund HBCUs and students attending HBCUs. Baskerville is a constitutional rights lawyer, an accomplished small business and association senior executive, who is a recognized expert and author on equal educational and employment opportunity, education excellence, access/success/finance; pipeline issues, minority student persistence, diversity issues, and campaign design/direction.

Ms. Baskerville is recognized by STEMconnector® as one of "100 Women Leaders in STEM;" by Diverse Issues in Higher as one of "25Women Making a Difference;" by AOL Black Voices as one of the nation's "Top 10 Black Women in Higher Education;" and by Ebony Magazine for six consecutive years as one of America's Top 100 Most Influential Association Leaders. Baskerville is acknowledged in The History Makers as a distinguished lawmaker. Baskerville holds a Bachelor of Arts degree, with honors from Douglass College, Rutgers University, and was inducted into its Hall of Fame in recognition of her unstinting commitment to improving the quality of life of vulnerable populations. Attorney Baskerville holds a Juris Doctorate with honors from Howard University School of Law, an Honorary Doctorate of Laws from Benedict College, and a Doctorate of Humane Letters from Shaw University.

CHAPTER THIRTEEN

A Global Perspective

"Given the rapid speed of change in today's global marketplace, a country must invest in its greatest asset – its people - and train them to excel in science, engineering, and math."

-John Chambers, Chief Executive Officer
Cisco Systems

Excerpt from *100 CEO Leaders in STEM,* a publication by STEMconnector®

Advancing a Jobs–Driven Economy:
Corporate Social Responsibility Takes a Different Form
By: Michael Norris, Chief Operating Officer, President of the Corporate Services Market, Sodexo North America

History tells us that change, progress and long–term success trace their origins to necessity, vision, and passionate commitment. I believe our economy, our nation and the global marketplace are converging at an intersection that requires change, demands that progress be made, and offers the promise of long–term success. I am passionately committed to developing the next generation of STEM leaders, and for that matter, helping to prepare all young leaders entering our workforce to be successful. With the global marketplace expanding at unprecedented rates, demographic shifts and emerging global trends playing an ever–increasing role in the American economy, it has become increasingly apparent that we as business leaders, industry experts and academics can offer a more comprehensive approach to preparing our future leaders to successfully enter the workforce.

The numbers speak for themselves. My company alone plans to add nearly 100,000 jobs over the next 10 years. When considering those kinds of growth targets, a focus on identifying, attracting and retaining the best talent is required. How then, do we develop and employ a strategy that ensures the next generation of STEM educated leaders are prepared for the jobs of tomorrow? Benjamin Franklin noted, "Tell me and I forget, teach me and I may remember, involve me and I learn.' Clearly, the key to effecting change, spurring progress and creating long–term success lies in a strategy based on and driven by meaningful engagement.

STEMconnector®'s Innovation Task Force & the STEM 2.0 Initiative
I would argue that such a strategy begins with reaching future employees long before they are ready to enter the workforce. One group that I've had the pleasure of working with over the last year is aiming to accomplish exactly that. STEMconnector®'s Innovation Task Force, a thirty–plus member consortium of leaders from industry, government, education, and the non–profit sectors are working towards identifying new pathways to STEM careers.

The task force has made STEM 2.0 its primary focus for 2014–2016. The STEM 2.0 initiative seeks to identify a number of critical new capability platforms that our next generation of talent needs in order to be successful in the future. The first three capability platforms (CPs), employability skills, innovation excellence, and digital fluency are applicable to all STEM fields and comprise the foundation of the initiative. The fourth "Hard Skills" platform will identify skills that are applicable to certain industries, including but not limited to: information technology; food and agriculture; and advanced manufacturing.

STEMconnector®'s Innovation Task Force is actively seeking partnerships to scale–up the STEM 2.0 initiative in the United States and globally. We are embracing the education community, aligning to state–level standards, involving teachers, and connecting to youth development organizations with strong STEM programming. We know that in order to make STEM 2.0 a reality, we must leverage the exponential power of the business sector.

The Applicability of STEM 2.0

My perspective has been shaped by a range of experiences across different industry sectors over the past 30 years. And from that experience, I have gleaned five essential ways business leaders can better support students considering a career in the STEM fields. I hope my recommendations open a dialogue among stakeholders who are committed to creating a stronger and more sustainable economy.

1. **Applying Theory to Practice**

   STEM students need exposure to practical applications of their subject matter. This is particularly relevant to the STEM fields. For example, Sodexo's National Research Director, Dr. Rachel Permuth, has a degree in Mathematics and another in Biostatistics. While Rachel loved math as a student, she didn't completely grasp the idea that it could inform business decisions until she entered the workforce. I am convinced that no age is "too early" to expose children to how education aligns with jobs. One way of introducing this to students is STEM Career Accelerator Day, a nationwide event that brings students into major STEM facilities to experience firsthand the excitement and rewarding potential of a STEM career.

2. **Moving Beyond People Skills: Instructing Students on the "Art" of Social Influence and Persuasion**

   Young students may be natural negotiators, but there are finer points to being influential in the workplace that can be taught and cultivated. In terms of STEM 2.0 priorities, I firmly believe that the ability to be persuasive – as well as using social influence appropriately and ethically are some of the key skill–sets today's students need to be successful in the future. The art of social influence and persuasion will be explored within the Employability Skills CP, and I would argue for the following to also be included:
   - Goal Setting
   - Making evidence–based decisions
   - Data Visualization
   - Story Telling (as an art of persuasion)

3. **Staying Relevant**

   In order to cultivate student interest in STEM fields, we – business leaders, industry experts and academics – share a responsibility for providing relevant and exciting examples of STEM job opportunities to impressionable students. Recently, I spoke to the head of the National Facilities Management Association, who noted that if we provide a "big picture" simulation of the roles and responsibilities of engineers and facilities managers, this could generate more interest in the field, rather than simply describing the tactical aspects of the day–to–day job as if we were reading from lesson plans.

   Case in point, a student learning how to design and manage huge complexes where people will learn and work in the future, and how to make them comfortable and productive – bringing a wide array of technological advances to bear – provides a vision and roadmap for how we should be explaining the field of facilities management (as opposed to a rote, tactical understanding of how boilers work, or how to adjust building temperature, etc.).

4. **Actively Seeking Educational Partnerships**

Educational institutions within our communities typically welcome the opportunity to engage with local businesses. However, it takes time to develop relationships between different types of organizations (such as education and non–profits) and even longer to develop a level of trust. The first step for any business leader is an earnest commitment to understand the missions, goals and strategies being pursued by potential partner organizations. Visiting high schools, vocational schools, and community colleges is a must. Listening to the administrators, teachers, and students discuss their frustrations and aspirations is required. Then, looking for ways to establish mutually beneficial partnerships is possible.

From our experience and learning, Sodexo has numerous internship and fellowship programs that allow students to experience STEM in action. For instance, one of our high–school sophomores is working with our Healthcare team on developing community health strategy; a freshman is college is developing a research study to understand Quality of Life factors among manufacturing workers. These are first–hand experiences that the students would not receive without active partnerships between Sodexo and educational institutions at many levels.

5. **Being a Mentor!**

Research on mentor–student relationships has shown dramatic impact on a mentee's (or an apprentice's) performance. Perhaps more importantly, is how those relationships are framed. We have to ask ourselves whether we are challenging students (at the appropriate level) with meaningful engagement. Are we treating them with respect and soliciting their ideas? Do we provide constructive feedback to students? Conversely, do we give accolades for great performance and innovation?

I am so enthusiastic about the promise of our future leaders and the opportunity we, as today's leaders, share to serve as catalysts for change, progress and long–term success. While the future will be lived by today's youth, the conditions of that future can be shaped and set by our current generation of leaders – you and me – and defined by our level of commitment toward meaningful engagement. My hope is to capture the attention and imagination of those young, creative minds, and help lead them to the STEM disciplines. By doing this, we act on our responsibility to create a better future – with a more engaged workforce, stronger communities and a vibrant, level global marketplace.

About Sodexo

Sodexo, Inc. is a world leader in Quality of Daily Life Solutions in the U.S., Canada and Mexico, with $8.0 billion (USD) in annual revenue   (FY2010) and 120,000 employees in North America. Sodexo, Inc. serves   more than ten million consumers daily in corporations, health care, long term care and retirement centers, schools, college campuses, government and remove sties.

Sodexo, Inc., headquartered in Gaithersburg, MD, is a member of Sodexo Group, and funds the Sodexo Foundation, an independent charitable organization that, since its founding in 1999, has distributed more than 945 grants, totaling more than $15   million to hunger–related organizations.

About the Author

Michael Norris was appointed Chief Operating Officer of Sodexo North America, an $8 billion solutions provider, and Market President of the Corporate Services Market in June 2005. Mr. Norris has also served as President of Sodexo's International Large Accounts market, representing 32 of the largest global accounts and is the market champion for Sodexo's Global Business & Industry Group.

Michael brings proven leadership experience in the food service and facilities management sector with a global business perspective. Michael is also an Executive Sponsor of Sodexo's Pan–Asian Network Group (PANG), the Women's Network Group (WiNG) and the Cross Market Diversity Council.

He has direct reporting responsibility to President and Chief Operating Officer George Chavel and Mr. Norris has an extensive background in driving sales growth and increasing market share and currently oversees Sodexo's B&I portfolio that has annual revenues of more than $1.4 billion and serves more than 1,800 client locations nationwide. Mr. Norris has also served as President of Sodexo's International Large Accounts market, representing 32 of the largest global accounts and is the market champion for Sodexo's Global Business & Industry Group.

Mr. Norris, in 2015, became the CEO of Sodexo North America Health Care.

Building a Global Action Platform for Jobs:
One Million Start–Ups for One Billion Jobs

By: Dr. Scott T. Massey, Chairman and Chief Executive Officer, Cumberland Center

From concerns in the U.S. and Europe over income disparities, to the bankruptcy of Detroit, continued turmoil across the Mideast, to sluggish growth in Japan and the EU, and the current slowing and rebalancing of the Chinese economy, there remain clear challenges to stimulating and sustaining a new round of economic growth in major regional economies and the world. The diverse challenges, like those just mentioned (among many others that could be listed) may appear disconnected, but in fact, are not. Instead, the various economic challenges we face to creating the jobs needed for the future are interconnected symptoms of an underlying economic dynamic.

Simply put, the world now faces an intensified need to create sustainable prosperity built on platforms of opportunity open to every person. The combination of globalization, mobile technology, free markets, global capital markets, and the increased speed of competition and change have created vast new opportunities for corporations and individuals, but this perfect storm of change has also disrupted economic systems "close to home" in which a majority of the world's population lives. Because of this, and as the human population grows toward nine billion, it is now urgent to put strategies in place that "re–localize" economies and create "new growth" at the regional level, like the new growth vegetation in an old growth forest.

In short, to move beyond the current spiral of economic crises, we need to take steps to create sustainable, shared, long–term prosperity; and to do this, we need to build dynamic innovation hubs in regions all around the world. Regionally based innovation hubs are the new engines of prosperity and platforms for broad–based economic opportunity and good jobs.

One new global effort to move toward this goal has been recently launched. In November 2012, four hundred leaders from ten nations, representing the corporate, research, government, finance, media, foundation, and NGO sectors convened at the Global South Summit in Nashville, Tennessee USA. The goal of this international gathering was to begin framing an agenda for abundance with a focus on three interconnected issues; food, health, and prosperity. At the conclusion of the inaugural Summit, an integrated approach to these three issues was defined as an urgent priority needing attention over the coming three to five years.

Why Food, Health and Prosperity?
Founding leaders in this new global initiative started with an economic concern –how to advance sustainable economic growth and prosperity for a growing world population. The organizers found strong interest in mobilizing cross sector leadership to find new paths and models for economic development aimed at sustainable job creation. Further, it became clear that the growing global challenges of food and health - basics for human capital - had to be addressed while developing ways to expand shared prosperity.

This vision of an economic future of sustainable growth and expanding opportunity for everyone requires a special lens. To balance growth, sustainability, and opportunity leaders identified a need for an adaptable model and tools, a nimble, neutral infrastructure well–suited for the fast–emerging, complex conditions of the 21st century.

The elements of this model include industry clusters, disruptive innovations, regional economies, platforms for collaboration, and strategy for competitiveness. New technologies, the internet, pervasive knowledge/training, and mobile devices are also key to the mix.

Today, the focus on food, health and prosperity has been further validated by the release of the new Sustainable Development Goals (that replace the Millennial Goals). The SDGs list the following as the top three priorities:

- To eliminate poverty everywhere (prosperity)
- To eliminate hunger, improve nutrition, and achieve sustainable agriculture (food)
- To provide a healthy life to all (health)

A Vision of Abundance

Instead of a focus on scarcity and conflict, this new initiative focuses on the creation of abundance as the central organizing idea. How can we focus economic activity in regional innovation hubs to expand opportunity and unleash innovation? How can the whole human population flourish —while also allowing the environment and ecosystems that make life possible also flourish?

Key drivers for innovation and prosperity are food and health. If economic growth requires a broad base of talented, innovative people working together, then food and health are critical. In fact, food and health are baseline measures of the asset strength of the major economic driver of today's economy—human capital.

Between the current state of affairs for healthcare and a major transformation of health systems lie thorny issues of realigning financial incentives while managing the demographic shifts toward an older population with greater health needs and while integrating large new populations to modern healthcare. As with economic and food issues, time is running out to address changes in healthcare; and under this pressure there is a growing sense of urgency to find transformative healthcare solutions and new financial models.

In terms of food, while the world currently produces enough food to feed everyone on the planet, the logistics and political consensus are missing to distribute what is produced. Food reserves have not been replenished since the 2010 drought, which puts the world on the brink of food shortages. Disputes are raging over the role of genetically modified foods, the composition of a healthy, nutritious diet, and the role of government to enforce diet, food policies, food safety, and government's role in funding research and food relief efforts.

Building a Global Action Plan

The challenge the world faces now is to frame long term solutions and innovations that have the capacity and promise to create abundant food, health, and prosperity for everyone on the planet. Solutions are simultaneously local, regional and global. In short, solutions require local cross–sector leaders to imagine, to explore - and to specify - how innovation can create abundance, and how we can efficiently and much more effectively connect and network invested leaders, research institutions and innovators to collaborate in fulfilling the promise of abundance.

The Global Action Platform has been created as a mechanism to connect and align efforts to create abundance through innovation. The Platform is built around four interconnected functions: Convene, Challenge, Connect, and Communicate. Through the Platform, an integrated series of financial investments, tied to leadership summits, action plans, and global multimedia communications are being implemented over the next five years.

Innovation for Abundance

The future welfare of both human beings and the planet depend on a distinctly human resource - innovation. Our emerging economies demand more timely solutions, access to innovation, improved efficiencies and high impact results. On this there is broad consensus. In order for societies to be innovative, people must be able to thrive; they need food, health, and the tools and systems of innovation that produce sustainable prosperity.

According to research reported by Jim Clifton of Gallup Poll, the U.S. economy needs to create one million successful new start–ups to sustain current economic levels and create one billion middle class jobs here and around the world. With a growing network of university–business–government–NGO–media partners, including STEMconnector®, the Global Action Platform aims to help launch one million start–ups to create one billion jobs, in short, to become a leading change agent for a world of abundance.

About Cumberland Center

Cumberland Center is a non–profit university–business alliance to build innovation hubs that transform innovation into prosperity, regionally and globally.

The Center executes its mission through the Global Action Platform. The Platform
- Advances a social leadership movement for abundance (Convene)
- Invests in innovation and new businesses (Challenge)
- Deploys online work groups (Connect)
- Delivers global communications to accelerate action (Communicate)
- Focuses on the intersection of food, health, and prosperity as prerequisites to future success and well–being

Global Action Platform is a neutral, collaborative platform to align resources and mobilize global corporations, universities, government agencies, NGOs, investors, and entrepreneurs to create abundance through innovation in food, health, and prosperity. Programs include an annual Global Action Summit; forums at the World Bank, National Press Club and Meridian International Center; multi–million dollar impact investments and awards; online services; a global Summit Fellows program for young leaders; publications and annual reports; content sharing with the G8, G20, APEC, and BRIC Summits; and a global corporate award program for shared value.

The programs of the Global Action Platform are operated by Cumberland Center, which is based at oneC1TY, a twenty–acre innovation hub being developed in Nashville, Tennessee (USA) to anchor a network of related campuses around the world. Cumberland Center serves as the think tank and concierge for the campus and its network.

About the Author

Dr. Scott T. Massey, Chairman and Chief Operating Officer of Cumberland Center. Cumberland Center is a university–business alliance to transform innovation into prosperity through the growth of regional innovation hubs. He is the immediate past President and Chief Operating Officer of The Meridian Institute (Indianapolis), a national think tank with programs in economics, education, and healthcare. His other prior roles include President and Chief Operating Officer, The Learning Collaborative, President and Chief Operating Officer, The Indiana Humanities Council, and Founding President and Chief Operating Officer of the Leonard Bernstein Center.

In addition to his leadership role at the Center, Dr. Massey is a Professor of Strategy and Competitiveness and a member of Michael Porter's Microeconomics of Competitiveness global network. He is a member of the Global Advisory Council of the Diplomatic Courier and a member of the STEM Higher Education Council. Recently Dr. Massey has also served as Strategic Advisor for the 50th Anniversary, Lincoln Center; as a member of the Advisory Board, Council on Competitiveness; and strategic advisor to YouScience, an educational software company.

Nationalizing Globalization: Saudi Arabia Prepares Future Leaders

By: Dr. Amal Fatani, Consultant and General Supervisor of Female Affairs,
Saudi Arabian Ministry of Higher Education

The Kingdom of Saudi Arabia shoulders the burden of a continuous need to nurture a futuristic climate ripe for entrepreneurial innovative overtures that will catapult their ambitious youth into the next technology–based millennium. This must be undertaken whilst maintaining its indigenous identity as a spiritual leader in the land that houses the two holy mosques. Fortunately, the Kingdom is endowed with an intrinsic alignment of its spiritual and scientific cultures, supporting the rapid change that is taking place. The Kingdom's efforts of progressive advancement in all sectors and particularly in the STEM fields will empower today's youth to become tomorrow's leaders strengthening the Kingdom, the region, and the world.

The region has previously had global impact. The first was in the 7th century when it became the cradle of Islam, becoming the center for learning and scientific advances. Muslim scholars made major contributions in many fields, including medicine, biology, philosophy, astronomy, arts and literature. Many of the ideas and methods pioneered by Muslim scholars became the foundation of modern sciences.

The second regional global impact began in the mid–20th century when the discovery of vast oil deposits propelled it into a key economic and geo–political role. The modern country's infrastructure and modern technological advancements were established constantly emphasizing the importance of diversifying its economy and an emphasis on promoting private enterprise and investment.

Saudi Arabia is boldly and proactively facing the demands of globalization. Our nation has achieved significant progress in its determined transformation into a knowledge economy, according to the Knowledge Economy Index (KEI) 2012 Rankings published by the World Bank. Ranking first worldwide in terms of progress made since 2000 and 50th on the knowledge economy index, advancing 26 places from its position in the 2000 report. The Kingdom recorded significant progress on the three indicators: advancing 30 positions on the education indicator, occupying the 58th place; advancing 17 positions on the economic incentives and institutional regime, occupying 60th place; and advancing 46 positions on the information and communication technology indicator, occupying 21st place. The financial and human capital investment as well as the national achievement represented by these figures is remarkable. These global rankings also spotlight Saudi Arabia's commitment to education as an important tool to achieve a viable knowledge economy.

The Saudi Arabian Higher Education sector has expanded exponentially during the last century, starting off with the establishment in 1925 of "the General Directorate of Education and the inauguration of the first government school in Saudi Arabia. In 1953 it evolved into the Ministry of Education undertaking the daunting task of setting up the modern systems of both general and higher education.

From a single university (King Saud University) established in 1957, to 569 universities and institutes of higher learning, with hundreds of thousands of registered students (1,358,312 students in 2013, 48 percent females), including specialized universities such as King Abdulla University for Science and Technology, a research–based world class University; as well as Princess Nora Bint Abdul Rahman University, the largest female University in the World.

The Ministry of Higher Education (MOHE), as a separate entity, was established in 1975. It assumes many tasks in implementing the state's educational policy in higher education including: complying with the regulations; supervising universities in terms of planning coordination, follow–up; observing concomitance between current and futuristic development and available personnel so as to optimize the use thereof; meeting the actual future needs in terms of national, technical and administrative competencies and specialties.

A pivotal policy of the Kingdom was enhancing its national efforts with international experiences and expertise. Therefore it established in (1928) schools for preparing its budding population for scholarships abroad. This has evolved during the last century culminating in the launch of King Abdullah Scholarship Program (KASP) in 2005, the largest program in history and in the world. Approximately 147 thousand students (1/4 females) are studying in universities all around the world in a multitude of specialties including Education (3.2 percent), humanities & arts (4.7 percent), social sciences, business & law (33.7 percent), science (16.4 percent), engineering, manufacturing & construction (21.7 percent), health & welfare (17.4 percent). The Ministry of Higher Education supervises the scholarship recipients through cultural attaché bureaus and a highly advanced portal. The Ministry also works towards consolidating cultural relations with academic and educational institutions and organizations abroad, and acquainting them with the development, civilization, and progress within the Kingdom.

The expansion of higher education and national economy presented many challenges in combination with the desired opportunities: the increasing demand for access to higher education, the need for correspondence levels between the capacity of its institutions and those of the production and service sectors in the field of scientific research and technical development, the necessity to keep up with modern and contemporary technological developments in education, the task of upgrading the performance level of its institutions at home, and the bolstering of compatibility levels between its outputs and the requirements of the development, and the job market needs.

The government responded to these challenges with increased funding providing the critical support necessary for both growth and the matching of requirements for the upcoming millennium. Currently higher education receives a substantial sum from the government's annual budget. Saudi Arabia has the highest percentage of public expenditure on higher education as a percentage of its gross domestic product, GDP (2.9 percent) as compared to the global average (0.8 percent).

Advancing a Jobs-Driven Economy

The Ministry of Higher Education met the specific challenges noted above and others by developing a progressive process within the higher educational system called the "Horizon" (Afaq) plan, formulated in alignment with the 20 year KSA National Science Technology and Innovation Plan (NSTIP), the national communication and information technology plan, and the comprehensive industrial national strategy. By taking into consideration the objectives and projects of the strategic plans of the government sectors affiliated to the Ministry, resources are maximized and synergies created strengthen all the stakeholders

In support of these comprehensive plans for the Kingdom that target matching requirements for the upcoming millennium, MOHE gives priority to scientific and technical disciplines through consolidating the infrastructure, such as research centers and advanced labs; developing and qualifying personnel, both scientifically and technically; and, expanding graduate and multidisciplinary programs.

The National Science Technology and Innovation Plan (NSTIP) is a multibillion Riyal undertaking involving over 190 programs and 62 government organizations. It aims to develop the Kingdom's human resources, promote R&D and innovation, support the commercialization of research and technology, and increase collaboration between academia, the private sector and industry. The integrated framework of guidance outlined in the plan intends to guarantee the continued efforts of all stakeholders to realize the Kingdom's long–term objective – the creation of the Kingdom of Saudi Arabia as a knowledge–based society and economy by the year 2025. Implementation of the plan is organized by the King Abdulaziz City for Science and Technology (KACST), an independent scientific organization administratively reporting to the Prime Minister.

Founded in 1977, KACST is both the national science agency for KSA and its national laboratories. KACST has a pivotal role in supporting and financing scientific research in universities; has a key role in related data collection and scientific publishing; and it manages the patent office. It has established Joint Centers of Excellence with leading R&D organizations around the world including: MIT, Stanford, Oxford, Cambridge, UCLA, UCSD, China Academy of Sciences, CSIR, NASA, Franhofer, EMPA, IBM, Intel, Boeing, Clariant, Selex and Si–ware.

The synergism between various entities will ensure that global demands of the future work force will be met effectively. Graduates of Higher Education should be highly productive individuals focusing on developing the necessary job market and social skills needed for the workforce. Thus a series of applied programs have been put into place and are meant to help qualify graduates for jobs that are much in demand in the local and global job market. Partnership with the industry and business sector are highlighted in a program geared to help ensure the improvement of creativity and research potential as well as the development of human resources by establishing links between universities and the industrial sector. There is a continued focus on bringing women into education and professional sectors through programs that diversify education opportunities for all, especially females. Moreover, higher education sectors, as well as public plus private sectors in the Kingdom, are undergoing an electronic transformation in order to raise efficiency and effectiveness, as well as provide easy and affordable services to all members of the community accessible anywhere, at any time.

This visionary plan for progressive advancement into the next millennium has been created for the Kingdom of Saudi Arabia under the leadership of King Abdullah. It is illuminated by thorough strategic planning, defined by the comprehensive coordination of key stakeholders, and enlivened by a committed responsiveness to the demands of the global arena. As a key stakeholder, the role of higher education is recognized as critical. The role of STEM education has been given priority. The Kingdom is answering the global call to action by preparing its youth to build and to lead in the economy of the future.

About the Author

Dr. Fatani currently serves as Consultant and General Supervisor of Female Affairs at the Ministry of Higher Education for the Kingdom of Saudi Arabia. Prior to that position, she held the position of General Supervisor of Female Sections in All Sectors in the Ministry of Higher Education. Dr. Fatani is a recognized thought–leader with a strong executive presence, she has served on numerous committees, authored several publications, and travels globally attending general and specialized events and symposia.

Previously, Dr. Fatani held three administrative positions as Dean of nine Scientific and Medical Colleges, Vice Dean of Pharmacy College and Vice Chairperson of the Department of Pharmacology and Toxicology at King Saud University (KSU) in Riyadh, KSA.

She continues to serve on the KSU faculty as an Associate Professor. Dr. Fatani's research has been published in dozens of journals including the Saudi Pharmaceutical Journal, The International Journal of Endocrinology, and the British Journal of Pharmacology. She was the Saudi Director of the Yale–King Saud international scientific twinning program that encouraged global cooperation on managing infectious diseases. Dr. Fatani was awarded the Rector Award for Excellence in Scientific Research and has published more than 28 specialized articles in renowned scientific journals. She currently serves as a board member of the Saudi Research Science Institute at King Abdullah University.

Dr. Fatani has been involved with key health organizations around the world, including The American Association of Pharmaceutical Scientists, the Zahra Society for Breast Cancer, the society for family safety, American Association of Pharmaceutical Scientists, The British Society for General Microbiology, the American Association for the Advancement of Science, the American Society of Health–System Pharmacists, and the International Society on Toxinology.

She is also a part time consultant for the King Abdulaziz and His Companions Foundation for Giftedness and Creativity (MAWHIBA), which mentors gifted and talented students throughout the Kingdom. She is very keen on networking with national and international, public and private sectors to promote social responsibility and sustainable development. Dr. Fatani holds a PhD in pharmacology and toxicology from the Department of Pharmaceutical Sciences at Strathclyde University in Glasgow, Scotland. Prior to her PhD, she obtained both her Master's and Bachelor's degrees in pharmacology at King Saud University.

CONCLUSION AND CALL TO ACTION

Conclusion & Call to Action

As substantiated by the expertise and insight from leading higher education, business, and community leaders, we are in critical need of rethinking and reimaging the system that supports STEM education and workforce preparedness. The often cited mismatch or skills gap reflects the opportunity to better align programs, policies, and practices that provide the foundation for student, institutional, and corporate effectiveness in support of local, regional, and national economic prosperity.

Higher education institutions, companies, communities, and policy makers must concurrently adopt a systems thinking and pipeline approach to STEM education and workforce development. Systems thinking reflects the understanding that each stakeholder's contribution shapes and is shaped by other sectors. The pipeline approach recognizes that STEM workforce readiness is the cumulative result of how students develop critical competencies as they progress through elementary, middle school, high school, and post–secondary education.

The result of the system redesign is nothing less than a revolution in the definition, development, and delivery of STEM education that equips students with the industry–defined skills and competencies necessary to thrive in the 21st century economy.

The Challenges
We cannot continue to stumble when it comes to the critical training necessary to support an increasingly STEM skills and jobs–based economy.

Workforce Preparedness
- Studies and testimony from educators and employers highlight the impact of the persistent misalignment between educational programs and workforce preparedness. Beyond the perception gap, business and higher education leaders must come together to ensure clear pathways from STEM education to employment in STEM careers. We must equip students with the skills and experience that companies require.

Workforce Sustainability
- In addition to addressing the effectiveness of education as a pathway to workforce readiness, the rapid pace of technology and demographic shifts necessitate additional focus on high-demand fields as well as an approach that broadens the appeal and engagement of underrepresented populations regarding the STEM workforce of the future. Ensuring a sustainable pipeline of STEM talent is fundamental to the health of companies and communities – we cannot afford to have millions of jobs remain unfilled. The relative dearth of women and minorities in STEM fields represents an opportunity to continue to grow and diversify the number of students who pursue STEM career pathways. While a demographic necessity, progress will require innovative approaches to policy and program outreach.

The Solutions

With the future of our communities and the economic prosperity of our country at stake, leaders across education, business, government, and communities must transcend boundaries and breakdown barriers to collaboration. Educators and employers must be active partners. Educators need to know and understand the needs of the business community. Businesses need to articulate their needs according to the skills and competencies they require. The necessary STEM education and workforce development revolution demands unprecedented cross–sector, multi–stakeholder collaboration, characterized by co–creation and co–ownership of curriculum development, student learning outcomes and workforce preparedness, and vibrant local economies.

Employers own STEM education as a critical driver of growth and innovation

- The jobs and employer–driven education and workforce system corroborated by business and education leaders alike requires that companies assume a leadership role in redefining a STEM education system that works. Companies and industries must clearly map specific skill and competency requirements, and desired credentials that they demand. In addition to actively participating in the reshaping of curriculum and programs, companies need to provide internships, apprenticeships, and project–based real–world opportunities for students to experience the application of academic coursework. Furthermore, support for ongoing teacher training and development ensures that educators remain abreast of both the technical requirements and real–life application of STEM subjects.

Educators embrace their roles as employment partners

- Increasingly supplemented by experiential, career–oriented learning, educational institutions need to actively engage in the dynamic STEM education ecosystem and supply the skills and competencies that align with industry demands. Often taking the form of specialized coursework that includes industry requirements, it is also important that training include portable credentials that will offer students options regarding career mobility and advancement. With the growing expectation that education impart career readiness and employment, secondary and post–secondary schools support better student outcomes with an ongoing regional assessment of high growth sectors, and the skills and competencies required. Roadmaps for higher learning institutions that align education and training with critical industry–defined skills and competencies offer concrete learning outcomes for defining STEM career pathways.

Community organizations and associations facilitate collaboration and scale

- When it comes to driving the effectiveness of the ongoing shift regarding STEM education and workforce development, there is strength in numbers. Bridging sector, industry, and geographic boundaries, community organizations and associations play a critical role in furthering the necessary transformation.

Government policy makers create an enabling environment for STEM education

- The aggregate voice of educators, employers, and communities is critical to informing and influencing enabling policies and scaling opportunities for public–private partnership. Policy and legislation that strengthens workforce development programs and underlying data, addresses higher education affordability, and supports underrepresented communities creates enabling environment for STEM education and accelerates workforce preparedness.

The Call to Action

A thriving STEM ecosystem will require collaboration and formal partnerships that bridge and align business, education, government, and community stakeholders. Ensuring that we are able to meet the demands of an increasingly STEM–based jobs–driven economy is the shared responsibility of education, business, community, and government leaders.

Align

- Assess and direct limited resources to high-growth sectors that require STEM skills

- Shift from a definition of success based on credit hours to the achievement of specific competencies, and from degree–defined to skills and competency–defined hiring criteria

Advance

- Develop and deploy STEM career roadmaps and toolkits that support structured educator and employer actions

- Pilot and scale immersive, skill and competency–based training to accelerate workforce readiness

Advocate

- All stakeholders must champion STEM education and STEM careers as critical to our sustainable economic prosperity

- Inform policy makers regarding the importance of continued investment in training to further develop the STEM talent pipeline in support of regional competitiveness

All hands on deck. The sustainable prosperity of our nation is at stake. Revolution demands STEM 2.0 and unprecedented, cross–sector collaboration.

As the STEM Workforce revolution is ongoing, we recognize that the opportunity to share and learn from one another does not end on the last page of this publication and cannot be limited to the physical confines of any book. What will support our continued success in honing and scaling innovative programs is our ability to remain connected and build on our shared knowledge in a dynamic and interactive manner.

The *Advancing a Jobs–Driven Economy's Virtual Community of Practice* provides an online platform, allowing our network to continue advancing the dialogue, programs, policies, and partnerships that are critical to an effective STEM education–to–employment system that is emerging in real time. Share your effective and innovative STEM Higher Education–Industry partnerships with us at
book.STEMconnector.org/SHEC.

About the STEM Higher Education Council Team
STEMconnector®

STEMconnector® is a consortium of companies, associations, societies, policy organizations, government entities, universities and academic institutions concerned with STEM education and the future of human capital. With several products and services, STEMconnector® is both a resource and a service, designed to link "all things STEM." STEMconnector®'s network includes organizations at the global, national, state and local levels. STEMconnector® focuses on the STEM workforce and jobs, with a particular emphasis on diversity and women. Our work spans the entire pipeline (Kindergarten to Jobs) and how STEM education experiences translate into careers.

STEMconnector®'s STEM Higher Education Council (SHEC) is the leadership forum of public and private colleges intently focused on STEM education and careers. SHEC envisions being the national catalyst for meeting the education and training needs of the global STEM workforce and educating the scientists, technologists, and innovators needed for a vibrant economy. SHEC hosted its inaugural event, Advancing a Jobs–Driven Economy: A National Summit, on October 8, 2014, at the Carnegie Institute for Science in Washington, DC. This unprecedented gathering brought together over 110 business and higher education leaders to showcase high impact cross–sector partnerships. SHEC members shared these Boundary–Breaking partnerships focused on improving the STEM ecosystem in higher education. A particular focus was on partnerships that lead to employment in STEM jobs. SHEC is committed to the highest levels of achievement and success for students, institutions, businesses and communities in all STEM related educational and professional endeavors.

Edie Fraser is CEO of STEMconnector® and Million Women Mentors (MWM), and a vice chair of Diversified Search, LLC. Edie has worked with more than 250 Fortune companies and associations to champion women's advancement. She has served on the boards of the University of Maryland Business School and the University of Tennessee School of Communications and Information. Edie has won 45 major awards for diversity and women's leadership, STEM, entrepreneurship and communications. She is the recipient of the Mosaic Woman Award and Lifetime Achievement Award from Diversity Woman Magazine. She has been inducted into the Enterprising Women Hall of Fame and is a founding member of C200. Edie was on the cover of *Women of Wealth Magazine* for her philanthropy and mentoring. She is the first woman to serve as Chairman of the World Affairs Council of DC and served on the national board of SCORE. Edie has written or served as publisher of many books, papers and articles. Examples include the *CEO Magazine, The Diversity Primer and The Diversity Officer.* Edie wrote a book, *Do Your Giving While You're Living,* with co-author Robyn Spizman, and another on women's entrepreneurship called *Risk to Riches: Women's Entrepreneurship in America.* Women and diversity support are at the core of Edie's work and values.

Edie built STEMconnector® with a dedicated team, starting officially in spring, 2011. Since then, STEMconnector® has grown to link with some 6600 organizations. The mission is to bring education, research, resources, best practices, communications and outreach—and provide resources such as the web site, *100 CEO Leaders in STEM, 100 Women Leaders in STEM*, STEMdaily, EdTech Weekly and STEM Results. STEMconnector® works with business, academia, government and nonprofit organizations, and media entities. Formerly, Edie built three best-practice initiatives: Diversity, Women and Corporate Communications. Edie is an entrepreneur having been president of a major PR Firm and a Public Affairs Firm and sold two companies throughout her career.

Dr. Talmesha Richards is Chief Academic and Diversity Officer at STEMconnector®. A vibrant scientist, she graduated from Johns Hopkins School of Medicine with a Ph.D. in Cellular and Molecular Medicine. Dr. Richards spent her undergraduate career at the University of Maryland Baltimore County (UMBC) as a Meyerhoff Scholar with a double major in Chemical Engineering and Mathematics, and also served as Captain of the Dance Team. She graduated Phi Beta Kappa, Magna Cum Laude, and as a Student-Athlete President's Scholar.

Nurturing both her academic and artistic sides, she danced as a National Football League Cheerleader for eight years and was Captain of the Washington Redskins Cheerleaders in 2012. Cheerleading afforded national and international travel, as well as combining her passions: community service, dancing, and science. As a Science Cheerleader, she participates in STEM mentoring, programming, and outreach. Dr. Richards' work with Science Cheerleader has been featured on various television programs including the Today Show.

In her role at STEMconnector®, Dr. Richards manages a portfolio of projects relating to the STEM Higher Education Council and Million Women Mentors. Prior to joining STEMconnector®, Dr. Richards advocated for the National Girls Collaborative Project, engaging stakeholders and representing national leadership. Her professional memberships include the American Association for the Advancement of Science (AAAS) and the Association for Women in Science (AWIS).

Dominik Sauter is Associate, Special Projects at STEMconnector®. He has a very diverse educational and cultural background as he grew up and went to school in 3 different countries: Germany, The Netherlands, and The United States. He is fluent in speaking, reading, and writing all three of the languages and he graduated from James Madison University Business School with a B.B.A. in International Business and a Marketing Concentration in 2014.

Ashley Post is Director, Projects at STEMconnector®. Graduating, with Honors, from George Mason University with a B.A. in Economics, Ashley spent her undergraduate studies pursuing her love of politics while interning in the offices of Senator Kirsten E. Gillibrand (D-NY) and Senator Mark R. Warner (D-VA). Prior to joining the STEMconnector® team, Ashley worked at CEB as a Business Development Representative.

Ted Wells is Vice President and Chief Strategy Officer at STEMconnector®. In his role at STEMconnector®, Ted manages a portfolio of projects relating to STEM K-12 education and workforce development. His clients include non-profit organizations, government entities and corporations. Key projects include the STEM Food and Ag Council, STEM Higher Education Council and STEMconnector®'s computer science education and maker outreach. He also has led the development of STEMconnector®'s Google+ On-Air Hangouts series that highlight issues in STEM education.

As the son of an engineer and an educator, this field is not far from his roots. He began his career as a French and Spanish teacher after attending Washington and Lee University. After 6 years as a teacher, Ted attended graduate school in International Affairs at the Elliott School at The George Washington University focusing on International Economic Affairs and International Development. He lives in the Columbia Heights neighborhood in Washington DC.

Resources

With several products and services, STEMconnector® is both a resource and a service, designed to link "all things STEM." The STEMconnector® website contains profiles of more than 20 categories of STEM–related entities and details 'Who is Doing What' on over 6,600 STEM–related organizations in all 50 states. STEMconnector®'s network includes organizations at the global, national, state and local levels. We encourage you to learn more about our STEMconnector®'s initiatives: STEM Higher Education Council, STEM Innovation Task Force, STEM Food and Ag Council and Million Women Mentors.

The STEMconnector® team advises and counsels our members and partners to ensure best STEM practices and scalable investments. STEMconnector® helps other organizations determine programs whose outcomes meet their desired objectives and needs.

STEMconnector® convenes its members and stakeholders through physical and virtual events, through STEM Councils and virtual STEM Town Halls, through Google Hangouts that regularly reach more than 500 thought leaders. As a free service from STEMconnector®, the STEMdaily newsletter provides nearly 17,000 diverse thought leaders in STEM education with a daily newsletter that increases connectivity across the nation and reaches over a million people through social media. STEMconnector®'s website has over 20,000 visitors a month. Finally, STEMconnector® recognizes leadership through its annual "100 Leaders in STEM" series, which has profiled over 176 organizations and executives, including 100 corporate CEOs.

If you are a college, university, skills training center, or business interested in advancing a jobs–driven economy, please contact us:

- STEM Higher Education Council website
  http://www.STEMconnector.org/higher–education

- 1200 New Hampshire Avenue NW
  Suite 820
  Washington, DC 20036

- Edie Fraser at Edie.Fraser@STEMconnector.org
  Office: (202) 296-5222

- Dr. Talmesha Richards at Talmesha.Richards@STEMconnector.org
  Office: (202) 304-1952

We will connect you with STEMconnector® members and other organizations that may be able to partner with you to meet your needs.

Appendix
Excerpts from 100 CEO Leaders in STEM,
a publication by STEMconnector®

"If the US truly wants to keep pace and remain competitive in the broader global economy, America's youth must be provided the education, skills and opportunity to discover, create and compete."

- Carlos A. Rodriguez, President and Chief Executive Officer
ADP

"Public-private partnerships are an essential component to creating a successful education-to-employment system because they allow for the marriage of supply and demand. Businesses can communicate their immediate and anticipated needs. Educational institutions and instructors can respond to the needs of the marketplace by structuring their programs and curricula around the local industries."

- Eric Spiegel, President and Chief Executive Officer
Siemens USA

"We have to encourage these students (women and underrepresented minorities) at home, at schools and in the community. It is critical that these students have access to, and interaction with, role models who can advise them of the wonderful career opportunities that will be available to them when they succeed."

- Dr. Wanda M. Austin, President and Chief Executive Officer
The Aerospace Corporation

"Developing partnerships with organizations that build and improve STEM programs allows Cargill to help educate the next generation of American scientists and engineers."

- Greg Page, Executive Chairman of the Board
Cargill

"There is a proven correlation between STEM jobs and GDP growth…STEM occupations are among the highest paying, fastest growing and most influential in driving economic growth…Caterpillar is competing not just for customers, but also for talent. We want the best talent in the world…"

- Doug Oberhelman, Chairman of the Board of Directors and Chief Executive Officer,
Caterpillar

"Industry must take a stronger stake in education by taking part in developing school's curriculum, creating internships for talented students and supporting communities with valuable education opportunities and resources…education is the single most important factor in achieving US innovative competitiveness globally."

- Tom Linebarger, Chairman and Chief Executive Officer
Cummins

"Corporations like Dow, which depend on a robust talent pipeline of skilled works, have a responsibility to invest their resources and expertise in improving STEM education in the United States."

- Andrew Liveris, President, Chairman, and Chief Executive Officer
The Dow Chemical Company

"We are proud to partner with organizations and fund efforts to expand STEM education. Like any company, we look to the return on investment with every capital allocation we make. By investing in human capital, STEM education and the workforce of tomorrow, the return on investment is clear and will ultimately create leaders who apply their skills to making healthcare better for everyone."

- George Paz, Chairman and Chief Executive Officer
Express Scripts

"The economy of the future will be driven by knowledge and ideas. Science, technology, engineering, and mathematics are going to be really important for everyone in this future, so we continue having great new companies and products that create more jobs and growth."

- Mark Zuckerberg, Founder and Chief Executive Officer
Facebook

"We need more mentors and role models for our students…people who can advise them about a STEM career and help them get on the right track." "Simply put, it takes lots of good people who can interact with students and guide them toward a STEM career."

- Marillyn Hewson, Chairman, President, and Chief Executive Officer
Lockheed Martin Corporation

"We live in a world where continuous change is the norm, and we need people skilled in science, technology, engineering and math to develop the innovative products and ideas that will allow us to keep up with the rapid pace of change. STEM subjects form the basis for innovation, which is the driver of economic growth and progress.".

,

- Indra Nooyi, Chairman and Chief Executive Officer
PepsiCo

References

1. Carnevale, A., Hanson, A.R., & Gulish, A. (2013, September). Failure to launch: Structural shift and the new lost generation. Retrieved from Georgetown University Center on Education and the Workforce https://cew.georgetown.edu/failuretolaunch/

2. Greenstone, M., Looney, A., Patashnik, J., & Yu, M. (2013, June). Thirteen economic facts about social mobility and the role of education. Washington, D.C.: The Hamilton Project: Advancing Opportunity, Prosperity, and Growth (Figure 7, p. 11). Retrieved from http://www.hamiltonproject. org/files/downloads_and_links/THP_13EconFacts_FINAL.pdf

3. Opportunity, Prosperity, and Growth (Figure 7, p. 11). Retrieved from http://www.hamiltonproject.org/files/ downloads_and_links/THP_13EconFacts_FINAL.pdf

4. National Academy of Sciences (US), National Academy of Engineering (US), and Institute of Medicine (US) Committee on Underrepresented Groups and the Expansion of the Science and Engineering Workforce Pipeline. (2011). Expanding underrepresented minority participation. Washington, DC: National Academies Press, p. 35. Retrieved from http://www.ncbi.nlm.nih.gov/books/NBK83370/

5. Kochan, T., Finegold, D., & Osterman, P. (2012, December). Who can fix the "middle-skills" gap? Harvard Business Review. Retrieved from https://hbr.org/2012/12/who-can-fix-the-middle-skills-gap

6. U.S. Census Bureau. (2014, January 29). Educational attainment in the United States: 2013 – Detailed tables. Retrieved from http://www. census.gov/hhes/socdemo/education/data/cps/2013/tables.html

7. U.S. Department of Education, Institute of Education Sciences, National Center for Education Statistics. 992 National Adult Literacy Survey and 2003 National Assessment of Adult Literacy (2003). National assessment of adult literacy (NAAL). Retrieved from http://nces.ed.gov/naal/kf_demographics.asp#2

8. American Academy of Arts and Sciences (2014). Restoring the Foundation: The Vital Role of Research in Preserving the American Dream. Cambridge, MA

9. Currall, S.C., Frauenheim, E., Perry, S.J., & Hunter, E.M. (2014). Organized Innovation: A Blueprint for Renewing America's Prosperity. Oxford, UK: Oxford University Press.

10. Block, F. & Keller, M.R. (2011). State of Innovation: The U.S. Government's Role in Technology Development. Boulder, CO: Paradigm Publishers.

11. Hunter, E.M., Perry, S.J., & Currall, S.C. Inside Multi-Disciplinary Science and Engineering Research Centers: The Impact of Organizational Climate on Invention Disclosures and Patents. Research Policy 40 (2011). 1226-1239.

12. Perry, S.J., Currall, S.C., & Stuart, T.E. (2007). The Pipeline from University Laboratory to New Commercial Product: An Organizational Framework For Technology Commercialization in Multidisciplinary Research Centers. In M. Epstein, T. Davila, & R. Shelton (eds.) The Creative Enterprise. Westport, CT: Praeger Publishers/Greenwood Publishing Group, pp. 85-105.

13. Baker, Stephen. "Putting a Price on Social Connections." Bloomberg Business Week. April 8, 2009. Accessed January 22, 2015. http://www.businessweek.com/stories/2009-04-08/putting-a-price-on-social-connectionsbusinessweek-business-news-stock-market-and-financial-advice.

14. "The Skills Gap and the State of the Economy." Recruiting Career Blog. October 29, 2013. Accessed January 22, 2015. http://blog.adeccousa.com/the-skills-gap-and-the-state-of-the-economy/

15. "The Talent Shortage Continues: How the Even Changing Role of HR Can Bridge the Gap," Manpower Group, 2014, p. 4, http://www.manpowergroup.us/campaigns/talent-shortage-2014/assets/pdf/2014_Talent_Shortage_WP_US.pdf

16. "Recovery: Job Growth And Education Requirements Through 2020." Georgetown University. Accessed January 22, 2015. https://cew.georgetown.edu/recovery2020.

17. "Half of New Graduates Are Jobless or Underemployed." USA Today. Accessed January 22, 2015. http://usatoday30.usatoday.com/news/nation/story/2012-04-22/college-grads-jobless/54473426/1.

18. "Managing the Talent Pipeline: A New Approach to Closing the Skills Gap," U.S. Chamber of Commerce Foundation, 2014, p. 13. Accessed January 22, 2015. http://www.uschamberfoundation.org/sites/default/files/Managing the Talent Pipeline.pdf.

19. "Talent Pipeline Management - Case Studies." U.S. Chamber of Commerce Foundation. Accessed January 22, 2015. http://www.uschamberfoundation.org/talent-pipeline-management-case-studies.

20. "Bill Gates - U.S. House of Representatives Committee Hearing." Bill & Melinda Gates Foundation. Accessed January 22, 2015. http://www.gatesfoundation.org/media-center/speeches/2008/03/bill-gates-us-house-of-representatives-committee-hearing.

21. "Task Force on American Innovation." Accessed January 22, 2015. https://www.ieeeusa.org/policy/policy/2014/031214.pdf

22. "Preparing The Next Generation Of STEM Innovators: Identifying and Developing Our Nation's Human Capita." National Science Foundation. Accessed January 9, 2015. http://www.nsf.gov/nsb/publications/2010/nsb1033.pdf

23. "The Best Jobs For 2014." Forbes. Accessed January 9, 2015. http://www.forbes.com/pictures/mkl45efdek/the-best-jobs-for-2014/

24. "Numbers of U.S. Doctorates Awarded Rise for Sixth Year, but Growth Slower." Nsf.gov. Accessed January 22, 2015. http://www.nsf.gov/statistics/infbrief/nsf10308/.

25. Ibid.

26. Ibid.

27. "Labor Force Statistics from the Current Population Survey." U.S. Bureau of Labor Statistics. Accessed January 22, 2015. http://www.bls.gov/cps/.

28. Lotto, Jill. Are They Really Ready to Work?: Employers' Perspectives on the Basic Knowledge and Applied Skills of New Entrants to the 21st Century U.S. Workforce. United States: Conference Board :, 2006.

29. Landis, Jim. "FOCUS: Job Skills Gap Widens at High Cost to U.S. Economy." The Herald News, Fall River, MA. January 1, 2013. Accessed January 22, 2015. http://www.heraldnews.com/article/20131220/News/312209922.

30. Cook, Dan. "Employers Spending More on Training." Employers Spending More on Training. January 1, 2014. Accessed January 22, 2015. http://www.benefitspro.com/2014/01/16/employers-spending-more-on-training.

31. Cleckler, Bob. "The Business of Illiteracy." Ending English Functional Illiteracy. January 1, 2012. Accessed January 22, 2015. http://www.englishliteracyinfo.com/the-business-of-illiteracy-3/.

32. Rothwell, Jonathan. "The Hidden STEM Economy." The Brookings Institution. June 10, 2013. Accessed January 22, 2015. http://www.brookings.edu/research/reports/2013/06/10-stem-economy-rothwell.

33. For purposes of this discussion, postsecondary includes two and four year credit-awarding educational institutions as well as credentials that are either for credit or non-credit offerings.

34. "What America Needs to Know About Higher Education Redesign." Gallup-Lumina Foundation Report. January 1, 2014. Accessed January 22, 2015. http://www.gallup.com/services/176759/america-needs-know-higher-education-redesign.aspx.

35. Alssid, Julian. "A New Gallup Survey Says Colleges and Employers Disagree About How Workforce-Ready Graduates Are -- Who's Right?" The Huffington Post. January 1, 2014. Accessed January 22, 2015. http://www.huffingtonpost.com/julian-l-alssid/a-new-gallup-survey-says-_b_4862669.html.

36. "Accenture 2013 Skills and Employment Trends Survey: Perspectives on Training." Accenture. January 1, 2013. Accessed January 22, 2015. http://www.accenture.com/us-en/Pages/insight-accenture-2013-skills-employment-trends-survey-perspectives-on-training.aspx.

37. "Employment Projections: 2012-2022 Summary." U.S. Bureau of Labor Statistics. December 19, 2013. Accessed January 9, 2015. http://www.bls.gov/news.release/ecopro.nr0.htm

38. "Manufacturing Industry Making a Comeback." The Daily News of Newburyport. Accessed January 9, 2015. http://www.newburyportnews.com/news/manufacturing-industry-making-a-comeback/article_75e4dc8b-3155-5303-a6f8-fdc6c1a21ce3.html.

39. "Education at a Glance: 2014." OECD. 2014. Accessed January 22, 2015. http://www.oecd.org/edu/Education-at-a-Glance-2014.pdf.

40. "The Employment Situation - December 2014." Bureau of Labor Statistics. January 1, 2014. Accessed January 22, 2015. http://www.bls.gov/news.release/pdf/empsit.pdf.

41. "Four Year Myth: Make College More Affordable." Complete College America. 2014 Accessed January 22, 2015. http://completecollege.org/wp-content/uploads/2014/11/4-Year-Myth.pdf.

42. "STEM 2.0: Innovation Critical for Workplace Skills Development." STEM 2.0: Innovation Critical for Workplace Skills Development. Accessed January 9, 2015. http://www.diplomaticourier.com/news/sponsored/1976-stem-2-0-innovation-critical-for-workplace-skills-development

43. "For Profit Higher Education: The Failure to Safeguard the Federal Investment and Ensure Student Success." United State Senate. Accessed January 9, 2015. http://www.help.senate.gov/imo/media/for_profit_report/PartI-PartIII-SelectedAppendixes.pdf.

44. "Students Still Lag in International Comparisons." US News. September 1, 2014. Accessed November 22, 2014. http://www.usnews.com/news/articles/2014/09/11/us-chamber-of-commerce-students-still-lag-in-international-competitiveness.

45. Beach, Gary J. The U.S. Technology Skills Gap: What Every Technology Executive Must Know to save America's Future. Hoboken, New Jersey: John Wiley & Sons, 2013.

46. Kidder, Tracy. The Soul of a New Machine. Boston: Little, Brown, 1981.

47. Carnevale, A.P., Rose, S.J., Hanson, A.R. (2012), Certificates: Gateway to gainful employment and college degrees. Georgetown Center on Education and the Workforce, Washington D.C. Retrieved from http://knowledgecenter.completionbydesign.org/sites/default/files/388%20Carnevale%20Rose%202012.pdf

48. Carnevale, A.P., Rose, S.J., (Winter 2012). Issues in Science and Technology, Forum, p. 16.

49. "Rockit FullStack Web Development Bootcamp." Rockit Bootcamp. Accessed November 20, 2014. http://www.rockitbootcamp.com.

50. Course Report. (November 2014). Alumni Spotlight.

51. "Job Openings and Labor Turnover - November 2014." Bureau of Labor Statistics. U.S. Department of Labor. Web. 21 Jan. 2015. http://www.bls.gov/news.release/pdf/jolts.pdf

52. Jolly, E. J., Campbell, P. B., & Perlman, L. K. (2004). Engagement, capacity and continuity: A trilogy for student success. Report commissioned by the GE Foundation. Retrieved July 3, 2010 from http://www.campbell-kibler.com/trilogy.pdf

53. "The National Higher Education and Workforce Initiative: Forging Strategic Partnerships for Undergraduate Innovation and Workforce Development." Business Higher Education Forum. June 1, 2013. Accessed December 2, 2014. http://www.bhef.com/sites/g/files/g829556/f/201308/2013_report_playbook.PDF.

54. Boykin, A. W. The effects of movement expressiveness in story content and learning context on the analogical reasoning performance of African-American children. Journal of Negro Education 70 (2002). 72–81.

55. Jarvela, S., Lehtinen, E., & Salonen, P. Socio-emotional orientation as a mediating variable in the teaching-learning interaction: Implications for Instructional Design. Scandinavian Journal of Educational Research 44(3) (2000). P. 293.

56. Ladson-Billings, Gloria. "But That's Just Good Teaching! The Case For Culturally Relevant Pedagogy." Theory Into Practice, 1995, 159-65.

57. Bracey, J. M. (2013). The culture of learning environments: Black student engagement and cognition in math. In J. Leonard &D.B. Martin (Eds.), The brilliance of Black children in mathematics: Beyond the numbers and toward new discourse (pp. 171-194). Charlotte, NC: Information Age Publishing.

58. Patterson, Eann A., Patricia B. Campbell, Ilene Busch-Vishniac, and Darrell W. Guillaume. "The Effect of Context on Student Engagement in Engineering." European Journal of Engineering Education, 2011, 211-24.

59. Hailey, C; Stallworth, Chandra Austin; Denson, Cameron; and Householder, Daniel L., "The Influence of MESA Activities On Underrepresented Students NSF DR K-12 Proposal 1020019". Mechanical and Aerospace Engineering Faculty Publications. Paper 71 2014. Retrieved from http://digitalcommons.usu.edu/mae_facpub/71/

60. Brown, J. S., A. Collins, and P. Duguid. "Situated Cognition and the Culture of Learning." Educational Researcher, 1989, 32-42.

61. "Pre-Collegiate Development Program | University of Colorado Colorado Springs." Pre-Collegiate Development Program | University of Colorado Colorado Springs. Accessed January 22, 2015. http://www.uccs.edu/~pcdp/.

62. Anschutz Foundation Report. Obtained 11/18 from Tom Dewar, development

63. "CISCO, UCCS Partnership Shared with Global Audience." UCCS Communique. January 21, 2011. Accessed September 22, 2014. Retrieved from http://communique.uccs.edu/?p=2717

64. Lowell, Linsday B., Hal Salzman, Hamutal Bernstein, and Everett Henderson. "Steady as She Goes? Three Generations of Students through the Science and Engineering Pipeline." October 1, 2009. Accessed September 30, 2014. http://policy. rutgers.edu/faculty/salzman/SteadyAsSheGoes.pdf.

65. Hrabowski III, F. A. Broadening Participation in the American STEM Workforce. BioScience 62(4), (2012), 325-326.

66. Kaye, Husbands Fealing, and Myers Samuel. "Pathways v. Pipelines to Broadening Participation in the Stem Workforce." ResearchGate. January 13, 2012. Accessed November 6, 2014. http://www. researchgate.net/publication/256014812_Pathways_v._Pipelines_ to_Broadening_Participation_in_the_Stem_Workforce.

67. Adkins, Rodney. "America Desperately Needs More STEM Students. Here's How to Get Them." Forbes. July 12, 2012. Accessed December 13, 2014. http://www.forbes.com/sites/forbesleadershipforum/2012/07/09/ america-desperately-needs-more-stem-students-heres-how-to-get-them/.

68. Eccles, Jacquelynn S.e. "Where Are All the Women? Gender Differences in Participation in Physical Science and Engineering." January 1, 2007. Accessed November 20, 2014. http:// www.rcgd.isr.umich.edu/garp/articles/eccles07.pdf.

69. Jones, Ann C., Eileen Scanlon, and Gill Clough. "Mobile Learning: Two Case Studies of Supporting Inquiry Learning in Informal and Semiformal Settings." Computers & Education, 2012, 21-32.

70. Rennie, L. J., Feher, E., Dierking, L. D., & Falk, J. H. Toward an Agenda for Advancing Research on Science Learning in Out-of-School Settings. Journal of Research in Science Teaching 40(2), (2003). 112-120.

71. Bevan, Bronwyn, and Robert J. Semper. "Mapping Informal Science Institutions onto the Science Education Landscape." January 1, 2006. Accessed January 22, 2015. http://cils.exploratorium. edu/pdfs/CILS BAI_Bevan & Semper_Mapping ISIs.pdf.

72. Lynch, M. G. (2012). Educating America's Talent in Science, Technology, Engineering, and Mathematics: an Analysis of the Effects of Parental and High School Factors on Females' and Males' Decisions to Enter STEM Fields of Study.

73. Legewie, Joscha, and Thomas A. DiPrete. "High School Environments, STEM Orientations, and the Gender Gap in Science and Engineering Degrees." February 21, 2012. Accessed October 19, 2014.

74. Lynch, M. G. (2012). Educating America's Talent in Science, Technology, Engineering, and Mathematics: an Analysis of the Effects of Parental and High School Factors on Females' and Males' Decisions to Enter STEM Fields of Study.

75. Bevan, Bronwyn, and Robert J. Semper. "Mapping Informal Science Institutions onto the Science Education Landscape." January 1, 2006. Accessed January 22, 2015. http://cils.exploratorium. edu/pdfs/CILS BAI_Bevan & Semper_Mapping ISIs.pdf

76. Durant, J., & Ibrahim, A. Celebrating the Culture of Science. Science 331(6022), (2011). 1242-1242.

77. Bell, Philip. Learning Science in Informal Environments People, Places, and Pursuits. Washington, D.C.: National Academies Press, 2009.

78. Bultitude, Karen, Dominic Mcdonald, and Savita Custead. "The Rise and Rise of Science Festivals: An International Review of Organised Events to Celebrate Science." International Journal of Science Education, Part B, 2011, 165-88.

79. Labov, Jay B. "Science Learning Can (and Should) Be Everywhere." BioScience, 2011, 173-74.

80. Bennett, George K., Harold G. Seashore, and Alexander G. Wesman. "Aptitude Testing: Does It "Prove Out" In Counseling Practice?" Occupations: The Vocational Guidance Journal, 2012, 584-93.

81. Hudson, Peter, Lyn D. English, and Les Dawes. "Catapulting into STEM Education: Female Students' Interactions within a." 2 Nd International STEM I N Education Conference. 2012. Accessed December 2, 2014. http://stem2012.bnu.edu.cn/data/long paper/stem2012_08.pdf.

82. Heyman, Gail D., Bryn Martyna, and Sangeeta Bhatia. "Gender and Achievement-Related Beliefs Among Engineering Students." Journal of Women and Minorities in Science and Engineering 8 (2002): 41–52.

83. Wilson, Zakiya S., Sitharama S. Iyengar, Su-Seng Pang, Isiah M. Warner, and Candace A. Luces. "Increasing Access for Economically Disadvantaged Students: The NSF/CSEM & S-STEM Programs at Louisiana State University." Journal of Science Education and Technology, 2011, 581-87.

84. Herrera, Felisha, and Sylvia Hurtado. "Maintaining Initial Interests: Developing Science, Technology, Engineering, and Mathematics (STEM) Career Aspirations Among Underrepresented Racial Minority Students." Accessed November 22, 2014. http://www.heri.ucla.edu/nih/downloads/ AERA 2011 - Herrera and Hurtado - Maintaining Initial Interests.pdf.

85. Rothwell, Jonathan. "The Hidden STEM Economy." The Brookings Institution. June 10, 2013. Accessed January 22, 2015. http://www. brookings.edu/research/reports/2013/06/10-stem-economy-rothwell.

86. Ibid.

87. CAP analysis of U.S. Department of Education, 2003-04 Beginning Postsecondary Students (BPS) Longitudinal Study, Second Follow-up (BPS:04/09), National Center for Education Statistics, 2014, available at http://nces.ed.gov/datalab/ postsecondary/index.aspx (last accessed December 12, 2014)

88. "The National STEM Report." The Condition of STEM 2014. 2014. Accessed December 17, 2014. http://www.act.org/stemcondition/14/.

89. CAP analysis of U.S. Department of Education, 2003-04 Beginning Postsecondary Students (BPS) Longitudinal Study, Second Follow-up (BPS:04/09), National Center for Education Statistics, 2014, available at http://nces.ed.gov/datalab/ postsecondary/index.aspx (last accessed December 12, 2014)

90. "UMB Creates New Program to Steer Children Into Health Careers, with NCI Grant." UMB News. October 28, 2014. Accessed December 17, 2014. http://www.oea.umaryland.edu/communications/ news/?ViewStatus=FullArticle&articleDetail=23509.

91. Olsen, Robert, Neil Seftor, Tim Silva, David Myers, David DesRoches, and Julie Young. "Upward Bound Math-Science: Program Description and Interim Impact Estimates." U.S. Department of Education. January 1, 2007. Accessed December 19, 2014. http://www2.ed.gov/ rschstat/eval/highered/upward-math-science/complete-report.pdf.

92. "The National STEM Report." The Condition of STEM 2014. 2014. Accessed December 17, 2014. http://www.act.org/stemcondition/14/.

93. "The Economic Cost of Unfilled Jobs in the U.S." Indeed. November 1, 2014. Accessed December 15, 2014. http://press.indeed.com/ wp-content/uploads/2014/11/Report-Empty-Desk-Final-.pdf.

94. "Boiling Point? The skills gap in U.S. manufacturing," The Manufacturing Institute. October 17, 2011. Accessed December 8, 2014. http://www.themanufacturinginstitute. org/News-Articles/2011/10/17-2011-Skills-Gap.aspx.

95. Cappelli, Peter. "The Skills Gap Myth: Why Companies Can't Find Good People." Time. June 4, 2012. Accessed October 30, 2014. http://business.time.com/2012/06/04/the-skills- gap-myth-why-companies-cant-find-good-people/.

96. "Changing Lives, Building a Workforce." ACT. 2012. Accessed October 31, 2014. http://www.act.org/research/policymakers/pdf/changing_lives.pdf.

97. "2014 State of the Industry Report: Spending on Employee Training Remains a Priority." Association for Talent Development. 2014. Accessed October 21, 2014. https://www.td.org/Publications/ Magazines/TD/TD-Archive/2014/11/2014-State-of-the-Industry- Report-Spending-on-Employee-Training-Remains-a-Priority.

98. "Community Colleges Expand Partnerships to Develop Innovative Models for Small Business Growth, Economic Development and Job Creation." American Association of Community Colleges. 2013. Accessed November 28, 2014. http://www.aacc.nche.edu/Resources/aaccprograms/ cwed/Documents/CC Small Bisiness White Paper_6262013.pdf.

99. Coy, Peter. "Job Training That Works." Bloomberg Business Week. November 20, 2014. Accessed January 22, 2015. http:// www.businessweek.com/articles/2014-11-20/job-training- that-works-where-certificates-replace-degrees.

100. "Talent Pipeline Management - White Paper." U.S. Chamber of Commerce Foundation. 2014. Accessed November 30, 2014. http://www.uschamberfoundation.org/talent-pipeline-management-white-paper.

101. "2014 Community College Fact Sheet." American Association of Community Colleges. 2014. Accessed December 5, 2014. http://www.aacc.nche.edu/AboutCC/Pages/fastfactsfactsheet.aspx.

102. O'Connell, A.J. "Community Colleges & Business Tackle Workforce Training." SkilledUp. October 6, 2014. Accessed December 22, 2014. http://www.skilledup.com/insights/community-colleges-and-corporate-america-tackle-workforce-training/.

103. " Community College-Industry Partnerships ." American Association of Community Colleges. Accessed September 18, 2014. http://www.aacc.nche.edu/AboutCC/Pages/college-industry_partnership.aspx.

104. "Workforce: Skills Certifications." The Manufacturing Institute. Accessed October 5, 2014. http://www.themanufacturinginstitute.org/Skills-Certification/Skills-Certification.aspx.

105. Johnstone, Sally M., and Louis Soares. "Principles for Developing Competency-Based Education Programs." Change: The Magazine of Higher Learning, 2014, 12-19. Accessed January 22, 2015. http://www.changemag.org/Archives/Back Issues/2014/March-April 2014/Principles_full.html.

106. "Economic and Employment Projections." Bureau of Labor Statistics. December 13, 2013. Accessed November 8, 2014. http://www.bls.gov/news.release/ecopro.toc.htmhttp://www.bls.gov/emp/.

107. "Why so Few?" American Association of University Women. 2010. Accessed December 16, 2014. http://www.aauw.org/files/2013/02/Why-So-Few-Women-in-Science-Technology-Engineering-and-Mathematics.pdf.

108. "Women in STEM: A Gender Gap to Innovation." U.S. Department of Commerce. August 2011. Accessed November 28, 2014. http://www.esa.doc.gov/sites/default/files/reports/documents/womeninstemagaptoinnovation8311.pdf.

109. "Women in STEM Research." NRCCUA. June 1, 2014. Accessed October 22, 2014. http://www.nrccua.org/cms/press-room/2014/39/Women-in-STEM-Research-Gender-Gap-in-STEM-Majors-Career-Interests

110. Pollack, Eileen. "Why Are There Still So Few Women in Science?" The New York Times. October 5, 2013. Accessed January 22, 2015. http://www.nytimes.com/2013/10/06/magazine/why-are-there-still-so-few-women-in-science.html?pagewanted=all&_r=0.

111. Schorr, Melissa. "Still Missing: Female Leaders in the STEM Fields - The Boston Globe." The Boston Globe. November 3, 2013. Accessed September 9, 2014. http://www.bostonglobe.com/magazine/2013/11/02/still-missing-female-leaders-stem-fields/26A5BYzZn1RhDAAqlL0rDM/story.html.

112. "Global Diversity and Inclusion: Fostering Innovation Through a Diverse Workforce." Forbes Insights. July 2011. Accessed November 20, 2014. http://www.forbes.com/forbesinsights/innovation_diversity/index.html.

113. Barta, Thomas, Markus Kleiner, and Tilo Neuerman. "Is There a Payoff from Top-team Diversity?" McKinsey&Company. April 2012. Accessed December 20, 2014. http://www.mckinsey.com/insights/organization/is_there_a_payoff_from_top-team_diversity.

114. Chua, Roy Y.J. "Innovating at the World's Crossroads: How Multicultural Networks Promote Creativity." Harvard Business School. May 24, 2011. Accessed November 22, 2014. http://hbswk.hbs.edu/item/6645.html.

115. "Bridging the Skills Gap." Association for Talent Development. 2012. Accessed December 21, 2014. http://nist.gov/mep/upload/Bridging-the-Skills-Gap_2012.pdf.

116. "Bringing the Institution into Focus." National Survey of Student Engagement. 2014. Accessed December 13, 2014. http://nsse.iub.edu/NSSE_2014_Results/pdf/NSSE_2014_Annual_Results.pdf.

117. "Civic Engagement and Student Success: A Resonant Relationship." Diversity & Democracy, March 1, 2012.

118. Allendoerfer, C., Wilson, D., Bates, R., Crawford, J., Jones, D., Floyd-Smith, T., Plett, M., Scott, E. and Veilleux, N., Strategic Pathways for Success: The Influence of Outside Community on Academic Engagement. Journal of Engineering Education 101 (2012), p. 512–538.

119. "The New Global Mindset: Driving Innovation through Diverse Perspectives." Ernst & Young. 2014. Accessed August 19, 2014. http://www.acareerinminingbc.ca/sites/default/files/thenewglobalmindset_driving_innovationthroughdiverseperspectives.pdf.

120. OECD Employment Outlook 2014. Paris: OECD Publishing, 2014.

121. OECD Skills Studies What the Survey of Adult Skills Says. Paris: OECD Publishing, 2013.

122. Job Creation and Local Economic Development. S.l.: Oecd, 2014.

123. Ibid.

124. Ibid.

125. Froy, Francesca. Designing Local Skills Strategies. Paris: OECD, 2009.

126. Job Creation and Local Economic Development. S.l.: Oecd, 2014.

127. Expanding Underrepresented Minority Participation. Washington, D.C.: National Academies Press, National Academy of Engineering, and Institute of Medicine of the National Academies, 2011.

128. Ibid, p.2.

129. Ibid. pp.22-23.

130. Ibid.

131. Ibid, p.2.

132. Spriggs, William E., Professor of Economics, Howard University; Senior Economic Adviser, AFL-CIO; former Assistant Secretary of Labor 2010-2014. Presentation to the NAFEO Membership, Presidential Peer Seminar. July 2013.

133. Gasman, Marybeth. "Comprehensive Funding Approaches for Historically Black Colleges and Universities." University of Pennsylvania Graduate School of Education. 2013. Accessed December 22, 2014. http://www.gse.upenn.edu/pdf/gasman/FundingApproachesHBCUs.pdf.

134. "The Educational Effectiveness of Historically Black Colleges and Universities: A Briefing Report." U.S. Commission on Civil Rights. January 1, 2010. Accessed October 19, 2014. http://www.usccr.gov/pubs/HBCU_webversion2.pdf.

135. Neither the author nor the National Association for Equal Opportunity in Higher Education, the association at whose helm she serves, intend to intimate that the other diverse and comprehensive academic strengths of HBCUs are any less important for advancing the jobs-driven economy. To be sure, HBCUs are leaders in graduating excellent, diverse teaching professionals (50% of public school teachers), have exemplary departments, curriculum and programs in the arts and humanities, agriculture, energy, sustainability, security, transportation and infrastructure, entrepreneurship and the entire gamut of disciplines essential for a thriving jobs-driven economy, thriving communities and a just society. This article highlights the predominance of HBCUs in graduating some of the growing populations in STEM contextualized for this STEMconnector® publication.

136. NAFEO works in and through The Alliance for Equity in Higher Education, a formalized relationship with the national membership and advocacy associations for the Hispanic Serving Institutions (HSIs) Tribal Colleges and Universities (TCUs) and Asian American and Native American Pacific Islander-Serving Institutions (AANAPIs). To cast the widest net in educating the growing populations about the centrality of all of these institutions in meeting the national need for an excellent, diverse jobs-driven economy, NAFEO will explore the interest of these, its sister associations in partnering in this undertaking.